FAUQUIER
DURING THE
PROPRIETORSHIP

FRANCIS FAUQUIER. ESQUIRE. F. R. S. (1704-1768)

H. M. LIEUTENANT-GOVERNOR AND COMMANDER-IN-CHIEF OF VIRGINIA

1758-1768

FAUQUIER

DURING THE

PROPRIETORSHIP

---

*A Chronicle of the Colonization and Organization
of a Northern Neck County*

By
H. C. GROOME

CLEARFIELD

Originally Published
Richmond, 1927

Reprinted
Regional Publishing Company
Baltimore, 1969

Reprinted for
Clearfield Company, Inc. by
Genealogical Publishing Co., Inc.
Baltimore, Maryland
1989, 2000

Library of Congress Catalogue Card Number 77-88164
International Standard Book Number: 0-8063-4953-0

Made in the United States of America

To the Memory
of my Wife
Mary Groome

PREFACE

IN presenting this compilation of the early records of Fauquier, it is believed that the conditions under which the seating of the county occurred can not properly be understood without some reference to the land system of the proprietors and to the devolutions of the proprietary title which at times seriously confused contemporary conveyancing. The colonization of the county was also materially affected by the practice of the proprietors' agents, and later of Lord Fairfax himself, of taking grants for their personal accounts of large tracts of land which were held by them as 'manors,' and of which the occupation was deferred by the conditions of settlement until late in the eighteenth century. Furthermore, in the important litigation attending the dissolution of the proprietary, one of these manors, lying for the most part in Fauquier, formed the basis of a compromise which controlled the partition of the Northern Neck lands. This was Lord Fairfax's Manor of Leeds on which at one time he contemplated the erection of a great house the furniture for which was actually imported from England. That the house was never built and that he passed his last years on the frontiers of the colony actively engaged in the work of colonization, may explain the immunity granted him in the legislation of 1777 under which the quit rents, abolished elsewhere in Virginia, were during his lifetime retained in the Northern Neck.

A brief history of the Northern Neck grant, therefore, and of the influence of the proprietors in the development of the territory held under it, is offered as a suitable background to the settlement and organization of the county.

Many of the subjects dealt with in this book have been treated in a series of four *Bulletins* published by the Fauquier Historical Society, 1921-1924, of which the writer was the editor and perhaps a too frequent contributor, but as the edition in each case was limited, the numbers successively were soon out of print and are not now generally accessible. In 1924, also, a very thorough and comprehensive study of origins in the Piedmont region of the Northern Neck was anonymously published under the title of *Landmarks of Old Prince William*, and as Fauquier was included in the exhaustive discussion of the author's subject, there would appear to be little room for amplification. This important contribution to local history, however, was privately printed and its circulation on that account necessarily restricted.

Under these circumstances a more available edition of Fauquier's colonial history seems to be justified and it is hoped that this volume may prove acceptable to those to whom access to the earlier publications has been denied.

In conclusion, the writer has pleasure in taking this opportunity to thank Mr. Fairfax Harrison for invaluable assistance and advice in this and previous work.

H. C. G.

Airlie,
Fauquier County, Virginia,
April, 1927.

CONTENTS

CHAPTER I.

The Indian Occupation.

THE great rivers of Virginia, along whose banks the early settlements pushed westward and whose waters later bore rich cargoes of tobacco to the sea, were first used for voyages of exploration undertaken soon after the planting of the first colony at Jamestown and many years before access to their upper watersheds had been gained through the dense forests that clothed the land.

A contour line through the falls of these rivers marks the boundary between Tidewater Virginia and that region which, rolling upward to the foothills of the Appalachians, is today known as the Piedmont Plateau. To this line on the Rappahannock river came Captain John Smith[1] on a voyage of discovery in 1608.

Smith had landed with Christopher Newport's company in May, 1607, and although then only twenty-seven years of age, had already been tried in many perils by land and sea. A soldier of fortune, his career had well fitted him for the task now before him and to his resourcefulness in emergencies and the sagacity he displayed in dealing with the savages, the little colony eventually owed its preservation, while we are indebted to the boldness with which he pursued his explorations for much that is known of the location of the aboriginal tribes.

In Smith's voyages, also, the student of the early history of Fauquier's territory can trace the move-

2 FAUQUIER DURING THE PROPRIETORSHIP

ment southward of the tribes with which the first
settlers had to do, and whose influence materially
delayed the colonization of the Piedmont. Smith's
only contact with these people followed his adven-
tures in the Algonquin country, but he afterwards
gathered much knowledge of their activities from
the Manahoacs and from the Maryland Indians, all
of which is set forth in his narrative.

Of his explorations, the first was led by Newport in person before his return to England. Accompanied by Smith and twenty others, he sailed
up the James and in six days reached its falls. There
he discovered an Indian 'Towne called *Powhatan,*
consisting of some twelue houses, pleasantly seated
on a hill; before it three fertile Isles, about it many
of their corn fields, the place is very pleasant and
strong by nature, of this place the Prince is called
Powhatan and his people *Powhatans'.*[2] This was while
Jamestown was still building, and although on the
voyage the 'people in all parts kindly entreated
them,' they returned to find that the colony had
been attacked in their absence, many of their com-
rades wounded, and one slain.

Some time was then devoted to adequately protecting the fort with palisades, and thereafter
Smith sought to trade with the Indians for corn.
With this object in view and in the hope of discover-
ing the headwaters of the Chickahominy, he as-
cended that river in December, 1607, but 'having
proceeded so far that with much labour by cutting
of trees asunder he made his passage,' he landed
and, becoming separated from his companions, was
attacked by a large band of Pamunkeys and taken
prisoner. Their chief, Opechancanough, after sub-

jecting him to many hardships, brought him before
'The' Powhatan at Werowcomoco, where his life
was eventually saved by Pocahontas, 'the King's
dearest daughter,' and he was allowed to return to
Jamestown. 'Six or seven weeks those Barbarians
kept him prisoner, many strange triumphes and
coniurations they made of him, yet hee so demeaned
himselfe amongst them, as he not onely diverted
them from surprising the Fort, but procured his
owne libertie, and got himself and his company such
estimation amongst them, that those Salvages ad-
mired him more than their owne *Quiyouckosucks*'.[3]

Smith next undertook to explore Chesapeake
bay. He sailed June 2, 1608, in an 'open Barge
neare three tons burthen,' with a company composed of six gentlemen adventurers, a 'doctor of
Physicke' and seven soldiers, and after touching at
several places on the Eastern Shore, crossed to the
mouth of the Potomac, up which he proceeded to
the Indian town Petomek, on Potomac creek in
what is now Stafford county, and at that point was
a day's journey overland from the southern boundary of the future county of Fauquier. Fauquier,
however, was to be born of the Rappahannock and,
as the first attempt at settlement from the Potomac
proved ineffective, so this first approach to its territory failed to afford that knowledge of its native
tribes which Smith's next voyage supplied.

After recovering from an injury received during
his recent cruise, Smith essayed a second voyage of
discovery in Chesapeake bay, July 24, accompanied
this time by six gentlemen, including a 'chirurgeon,'
and six soldiers.[4] They sailed to the Patapsco and a
little farther up the bay encountered the dreaded
Massawomeks, the Iroquois[5] of our school books and

the scourge of the Maryland and Virginia tribes, of
whom Smith was to hear more from the people of
'the small rivers' above the falls. His meeting on
-this occasion, however, was a friendly one and he
was much impressed by the dexterity they displayed in handling their canoes and by the superior-
ity of their arms and equipment.[6]

Continuing his voyage he explored the Susque-
hanna (the 'Bolus' river of Smith's narrative),[7] and
on his return sailed up the Patuxent. On all sides
he heard complaints of the Massawomeks and was
importuned for aid against them. 'To this purpose,
they offered food, conduct, assistance, and con-
tinuall subiection'.

Smith, however, had work to do with which we
are more concerned and in August his barge entered
the Rappahannock[8] ('the changing stream'), of
which he says, 'it is an excellent, pleasant, well inhabited, fertill, and a goodly navigable river.' On
its lower reaches his party fell in with the Moraughtacund, a tribe of the Powhatan Confederacy, by
whom they were 'kindly entertained.' Here also
they met their 'old friend *Mosco*, a lusty Salvage of
Wighcocomoco vpon the river of Patawomek,' and
persuaded him to accompany them as guide.[9]

Passing the Rappahannocks, with whom they had
some hostile exchanges, they proceeded up the river
'so high as our Boat would float' and landed near
the present site of Falmouth, where, having set up
crosses and cut their names on trees in token of
possession, they scattered to examine the country.
While in this position they were attacked by 'an
hundred nimble Indians skipping from tree to tree,
letting fly their arrows as fast as they could.'
Smith's men also sought cover of the trees and,

stoutly assisted by Mosco, soon drove the Indians off, capturing one of their number who had been wounded in the knee. This savage, whose name was Amoroleck, was carefully tended by Master Bagnall, the surgeon of the expedition, and from him they learned that the Indians who had attacked them were Hassinungas, who with the Stegaraki, Tanxnitania and Shackaconia made up a large hunting party, the several tribes of which separated during the day and reassembled at night at Mahaskahod, a hunting village nearby. The Hassinunga, for instance, were fishing when Smith encountered them. These tribes, together with the Ontponea, Tegninateo and Whonkentia, which Smith mentions in a later work, were all tributary to the Manahoacs (Algonquin for 'they are very merry'), and formed what has since been styled the Manahoac Confederacy. Amoroleck on being asked why they had attacked the white men, who had come to them in peace and to seek their love, answered that 'they heard we were a people come from vnder the world, to take their world away from them,' a rumor certainly with some justification in fact.

"We asked him how many worlds he did know, he replyed, he knew no more but that which was vnder the skie that covered him, which were the *Powhatans,* with the *Monacans* and the *Massawomekes* that were higher vp in the mountains.

"Then we asked him what was beyond the mountaines, he answered the Sunne; but of any thing els he knew nothing; because the woods were not burnt."

On being pressed further the savage, who it appeared was a brother of the chief of the Hassinungas, told them that Mahaskahod was on the border between the country of the Manahoacs and the

Nandaughtacunds (a Powhatan tribe) who were their enemies, and that the Monacans were their neighbors and friends 'and did dwell as they in the hilly Countries by small rivers, liuing vpon rootes and fruits, but chiefly by hunting. The Massawomeks did dwell vpon a great water, and had many boats, and so many men that they made warre on all the world.'

That night Smith's party dropped down the river and was again attacked by the Manahoacs, but proceeding until a broader stretch of water was reached, the boat was anchored out of arrow shot for the night. The next morning Amoroleck held a long discourse with his tribesmen on the bank, in which he told them how well the white men had used him, how they wished to be friends and in that case would release him, and that in any event 'to do vs any hurt it was impossible.' Whereupon the Indians on the bank hung their bows and quivers upon the trees, while one came swimming to the boat with his bow tied upon his head and another with a quiver of arrows carried in the same way. Smith received the messengers of peace kindly and expressed the wish that the other chiefs in the party should perform the like ceremony so that the great King whose servant he was might be their friend.

"It was no sooner demanded but performed, so vpon a low Moorish poynt of Land we went to the shore, where those foure Kings came and recieued *Amoroleck;* nothing they had but Bowes, Arrowes, Tobacco-bags, and Pipes; what we desired, none refused to giue vs, wondering at every thing we had, and heard we had done: our Pistols they took for pipes, which they much desired, but we did content them with other Commodities. And so we left foure or fiue hundred of our merry *Monahoacs,* singing, dauncing, and making merry, and set sayle for Moraughtacund."[10]

The map of Virginia attributed to Smith[11] was published by him in 1612 with a geographical treatise entitled *A Map of Virginia, with a Description of the Countrey, the Commodities, People, Government and Religion.* On this map Mahaskahod is shown on the east bank of the Rappahannock above the falls, and opposite to it a cross is placed to mark the point to which Smith's party penetrated in 1608. The unexplored country northward to the mountains is assigned to the Manahoacs, the legend of the map stating that 'to the crosses hath bin discouered—what beyond is by relation.' The Great Fork of the river, the confluence of the North Fork (originally known as the Indian or Cannon River) and the Rapidan, is shown in this territory, and within it is displayed the 'king's house' of the Hassinunga. The Shackaconia appear opposite to the Hassinunga on the south bank of the Rapidan, while the Stegora (Stegaraki) are allotted to the lower side of that river but nearer its head. The Tanxnitania are placed on the east bank of the North Fork, and these Indians can be accepted as a native tribe of Fauquier. Recent research has identified the site of their village as that of the White Sulphur Spring on a high bank of the river near the mouth of Barrow's run. The Whonkentia have, by some authorities, also been assigned to Fauquier, but the position given them on the head of the Rappahannock[12] is apparently taken from Smith's general statement of the location of all the Manahoac tribes.

Our first knowledge of the territory of Fauquier and of its native Indians thus comes as a result of Smith's discoveries in 1608, although neither he nor any member of his party actually set foot on

its soil. We learn from him of the Powhatan tribes
that inhabited the Coastal Plain and the great rivers
to their falls; that they differed in language from
the people of the 'hilly countries by the small rivers,'
with whom they were constantly at war; that the
Monacans who dwelt on the headwaters of the
James were friends and allies of the Manahoacs and
spoke a kindred tongue, and that beyond the mountains dwelt the Massawomeks, the 'most mortall
enemies' of all the Virginia tribes.

Ethnologists are now agreed that the Manahoacs, as well as their allies the Monacans, were of
Siouan stock and that the prehistoric home of that
race was not on the prairies of the Middle West,
but among the western foothills of the Alleghany
mountains. It is believed that they were driven from
their original habitat and forced westward along
the Ohio or eastward over the mountains, in search
of game or by the pressure of hostile tribes.[18]
The Sioux were not an agricultural people;[14] they
lived by hunting, and the Virginia tribes at the time
of Smith's discoveries had, by the process of firing
the forests, cleared the river bottoms and adjacent
lands of timber, after which the spontaneous growth
of nutritious grasses in this favored region soon
supplied the buffalo and other herbivorous game
with luxuriant pasture and created for them a natural preserve.[15] Captain Argall, ascending the Rappahannock to the falls in 1613, says, that 'marching
into the Countries I found great store of cattle as
big as Kine, of which the Indians that were my
guides killed a couple which were found to be very
good and wholesome meate, and are very easie to
be killed in regard they are heavy, slow and not so

wilde as other beasts of the Wilderness.' Lederer, too, half a century later, describes this region as 'a pleasant and fruitful country, with open spaces clear of timber and abounding in game.'

According to their own tradition, the Manahoacs had not been the first inhabitants of the country in which they dwelt. They and the other Siouan tribes of the Piedmont districts of Virginia and Carolina, coming from the west, 'where the sun sleeps,' countless years before, had found an ancient people, very rude and barbarous who fed only on raw flesh and fish. The Siouan Indians had taught them how to plant corn and instructed them in its use, and later had apparently absorbed them, for the race, as the story ran, had long since become extinct. It is possible, however, that these people were purely mythical and creatures only of a tribal legend.[16]

A few years after Smith and Argall's visits the Manahoacs were dispossessed of their country and dispersed by the Iroquois. Merging with the Monacans and other related tribes, they eventually drifted as far south as Carolina, to return again to Virginia and take refuge for a time on an island in the Roanoke above the Occaneechi. There with their kinsmen they fell victims to Bacon's treacherous assault in May, 1676, while the survivors were again attacked and driven from their sanctuary by their implacable Indian enemy in 1681. After this, Governor Spotswood, for their own protection, herded them with other Siouan derelicts at Fort Christanna, where, according to Colonel Byrd, 'the daughter of the last king poisoned herself from distress at the degradation of her people.' Finally a pitiful few of our aborigines strayed north and were formally adotped by their racial enemies, the Cayuga, in 1753, but their happy temperament seems to have survived their misfortunes and as late as 1870 an ethnologist discovered in Canada at least one member of this race, 'a merry old man named Mosquito', who still spoke his inherited Siouan tongue and claimed the ownership of his tribal lands in Virginia.[17]

The Indians, then, with whom the early settlers of Fauquier had to deal were not the 'merry Manahoacs', but that ruthless race of northern savages who, as Massawomeks, had made their name terrible to the tribes that Smith encountered at the head of Chesapeake bay, as well as to the Sioux on the headwaters of the Virginia rivers. They belonged to a confederation known as the 'Five Nations' that had been formed about the year 1570 by the Cayuga, Mohawk, Oneida, Onandaga and Seneca of the Lake Champlain and Genessee River countries of New York, for the purpose of extending their political organization by the conquest and absorption of all alien tribes within the range of their hostilities.[18] So rapidly did they push their wars southward that as early as 1608 they were confronting the Susquehannocks (Conestoga) in Maryland and threatening the Indians of the Virginia Piedmont. Of the former, Smith, who calls them 'Susquesahannocks,' says, 'they can make neere 600 able and mighty men and are pallisadoed in their Townes to defend them from the *Massawomekes*, their mortall enemies.'[19]

Subsequently these Susquehannocks served the Dutch merchants of Manhattan Island as intermediaries in their trade in skins and furs with the Carolina Indians and incidentally opened a route

across the future territory of Fauquier which locally acquired historic importance. In 1662 the preamble to an act of the Virginia Assembly recited,
'that the Susquehannock and other Northern Indians
in considerable numbers frequently came to the
heads of our rivers whereby plain paths will soon
be made which may prove of dangerous consequence';[20] and the act then proceeded to interdict
the traffic. This law, however, could not be enforced
and only served to excite the enmity of the Indians
against whom it was directed.

The Susquehannocks continued to use their 'plain
paths', but now showed their resentment against
the Virginia government by committing depredations on the white settlements of the Potomac and
Rappahannock as they journeyed north and south.
In 1675, their last stronghold in Maryland having
fallen before the final assault of the Iroquois, the
'mortall enemy' whose attacks they had so long
withstood, they established themselves on the
Roanoke and in the Susquehannock war which en-
sued, proved pitiless enemies of the English.

The Iroquois, in the meantime, had occupied the
Manahoac country, their sachems informing Governor Spotswood at Albany in 1722, that 'they had
never intended to live there but the whole world
knew that they had conquered that land and that
it was their hunting preserve.'[21] That the buffalo
and deer of the Piedmont were not their only
quarry, however, Lord Baltimore testifies in 1681,
in a letter describing some recent outrages committed by them against settlers of the upper Potomac. He says:

"These Northern Indians pretend no desyne of mischiefe
towards the English, but tell us they're resolv'd to destroy all

our neighboring indians, whome when they're subdued, conquered and destroyed, I believe their next desyne will be against
the Inhabitants of both these colonies, whose stocks of cattle
and hoggs they already make bold with; and especially in Virginia, where these savages kill and destroy hoggs and cattle
afore the faces of the Owners of them, and if the English
make any opposition they're immediately fir'd at by these Indian
villians."

This indictment is repeated by Nicholas Spencer
in 1683, who refers to the Iroquois as 'Senecas', the
name by which they were generally known in Virginia and Carolina:

"The inhabitants of the extreme parts are in great fear of
the Senecas who have inflicted many insolences and injuries,
robbed the houses, frightened the people and wantonly and
maliciously killed the stock. Either they wish to provoke the
inhabitants against them, or they wish to show by sheer mischiefe, how little they regard us. The consequences in either
case be bad. The Senecas are so remote a people that we cannot hope to reach them at home, while it is equally difficult to
find them abroad. The hazard too is great. It is a stout,
numerous, rapacious people composed of many nations, receiving all sorts of outlying indians and, therefore, an un-
governed people, with whom no treaty can be depended on".[22]

The treaty Spencer referred to was one of al-
liance with the Long House of the Iroquois made
at Albany in 1679, by representatives of the Virginia and Maryland governments, and that his
skepticism was justified seems to have been proved
by a raid made shortly afterward by a war party of
Senecas into the Northern Neck, ending in a pitched
battle with a tribe of Rappahannock Indians tributary to the colonial government.

Lord Howard of Effingham, on becoming governor of Virginia, undertook in 1684 to put an end
to such disturbances and for this purpose went to

Albany in person. The result of his mission was
another treaty by which the Five Nations engaged,
'that because of the mischief that has been done to
the People and Castles of Virginia and Maryland,
we must not come near the Heads of your Rivers,
nor near your Plantations, but keep at the foot of
the mountains';²³ an agreement which, in effect,
constituted a cession of the eastern slopes of the
Blue Ridge, and the country west of that range, to
the Iroquois in return for immunity from molestation to the settlements already established below
the falls of the rivers. This covenant, while it remained in force, checked colonization in the Piedmont, as the Indians regularly frequented the
territory they had acquired and establishing a path
south which crossed the Blue Ridge at the Indian
thoroughfares of Ashby's and Williams' gaps, continued to menace the frontier plantations. Colonel
Joshua Fry, in his *Description of Virginia*, written in
1751, says, 'The Indians had been ever since the
year 1684 in Possession of a Road by Treaty on
the east side of the Blue Ridge and frequently hunted
on the Lands between the Falls of the Rivers and
the Mountains'.²⁴ It was beside this 'road' and
under these conditions that the Brent Town block
house in lower Fauquier was built in 1686 as a de-
fense against the far wandering bands of the
Iroquois.

The use these marauders made of their southern
path and the wide range of their depredations is
attested by John Lawson, the surveyor-general of
Carolina, in 1701. In that year he made a journey
through the interior of the colony from Charleston
to Pamlico sound and in his journal states, 'that the
Saponas had (about ten days before we came

thither) taken five prisoners of the *Sinnagers* [Sene-
cas] or *Jennitos*, a sort of people that range *several
thousands of miles*, making all prey they lay their
hands on. These are feared by all the savage nations I ever was among, the Westward Indians
dreading their approach. They are all sorted in,
and keep continual spies and outguards for their
better security'.[25] In another place he says, 'This
day we met with seven heaps of stones, being the
monuments of seven Indians that were slain in that
place by the *Sinnagers* or *Troquois*'.[26]

[1] John Smith was the eldest son of George Smith, a well-to-do tenant
farmer on the estate of Lord Willoughby de Eresby, in Lincolnshire,
where Smith was born in 1579. His mother, Alice, had some claim to
gentle blood, and his father's family may be said to have belonged to a
class that differed little from the small county gentry of that day.
Young Smith was educated at the free schools of the neighborhood and
afterward apprenticed to Thomas Sendall, a merchant of Lynn. Finding the counting house little to his liking and with a soul primed for
adventure, he made his way to London after his father's death in 1596.
From there he journeyed to Paris and took service under an English
captain of free lances, with whom he served for several years in
Flanders. Thrown out of employment by the ensuing peace, he suffered
shipwreck on a voyage to Scotland and after an illness caused by ex-
posure, visited Edinburgh, where he was well received. He was then
twenty years of age. After this he returned home to Willoughby
'where within a short time, being glutted with too much company
wherein he took small delight, he retired himself into a little woody
pasture a good way from any town, environed with many hundred acres
of woods. Here by a fair brook he built himself a pavillion of boughs
where only in his clothes he lay. His study was Macchiavelli's Art of
War and Marcus Aurelius; his exercise a good horse, with lance and
ring; his food was thought to be more of venison than anything else,
what [else] he wanted his man brought him'.
 In this somewhat eccentric solitude he was approached by one Pola-
loga, an accomplished Italian gentleman in the service of the Earl of
Lincoln, whose languages and good discourse and exercises of riding
drew Smith to stay with him at Tattersall'. Soon growing restive
in the Earl's service, he announced himself as desirous to see more of
the world and to try his fortune against the Turks.
 Next came his wanderings through France from Picardy to Mar-
seilles, where he took ship for Italy in a vessel full of pilgrims on their
way to Rome. A fierce storm arising, the Catholics cursed him for a
heretic and saying there would be no good weather while he was aboard,
threw him, like a Jonah, into the sea. He saved himself, however, by
swimming to a small island nearby from which he was presently rescued
by a Breton ship, whose captain treated him kindly, and with him Smith

sailed to Egypt and the Levant. On the return voyage they met a Venetian argosy laden with velvet, silks and treasure, which they fought and captured. Smith's share of the booty was 500 sequins and with this sum he was put ashore at a small port in Italy. He then proceeded to Rome, where he saw Pope Clement, and passing thence through Tuscany and Venice came to Gratz, in Styria. Here Ferdinand, Archduke of Austria, lay, and from his officers Smith learned much of the Turks who were then overrunning Hungary. Confirmed in his purpose to measure swords with them, he passed on to Vienna and took service under the Emperor Rudolph II. He participated in the bloody campaigns of 1601-1602, as captain of two hundred and fifty horse in the regiment of 'Earl' Meldritch, a command subsequently transferred to the service of Sigismund Bathori, Prince of Transylvania.

During the siege of Regal he fought and slew successively in single combat three Turkish champions and for this feat later received a grant of arms from Sigismund.

At the battle of Rothenthurm, November, 1602, in which Meldritch led his regiment against an overwhelming force of Crim-Tartars, Smith was wounded and left on the field for dead. In this plight he was taken by the enemy, sold as a slave, and then marched to Constantinople where he passed into the service of the lady Charatza Tragabigzanda, whose regard he won. Fearing lest her mother should sell Smith, she sent him to her brother on the Don to be well treated 'until time made her master of herself'. But the rude pasha paid no heed to his sister's message and 'so beat, spurned and reviled him', that one day in the harvest field Smith, although in irons, slew his captor with his 'threshing bat' and made his escape after many hardships, to a Muscovite outpost where his irons were removed and his wants supplied.

Thence journeying through Muscovy, Hungary and Austria, and attracting much sympathy as an escaped Christian slave, he finally reached Leipzig in December 1603, where he found his old leaders Prince Sigismund and Meldritch and was welcomed as one returned from the dead. It was at this time that he received his grant of arms, together with 500 ducats in gold and a letter of safe conduct. He then travelled through Germany, France and Spain and made a voyage to Morocco, during which the captain of his vessel encountered two Spanish ships which he fought and captured, so that Smith increased his store of gold and returned home to England in 1605 with a thousand ducats in his purse.

Twenty-five years old and certainly mature in experience, his strong geographical curiosity was attracted by the expeditions then being planned to America and, as we know, he eventually joined Newport in his voyage to Virginia in 1607. How he served the new colony, how he was chosen its President in September, 1608, and how, wounded by an accidental explosion of gunpowder, he returned to England in October, 1609, are matters of general knowledge which need not be discussed in this note.

The rest of Smith's life can be briefly touched on. 1610-1617 was spent in explorations to New England, during which the Western Company for North Virginia gave him the title of 'Admiral of New England'. His last years were chiefly devoted to authorship, and in this period he published his most important work, 'The General Historie of Virginia, New England and the Summer Isles'. John Smith died June 21, 1631, and was buried in St. Sepulchre's Church, London. (*Smith's Works*, ed. Arber, 1910, pp. i-xxvi, and 821-880.)

² *Ibid.*, p. 387. The Powhatans were a confederacy of Virginia tribes of Algonquin stock whose villages at one time numbered nearly two

hundred. Their territory included all of eastern Virginia south of the Potomac and extended inland as far as the falls of the James and Rappahannock rivers. (*Handbook Am. Indians*, II, p. 299.)

[3] *Smith's Works*, p. 395.

[4] *Ibid.*, p. 421. Smith's party on this voyage consisted of:

'Nathaniel Powell	Jonas Profit
Thomas Momford	Anas Todkill
Richard Fetherston	Edward Pising
Michell Sicklemore	Richard Keale
Iames Bourne	James Watkins
Anthony Bagnall, Chir.	William Ward
Gentlemen	Souldiers'

Of the above, Nathaniel Powell was a surveyor who had come out with Newport in 1607, and with him had explored the James river in the early summer of that year. He was killed in the massacre of 1622.

[5] *Handbook Am. Indians*, I, p. 618.

[6] *Smith's Works*, p. 72. 'Seven boats full of these *Massawomeks* the discouerers encountered at the head of the Bay; whose Targets, Baskets, Swords, Tobaccopipes, Platters, Bowes and Arrowes, and euery thing they shewed, they much exceeded them of our parts'.

[7] 'Thirty leagues norward is a river not inhabited [the Susquehanna], yet navigable, by reason of the red earth or clay resembling bole-armoniack; the discoverers called yt Bolus.' (Wm. Strachey, *Historie of Travaille into Va. Brittania*, ed. Hakluyt Society, 1849, p. 39.)

[8] Strachey thus describes the Rappahannock river: 'The third navigable river by the Naturalls of old was called Opiscatumeck, of late Toppahanock, and we the Queen's River; this is navigable some one hundred and thirty miles. At the top of yt inhabite the people called Mannahoacks, amongst the Mountaynes, but they are above the place described in Captain Smithe's mapp'. (Strachey, *Va. Brittania*, p. 37.)

The James was called 'the King's River'; the York, 'the Princes River'; the Potomac, 'Elizabeth River', and the Patuxent, 'the Dukes River'.

[9] *Smith's Works*, p. 424. Of Mosco, Smith says, 'We supposed him some *French* mans sonne, because he had a thicke blacke bush beard, and the Salvages seldome haue any at all; of which he was not a little proud.'

[10] *Ibid.*, pp. 426-429.

[11] The authorship of this map is doubtful. Smith himself makes no claim to it, nor is it referred to by his contemporaries as his handiwork, moreover there is evidence to show that Smith himself had no skill as a draughtsman. It may be inferred, therefore, that the map was drawn by some one from data furnished by Smith as a result of his observations and discoveries. The theory has been advanced that the maker of the plat from which the map was engraved was one Nathaniel Powell, a surveyor, who, as stated in a previous note, accompanied Newport in his expedition up the James in 1607, and in 1608 explored Chesapeake bay with Smith. In 1641 Robert Evelyn, in an advertising tract, refers to 'Captain Powel's map' of this region and as this map has not been otherwise identified, it may have been the map which Smith put forth in 1612.

The so-called Smith map was prepared from material obtained between the years 1608 and 1612, and was engraved by William Hole. On the first issue the words 'Discouered and Discribed by Captayn John Smith and 'Grauen by William Hole' are found under the scale, and in the second issue the year '1606' was inserted under the name 'Smith'. This inscription has persisted in the eight subsequent states, or issues, of the map, the last, or 10th, of which was made from the Hole plate in 1632. It is from this last state that the modern representations are copied. (Amer. Geographical Society, *Geographical Review*, July, 1924, pp. 433 *et seq.*)

[12] *Handbook Am. Indians*, II, p. 946.

[13] Mooney, *Siouan Tribes of the East*, p. 9.

[14] Smith describes the Manahoacs and Monacans as 'very barbarous, liuing for the most part on wild beasts and fruits'. (*Smith's Works*, p. 367.)

[15] Of the practice of burning the forests to create grass lands, a statement is found in *The Use and Abuse of Forests by Va. Indians*, (*W. & M. Quarterly*, xix, p. 103) : 'Virginia between its mountains and the sea was passing through its fiery ordeal and was approaching a crisis at the time the colonists snatched the fagot from the Indian's hand. The tribes were burning everything that would burn, and it can be said with at least as much probability of Virginia as of the region west of the Alleghanies that if the discovery of America had been postponed five hundred years, Virginia would have been a pasture land or desert'. (*Landmarks of Old Prince William*, I, p. 32.)

[16] Mooney, *Siouan Tribes, etc.*, p. 29.

[17] *Old Prince William*, I, p. 33.

[18] *Handbook Am. Indians*, I, p. 617.

[19] *Smith's Works*, p. 54.

[20] Hening, II, p. 153.

[21] *Old Prince William*, I, p. 27.

[22] *Ibid.*, p. 78.

[23] *Ibid.*, p. 80.

[24] *Ibid.*, p. 89.

[25] Lawson, *History of North Carolina*, London, 1714, reprint Raleigh, N. C., 1860, p. 82.

[26] *Ibid.*, p. 78.

An incident in the Iroquois tenure of the Virginia Piedmont occurs in the temporary occupation of the valley north of the Pignut in Fauquier, by the Piscataways (Conoy), between the years 1697 and 1699. The Piscataways were a Maryland tribe of the Algonquin family that had incurred the hostility of the Iroquois by taking sides with Maryland in the Susquehannock war of 1676, and afterwards were granted permission by the government of that colony to move back from the north bank of the Potomac to Zachaia swamp, on Mattawoman creek, where among the white inhabitants they might find security from their enemy. Here they were followed in 1681, but successfully withstood a siege laid to their fort by the Iroquois, who then taunted them with their protection by the whites and invited them to join forces with those 'who would and could make men of them'. (*Old Prince William*, I, p. 94.) Later the young men of the tribe were won by these representations and the migration to the Iroquois territory of northern Virginia took place. The Piscataways, however, were fishermen and doubtless missing in their new home their spring diet of Potomac river shad, were soon induced by the Maryland and Virginia governments to remove themselves from Iroquois domination and return to Maryland.

CHAPTER II

Explorations and Early Settlements

THE curtain that had lifted for a moment to reveal to Smith the aboriginal Indians of the Piedmont and to give Argall a glimpse of the buffalo feeding on its pastures, had fallen again and for half a century the wilderness life was undisturbed by the intrusion of any white man. This period, however, had witnessed the passing of a race and when John Lederer entered the Manahoac country at the head of an overland exploring party in 1670, he found an apparently uninhabited region, on the beauties of which he thus discoursed:

"We travelled thorow the Savanae amongst vast herds of red and fallow deer which stood gazing at us; and a little after, we came to the Promontories or spurs of the Apalataen mountains.

"These Savanae are low grounds at the foot of the Apalataeans, which all the winter, spring and part of the summer, lie under snow or water, when the snow is dissolved, which falls down from the mountains commonly about the beginning of June; and then their verdure is wonderful pleasant to the eye, especially of such as having travelled through the shade of the vast forest, come out of a melancholy darkness of a sudden, into a clear and open skie. To heighten the beauty of these parts, the first springs of most of those great rivers which run into the Atlantick ocean, or Chesapeack bay, do here break out, and in various branches interlace the flowry meads whose luxurious herbage invites numerous herds of red deer (for their unusual largeness improperly termed elks by ignorant people) to feed".[1]

Lederer, who was described by a contemporaneous writer as a 'German Chirurgeon', had made two previous 'marches' to the mountains under a commission of discovery from Sir William Berkeley, then governor of the colony, and on this journey, the third and last, he was accompanied, as he states in his report, by Colonel John Catlett[2] 'with nine English horse and five Indians on foot'. They left the house of Robert Taliaferro, on the south bank of the Rappahannock, on the morning of August 20th, and that night reached the falls, 'in Indian, *Mantapeuck*'. The next day his party entered what is now Stafford county and passing through the lower edge of Fauquier, crossed the North Fork into Culpeper. Thence keeping the river to the east of them they followed it until it became 'so shallow that it only wet our horses hoofs'. On the 26th they reached the Blue Ridge mountains, 'where finding no horseway up, we alighted, and left our horses with two or three Indians below, whilst we went up afoot. The ascent was so steep, the cold so intense [*sic*], and we so tired, that having with much ado gained the top of the highest, we drank the King's health in brandy, gave the mountain his name ['mons. Car. Reg.', on Lederer's map], and agreed to return back again, having no encouragement from that prospect to proceed to a further discovery; since from thence we saw another mountain, bearing north and by west to us, of a prodigious height: for according to an observation of the distance taken by Colonel Catlett, it could not be less than fifty leagues from the place we stood upon'.[3]

Another account of this expedition, written by Thomas Glover in 1676, reveals its purpose and in-

cidentally discloses the geographical confusion of
the time:

> "There was one Colonel Catlet, that was a good Math-
> ematician, who with some other Gentlemen took a Journey to
> make some further discoveries of the Country to the West-
> ward, and arriving at the foot of the Mountains early in the
> morning, they left their horses, and endeavored to gain the tops
> of the Mountains, which they accomplished about four of the
> Clock in the afternoon, and then looking further forward they
> discovered other Mountains, whereof they took the altitude
> and judged them inaccessible; which discouraged them from
> any further attempts, their design being chiefly to discover
> whether there were any Rivers that ran into the South-ocean".[4]

Although no waterway to the 'South-ocean' was
discovered, this journey first disclosed to the explorer the forests, streams and plains of the Piedmont country, and in its progress the territory of
Fauquier was first entered by white men and its
soil first trod by a horse's hoof. Other explorations
soon followed, notably that of Cadwalader Jones
in 1682.

Jones had taken up land on the south side of the
Rappahannock in 1673, and for the next few years
figured prominently in the activities of the frontier.
He held his plantation against the Indians during
the raids following the Susquehannock war and in
1679 commanded a fort near the site of Fredericksburg which had been built under Berkeley's act of
1675, to establish forts 'on the heads of the rivers
and other places fronting the enemy'.

The value of his services in protecting the upper
settlements in these difficult times, was acknowledged by the Council in 1680, when his petition for
indemnity for losses inflicted by the Indians was
granted. The order stated that, 'the Sufferings of

the Petitioner are most apparent and his resolute-
ness to abide his plantation ag't all attempts and
conspiracies of our Indian enemies for many years
hath (as may well be supposed) maintained us in
the seatment of the upper parts of Rappahannock
for many miles'.[5]

In 1682, commanding a company of the Rappahannock Rangers, he ranged the Great Fork and
explored the headwaters of both its branches. John
Taliaferro, a son of the Robert Taliaferro who had
accompanied Lederer in 1670, testified in 1706, that
he had been a member of Jones's party on this expedition and that 'we traviled up the South river
[Rapidan] till we came to sev[ll] small mountains &
so to the North River [Hedgmans]. In our travills
we were sev[ll] times on the North River and went
up the South River to the great mountains where
we discovered the South River's Springs to head
into the Mountains. All our Judgm[tt] was the South
river to be the bigest and were inform'd so by all
the Indians y[t] was our Pilotts; and saw an Indian
y[t] made a periauger at the mountain and brought
her down to the Garison with Skins and venison,
where the said Jones Commanded'.[6]

With the white settlements creeping up the Rappahannock toward the falls and the country beyond
unfolded by these explorations, an early movement
into the territory might have been expected but for
Lord Howard of Effingham's agreement with the
Long House, which, as we have seen, was effected
within the next two years. This gave the Piedmont
to the Iroquois and beyond a well defined trail which
traversed the southeast corner of Fauquier, no colonization was possible until the Treaty of Albany
was negotiated in 1722. Behind this trail in Staf-

ford and Prince William, however, an attempt was made to settle a large tract of land with Huguenots, and in the effort the first outpost of civilization was established in Fauquier.

After the revocation of the Edict of Nantes and upon the arrival in England of the first batch of Huguenot refugees, Nicholas Hayward, a notary public of London and the son of a merchant in the Virginia trade, conceived the plan of utilizing these desirable emigrants to colonize a tract of land that he had recently acquired on the Potomac, adjoining William Fitzhugh.

Fitzhugh, on learning of Hayward's purpose, seemed impressed by the possibilities of the scheme and in a letter to Hayward, May 20, 1686, offered to seat 150 to 200 of these families on a large tract of his own, and incidentally to take Hayward's land off his hands. He writes, 'if your Intentions therein be as well led by charity to help the distressed, as p advantage to make profit of your Purchase, I believe it may lay in my power to answer both or either of them for if you are designed for sale, if you please to give me the offer, and to set your lowest price I will accept and make you punctual and good payment either in money or Tob°'.[7]

Hayward, however, declined this proposal, but realizing from Fitzhugh's representations that the tract he had at first intended to colonize was too small for the purpose, he formed a partnership with Richard Foote, his brother-in-law, and Robert Bristow, both merchants of London, and George Brent of Woodstock, Virginia, to purchase from Lord Culpeper, then proprietor of the Northern Neck, a tract of 30,000 acres 'in the forest' of what was then

Stafford county. The grant, dated January 10, 1686/7, described the land as, 'All that tract, Territory or parcel of Land Containing by estimation thirty thousand Acres be the same more or less, Scituate, lying and being in or near the said County of Stafford in Virginia aforesaid, Between the Courses of the said Two Rivers, Rappahannock and Potowmack, backwards, at least six miles Distant from the said Main River and from any Land already seated and inhabited, and upon and Between the Southwest [Cedar Run] and Northeast [Broad Run] Branches of Ocaquan Creek and from thence towards the Mountains'.[8]

Hayward then obtained a dispensation from James II granting to the proposed colonists permission to freely exercise their religion. The warrant directed, to 'our Righty Trusty and well beloved Francis, Lord Howard of Effingham our Lieutenant & Governor Generall of our Collony & Dominions of Virginia in America and to our chiefe Governor or Governors there for the time being', and dated February 10, 1686/7, read:

"Whereas our Trusty and well beloved George Brent of Woodstock, in our County of Stafford in that our Collony of Virginia, Richard Foote and Robert Bristow of London, Merchants, & Nicholas Hayward of London, Notary Publick, have by their humble Petition informed us that they have purchased of our right trusty and well beloved Thomas Lord Culpeper a certain tract of land in our said Colony between the Rivers of Rappahannock and Potomac containing of estimation Thirty thousand acres lying in or near our said County of Stafford some miles distant from any present settlement or Inhabitants and at or about Twenty Miles from the foot of the mountains, upon part of which Tract of Land the Pet'rs have projected and do speedly designe to build a Towne with convenient fortifications, and doo therefore pray that for the encouragement of Inhabitants to settle in the said Towne and plantation wee

would be pleased to grant them the free exercise of their
Religion, wee have thought fitt to condescend to their humble
request and wee do accordingly give and grant unto the Pet'rs
and to all and every the Inhabitants which are now or hereafter shall bee settled in the said Towne and Tract of Land
belonging to them as is above mentioned, the free exercise of
their Religion without being prosecuted or molested upon any
penall laws or other account for the same, which wee do hereby
signifie unto you to the end you may take care and give such
orders as may be requisite. That they enjoy the full benefit
of these our gracious intentions to them.

"Provided they behave themselves in all civill matters so
as to become peaceable and Loyall subjects, and for so doing
this shall your warrant and so wee bid you heartuly farewell".[9]

The 'towne' so to be established, received the
name of Brent Town, and a block house was built
on the lower side of Town run in the southeast corner of Fauquier, not far from the modern village of
Sowego. This position had the strategic advantage
of 'overlooking' the Iroquois trail which followed
the original 'plain path' of the Susquehannocks between their trading posts on Conoy island in the
Potomac and Occaneechi island in the Roanoke,
and, as a frontier fort, was locally important during
the period of the Iroquois occupation of that portion
of the Piedmont.

George Brent now lost no time in the development of the property and to provide access to it, cut
the 'Brent Town road' from the Potomac up the
Beaverdam branch of Aquia and across Dorrell's run
to the new town site, where, by June 1, 1688, he
had established a few pioneers.[10] Hayward in London, however, was less successful. In his efforts to
secure the Huguenots as colonists he encountered
the organized competition of Carolina and other
states, and although a few families were planted

in the end his project to settle the tract with French Protestants failed. One of his 'broadsides' written in French and circulated in London in the early summer of 1687,[11] explains the terms under which colonization was invited:

"The proprietors of the land * * * make the following propositions for the encouragement of persons who plan to emigrate into that country and there make a permanent establishment, that is to say,

'To the first to present themselves they will sell, for the sum of ten pounds sterling cash, at four *écus* to the pound sterling, 100 acres of land near enough to the town to build a house upon it. Under this offer the purchasers, and their heirs, will become proprietors of the said land in perpetuity, subject only to a quit rent of four shillings sterling per annum i. e. double the proprietary quit rent. * * * *

'For the further encouragement of such families as shall first present themselves, who cannot or do not wish to pay cash, and who desire to be assisted by these proprietors, they offer to lease to such persons 100 acres of land for a farm and one acre in the said town for a house, and to furnish to each family nails and other hardware in sufficient quantity to build a house in size 26 to 28 feet long and 14 to 16 feet wide, and 15 bushels of indian corn for their subsistence the first year, all at an annual rent of 4 *écus* (or one pound sterling).

'If any shall find 100 acres too much or not enough, what they want may be leased on a basis in proportion to that stated above, but upon the same conditions'."

After the failure of Hayward's plan, Brent, who was a Roman Catholic, took occasion, on the succession of William and Mary in 1689, to offer the Brent Town tract as a refuge for his co-religionists in England. Whether his proposal was ever seriously considered seems doubtful, but it at least elicited the promise of Fitzhugh's support, who wrote to Hayward, April 1, 1689:

"What encouragement my poor Endeavors or Interest can give to your pleasing Establishment at Brenton, and a sudden commotion we have had (under the pretended expectation of Indians, of which Capt. Brent has given you a full, just and clear relation) gives me the present opportunity not only to assure the people but also to satisfie the Government that were full encouragement given and Immunity granted to that Town, which might be conducive to draw Inhabitants thither, the country would be indifferent secure from future alarms; and it would be a sure bulwark against real dangers, because either by them or within them must be the Indian Road. A good company of men there settled would be immediately called either to keep off the Enemy at his first approach or cut him short in his Return. This sudden turn of times in England may perhaps at present give a check to the Increment of Brenton from your French expectation, but I believe may be additionally supply'ed by those methods, (Capt. Brent intimates though not plainly expresses), by being a Refuge and Sanctuary for Roman Catholics, And I dare say, let it be increaced by whom it will, our government will give it all the Indulgences that can be reasonably required by reason of its convenient Scituation for a Watch and Defence agst. Indian Depredations and Excursions; neither do I believe that perswasion will be hindered from settling anywhere in this country, especially there where, being Christians, they may secure us against the Heathen."[12]

The final failure of the enterprise is intimated in a later letter of Fitzhugh, dated May 20, 1691. He wrote to Hayward, 'Sir I truly condole your unsuccessful (though chargeable and vigorous) proceeding about Brenton, the unsteadness of the times Since the first undertaking has been a great hindrance thereto, When or Whether they will end, for your advantageous perspect and Interest in that concern, I believe is uncertain. * * I am glad your

Hudson Bay interest makes you some compensation'.[13]

Nevertheless the town site in Fauquier was settled, if sparsely, and the block house served as a point of observation on the movements of the Iroquois and was frequently visited by the local 'Rangers'.

The organization of this force had been suggested by Lord Culpeper some years earlier, and when the Assembly from motives of economy, decided in 1682 to dismantle Berkeley's forts on the heads of the four great rivers, Culpeper's plan to organize and maintain bands of light horsemen to range the woods and guard against surprise attacks by the Indians, was adopted. What success this system of scouting at first had, does not appear, but in March, 1692, the Assembly passed an act which gave Governor Nicholson authority to raise 'one lieutenant, eleven soldiers and two Indians, well furnished with horses and other accoutrements * * * * levied, armed and mustered to range and scout about the great rivers and in such other places as shall be most likely to discover our enemies'.[14]

That the Potomac Rangers were actively employed in the summer of 1692 and that Brent Town was reached on one of their expeditions, we learn from the journal of David Strahan, their lieutenant. He reports:

"July the 3ᵈ: We ranged up Neapsico, and so back of the Inhabitants &c.

July 11ᵗʰ: We ranged up to Brent-towne and ther we lay &c.

The 19th: We ranged up Ackotinck & discovered nothing &c.

So we ranged once in the week until the 20ᵗʰ Septbr: then we marcht to Capt. Masone's & ther we met Capt. Housely

[Owsley][15] & his men, so we drawed out 12 of our best horses: & so we ranged up Ackotinck & ther we lay that night."[16]

Again in 1694 we find the colonial council sending instructions to the Rangers to give 'particular care to guard Brent Town.' After this date little is heard of the place until a controversy arose in 1720 over the boundaries of the original grant, which it appeared had never been marked. The Assembly in that year directed that the tract be surveyed within three years, but this order was apparently ignored and another effort to have its boundaries defined, made by Colonel Carter as agent of the Proprietors in 1723, proved equally futile. Finally, about 1736, the tract was surveyed by James Thomas for William Fairfax, who had succeeded Carter as proprietary agent, and a 'Mr. Savage', representing 'Messrs. Brent, Foote & Co.' When 'so delimited, the greater part of it was found to lie, as contemplated by the grant of 1686, in the fork between Broad and Cedar runs, extending west to a 'back line', which ran from the mouth of Walnut Branch of Cedar to the vicinity of the ford (since known as Linton's), by which the north fork of the Dumfries road crossed Broad run; but there was still included the town site of 1687 with a considerable area below Cedar reaching south between the mouths of Champ's and Dorrell's runs'.[17]

Brent Town appears on Cadwalader Jones' map of 1699, and the location of the tract is indicated on John Warner's Northern Neck map of 1737. The town site is one of three places in Fauquier county shown on John Henry's map of 1770, but is incorrectly placed south of Dorrell's run. It was suggested to the Council as the site of the second

Prince William court house in 1742,[18] and is referred to in the proceedings of the first court for Fauquier in 1759, at which John Catlett was appointed surveyor of the road 'from Brent Town to the Stafford line'.[19]

[1] Lederer, *Discoveries in Three Several Marches*, p. 27.

[2] John Catlett came to Virginia about 1650 from Sittingborne Parish, Kent, England, and took up land on the south bank of the Rappahannock below Robert Taliaferro's. 'He was a leading man on the frontier, and after 1665 was presiding justice of old Rappahannock county. Soon after he returned from the expedition with Lederer he was killed by Indians while serving against them with the militia'. (*Old Prince William*, I, p. 34.)

[3] Lederer, *Discoveries*, etc., p. 28.

[4] *Old Prince William*, I, p. 34.

[5] *Ibid.*, II, p. 608.

[6] *Ibid.*, I, p. 28.

[7] *Va. Magazine*, I, p. 408.

[8] *Old Prince William*, I, p. 178. 'The survival of this instrument [the Brent Town patent] has a curious history. Executed in London, it was acknowledged in Stafford court by William Fitzhugh as attorney for Culpeper and was there recorded, July 13, 1687. The record book is one of those which was lost, but when in 1737, William Byrd was arguing on behalf of the Virginia government that the Rappahannock river named in the final Northern Neck charter of 1688 was the north fork of that stream and not the Rapidan as was claimed by Lord Fairfax, he produced a copy of the Brent Town grant in support of his position and appended it to the report of the Virginia Commissioners which went to London. It is from that record we have rescued it'. (*Ibid.*, I, p. 191).

[9] *Va. Magazine*, XVII, p. 309.

[10] *Old Prince William*, I, p. 179.

[11] Translated from Hayward's original French. (*Ibid.*, I, p. 180.)

[12] *Va. Magazine*, II, p. 275.

[13] *Ibid.*, III, p. 259.

[14] Hening, III, p. 115.

[15] Alarmed by depredations supposed to have been committed by a wandering band of Maryland Indians, the Stafford court under instructions from Governor Nicholson, resolved that Strahan should 'continue his ranging in the upper Parts of the County and Freshes of Potomac' and that as a supplementary force 'ten men under the command of Capt. Thomas Owsley' should be appointed 'to range and scout from Occoquan to the head of the River'. (*Old Prince William*, I, p. 83.)

[16] *Ibid.*, I, p. 85.

[17] *Ibid.*, I, p. 185.

[18] *Va. Magazine*, XV, p. 384.

[19] *Fauquier Court Minute Book*, 1759-63, p. 1.

CHAPTER III

Northern Neck Land Titles[1]

THE territory lying between the Rappahannock and Potomac rivers in which the county of Fauquier is included, is historically known as the Northern Neck. Here, as in other parts of Virginia, the land system adopted at the time of the Jamestown settlement and continued throughout the entire colonial period, was the form of freehold tenure which in the seventeenth century prevailed in England and was generally styled 'free and common socage'.

Feudal land tenure, of which socage tenure was a survival, was based on the principle that the sovereign was the supreme lord of all the land and that everyone held under him as tenant. The terms were fealty and direct service to the Crown by the overlord who, so long as such service was faithfully discharged, held his fief, practically and in relation to all under tenants, as owner of the land.

The under tenant, in turn, held under his overlord by a military tenure, such as Knight's Service, or, in the case of the humbler obligations of the villein to his landlord, by labor performed for so many days in each week or by payment in kind from the produce of his land and stock. Servile tenure of the latter form gradually gave place to a system under which labor service was commuted into money payments, and contemporaneously all military tenures were abolished.

The incidents of socage tenure, or tenure in fee simple, thus evolved, were fealty and a fixed rent,

called the quit-rent, by the payment of which a
tenant was quit or free from all other feudal services. Although the render of this rent constituted
an acknowledgment of the higher title of the landlord, it in no way affected the freeholder's control
of his property or his right to alienate or bequeath
it subject to the terms of his own tenure.[2] In Virginia, titles to land held in free and common socage
were descendable fee titles absolute in the grantee
and subject only to the payment of the quit-rent,
which was reserved in the patent, or deed, and the
non-payment of which within a certain period,[3]
gave the grantor the right to resume possession of
the land as in the case of a leasehold.

The history of Northern Neck titles and the influences under which the land system was administered must be traced back to the first grant of land
to the Virginia Company in 1606. In this company's first charter, governmental as well as commercial and territorial control was reserved by the
Crown, the 'King agreeing that he would grant by
patent, to such persons and for such estates as its
[the Virginia Company's] council should appoint,
all the lands within the territory granted by the
charter, to be held of the Crown as of the Manor
of East Greenwich in Kent, in free and common
socage'.[4] This gave the grantees the status of free
tenants of a royal manor with the sovereign as
their direct overlord.

Under the charter of 1609, however, a different
system was created. The Company was incorporated and invested not only with the power to
grant land, but with rights of government as well,
Virginia thus being transformed into a proprietary
province with a commercial company as its over-

lord.[5] The Company was 'authorized and required
to distribute the lands under its common seal, from
time to time, among the adventurers and planters',[6]
who held under it as under a mesne lord, although
the tenure was the same as in the case of grants
under the previous charter.

When the Company's third and last charter
(1612) was revoked in 1624, all the rights and
powers held by the Company were resumed by the
Crown. The colony then became a royal province
with a governor and council appointed by the King.
Lands were now granted by the colonial government, the Governor being 'by his sacred Majestie's
instruction, authorized by and with the consent of
his Majestie's Council of Virginia to grant by patent, lands to all adventurers and planters', such
lands to be held 'of his Majestie in free and common
socage under the annual rent of one shilling for
every fifty acres'.[7] By this charter the direct overlordship of the Sovereign was re-established, the
Governor making grants of land and collecting fee
rents as agent of the Crown.

The demand of the colonists for greater freedom
and a more popular form of government, had at first
found little favor with the King (James I) who,
restive under parliamentary restraint at home, had
no desire to see the royal prerogative further curtailed by the establishment of liberal institutions
abroad. The Virginia Company, on the other hand,
controlled by Sir Edwin Sandys and his party,
adopted a more progressive policy and eventually
under the charter of 1612 the colony was granted
representative government. On the dissolution of

the Company this privilege was not at first renewed, but Charles I actuated by the favorable reports of Sir Francis Wyatt, then governor, finally yielded to the wishes of the people and the right of representation was restored. Under the Parliament, the House of Burgesses, in which the representatives sat, became the governing body of the colony and Virginia was at that time to all intents and purposes, a republic. Emancipation from court influence having thus been achieved and a substantial measure of independence obtained, it can be imagined with what indignation and chagrin the colonists learned that Charles II had granted a large slice of their territory to a half dozen, or so, of his impoverished followers to be held by them as proprietors under the Crown with all the rights and privileges of manorial lords.

The grant was made at St. Germain-en-Laye, September 18, 1649, Charles, after the death of his father, having assumed the royal title and been proclaimed King in Scotland and some parts of Ireland earlier in the year.[8] The territory granted was described in the charter as 'bounded by and within the head of the rivers of Tappahannock, *alias* Rappahannock, and Quirriough[9] or Pattawomecke Rivers, the Courses of the said Rivers as they are commonly called or known by the Inhabitants and Descriptions of those parts, and Chesapoyocke Bay'.[10] This was the Northern Neck of Virginia which had as early as 1639, attracted the attention of the Somers Islands Company as a convenient outlet for the overflowing population of the Bermudas.[11]

The grantees under this charter were Ralph Lord Hopton, Baron of Stratton; Henry Lord Jermyn,

Baron of St. Edmund's Bury (afterwards Earl of St. Albans); John Lord Culpeper, Baron of Thoresway; Sir John Berkeley (afterwards John Lord Berkeley of Stratton); Sir William Morton, described as one of the justices of the Court of King's Bench; Sir Dudley Wyatt, and Thomas Culpeper,[12] and although the grant remained without force until after the Restoration, it was renewed by Charles, August 3, 1663, and the patentees took steps to establish possession. Their agent, Sir Humphrey Hooke, however, at the outset encountered opposition both from the inhabitants of the granted territory and from the government of the colony, and on the proprietors appealing to the King, a new charter was issued at Westminster, May 8, 1669, which after reciting the death of Ralph Lord Hopton, John Lord Culpeper, Sir Dudley Wyatt and Thomas Culpeper, and the sale by Lord Hopton previous to his death, of his interest in the property to John Trethewy, regranted the territory to Henry Jermyn, Earl of St. Albans, John Lord Berkeley of Stratton, Sir William Morton and John Trethewy.[18]

The only part of the Northern Neck which was colonized and, therefore, at the time affected by this grant, was a narrow strip of land between the rivers, extending northwest toward the falls of the Rappahannock and originally known as 'Chicacoan' from the Indian tribe that had occupied it. It was settled in 1644 by refugees from Maryland who held themselves independent of Virginia and refused to acknowledge that government. However, these people were soon 'reduced' and in 1648 the Chicacoan district was erected into the county of Northumberland which then included the whole of the Northern Neck. Thereafter, the population rapidly

increased and Lancaster was formed from Northumberland in 1651, and Old Rappahannock from
Lancaster in 1656. On the Potomac river side Westmoreland was created in 1653 and Stafford in 1664.
The colonists who had seated these counties were
now greatly disturbed by the interposition of a proprietary overlord, with some justification, it must
be admitted, had the proprietors attempted to exercise all the privileges conferred by the new charter.
It invested them, for instance,

"with power to divide the said tract or territory of land into
counties, hundreds, parishes, tithings, townships, hamlets and
boroughs, and to erect and build cities, towns, parish churches,
colleges, chapels, free schools, almshouses and houses of cor-
rection, and to endow the same, at their free wills and pleasures; and [the King] did appoint them full and perpetual
patrons of all such churches so to be built and endowed with
power of electing, nominating and presenting, any fit person
to the office and place of master of any college, or schoolmaster of any school so to be founded and endowed; with
power also to divide any part or parcels of the said tract or
territory, or portion of lands, into manors, and to call the
same after their own or any of their names, or by other
name or names whatsoever, and within the same to hold a
court, in the nature of a court baron, and to hold pleas of all
actions, trespasses, covenants, accounts, contracts, detinues,
debts and demands whatsoever, where the debt or thing demanded exceed not the value of forty shillings of current
money of England, and to receive and take all amerciaments,
fines, commodities, advantages, perquisites and emoluments
whatsoever, to such respective court barons belonging, or in
any wise appertaining: And further to hold within the said
manors a court leet, and view of frank pledge, of all the
tenants, residents and inhabitants, of the hundreds within such
respective manors, to be holden twice in every year, and to
erect fairs, markets, courts of pipowder, with all things incident thereto."

The grantees, however, were required to recognize title to all lands taken up under head rights prior to September 29, 1661, and were prohibited from 'intermeddling' in military affairs within their territory: they were also made subject to the laws of the colony.[14]

In respect to the land the proprietors under this grant held of the Crown as tenant *in capite* and they and their heirs and assigns, were given license to 'give, grant, or by any ways or means sell or alien, all and singular the premises by these presents granted, and every part and parcel thereof, to any person or persons being willing to contract for or buy the same; to be holden of [the proprietors] as of any of their aforesaid manors, in free and common socage, by fealty only and by suit of court, or by any other lawful tenure or terms used within the kingdom of England, rendering and paying such rents and other lawful reservations, as shall seem fit and convenient to them'.[15]

Obnoxious as these terms were, the landholders particularly resented a further provision which required all persons who had obtained patents from the governor and council subsequent to September 29, 1661, to have their lands re-surveyed for the purpose of receiving new conveyances from the proprietors, and when Thomas Kirton, acting as agent, attempted to enforce this exaction the colonists protested, and a petition was addressed to the King begging a rescission of the more odious features of the grant.

Kirton's order issued September 18, 1672, to the surveyor of Westmoreland county, was in part as follows:

"Impˢ: you are to give notice to all yᵉ inhabitants of yᵉ county of Westmorelanᵈ yᵗ as soone as yᵉ land of yᵉ Northern tract shall be surveighed, yᵉ Hon:ᵇˡᵉ yᵉ pʳprietors intend to grant them Conveighances of all lands taken up since Michaelmas, 1661, upon yᵉ rent of two shill: pʳ hundred acres and under other reasonable covenᵗˢ, and that they shall hold of ther Lordsps in free & common soccadge & not by Knᵗˢ service or any other Terms or service, & yᵗ ther Lordsᵖˢ expect yᵗ all lands, w'soever in yᵉ sᵈ County, be forthwith surveighed at yᵉ Charge of all such as claime yᵉ sᵈ Land Respectively.

*   *   *   *   *

"3.   That for pʳsent, in respect of an addresse lately sent to his Maᵗⁱᵉ by yᵉ inhabitants of this tract, you suspend yᵉ surveighing of any lands untaken up till his Maᵗⁱᵉˢ pleasure be first known, but you may pʳceede to surveigh any lands in controversy or any lands taken up & in Actual possession for whᶜʰ yᵉ claimᵗ paies Rent".

On the above instructions being submitted for record, the General Court, March 25, 1673, after reserving any advantages from the pending petition, declared that 'the Court doth think it very hard that the Tennants who have been long seated and peaceably enjoyed their Estates should pay that Rent which they have formerly paid to his Maᵗⁱᵉˢ Treasurer or deputy according to his Maᵗⁱᵉˢ instructions, or that the said Tennants should be recharged to new survey their lands after so long Tyme of possession'.[16]

While this petition was pending, any hope the colonists may have had of its favorable reception was rudely upset by another grant made by Charles, February 25, 1673, this time of the entire colony for thirty-one years to two court favorites, Henry Bennet, Earl of Arlington, his Secretary of State, and Thomas 2nd Lord Culpeper, eldest son and heir of John Lord Culpeper. This grant included, also, the quit-rents which had accrued since the date of the second Northern Neck charter.[17]

When the news of this latest concession reached the colony, the people 'to their unspeakable griefe and Astonishment', felt that they were now 'reduced to a far worse condition than that wherein they had adventured their lives and fortunes for the planting that Country under the Company',[18] and the Assembly in October, 1674, dispatched commissioners to London to set forth 'the grievous pressures likely to grow upon us' and to seek the annulment of the recent grant and, if possible, of the Northern Neck charter as well.

The colonial representatives on their arrival conferred first with Lords Arlington and Culpeper, who readily enough agreed to relinquish their patent provided Virginia would offer no objection to a new grant assuring them the quit-rents and escheats. The Earl of St. Albans and his associates, who at that time appear to have been Thomas 2nd Lord Culpeper, John Lord Berkeley of Stratton, Sir James Morton, of Kidlington, county Oxford, Alexander Culpeper, Surveyor General of Virginia, and Anthony Trethewy, of St. Stephens in Brannel, county Cornwall,[19] were then approached and proving equally amenable, agreed to take £400 apiece for their interests in the Northern Neck under the charter of 1669.[20] All had gone well so far and the commissioners drew up a petition to the King for the incorporation of the colony under a new charter, which provided for the revocation of the grant of 1673, and gave the colonial government permission to purchase the Northern Neck. It also contained a provision that the governor and council should be consulted before any further proprietary grants could be made and declared that Virginia 'should have no other dependence than upon the Crown of England nor in future be cantonized into parcels by grants made to particular persons'. The petition was presented to the King in Council, June 23, 1675, and being favorably reported upon by the law officers of the Crown in October of that year, Charles ordered that the papers be prepared for his signature. Further delay occurred, but finally April 19, 1676, at the urgent request of the commissioners, the King directed that the new charter should pass under the Great Seal. Before this could be done, however, the news of Bacon's Rebellion had reached England and the order was revoked.[21]

The failure of these negotiations greatly irritated the colonists, who had been 'made desperately uneasie' by the heavy expense of the commission, 'especially when after a whole Years Patience they had no Encouragement from their Agents', and, after the disturbances of Bacon's Rebellion had subsided, they renewed their opposition to the proprietary grants. This effort also proved futile, and Culpeper, in addition to his other emoluments, had now become Governor of Virginia. He had received a commission July 8, 1675, to take effect on the death of Sir William Berkeley, and when that occurred in July, 1677, he immediately took the oath of office. Ordered to repair to his seat of government with all possible despatch, he, on one pretext or another, delayed his departure for over two years and did not arrive in Virginia until May, 1680. During a short stay in the colony he seems to have produced a favorable impression on the planters, and believing that their opposition could eventually

be overcome and, with their good will, the two concessions in which he was interested be made profit-
able, he returned to England to negotiate with his
fellow proprietors for the purchase of their shares.
He effected his purpose in the following summer,
receiving a deed July 21, 1681, which gave him
full control of the Northern Neck property, and on
Arlington's transferring to him his interest in the
charter of 1673, September 10th of the same year,
Culpeper became for the moment, both governor
and nominally sole proprietor of the entire colony.[22]

On his second visit to Virginia in December, 1682,
he took vigorous steps to assert his individual rights
as proprietor of the Northern Neck and to put an
end to the issue of patents in that territory by the
colonial council.[23] He was unsuccessful, however,
in establishing public confidence in the proprietary
as a source of title and his plans for the immediate
development of the property were frustrated by the
consequent disinclination of would-be settlers to
accept his grants.

Culpeper returned to England in May, 1683, in
disobedience of the order delivered to him before
going out to Virginia 'that noe Governor doe come
home into England from his Government' without
first obtaining leave from the King, and Charles,
weary at last of his neglect of duty, ordered an
inquisition to be held on his conduct, as the result
of which Culpeper was removed from office in August, 1683.[24] Fearing now that his Virginia invest-
ments might prove a loss, he succeeded in selling
the Arlington grant to the Crown, and by a deed
dated May 27, 1684, he surrendered this obnoxious
concession in consideration of a pension of £600 to

be paid to him annually for a period of twenty-one years.[25]

As proprietor, he next attempted to sell the Northern Neck charter to the colony, but failing in this, and on his representations to James II that local obstruction had hitherto prevented the settlement of the territory, he obtained a reaffirmation of his title by a grant made September 27, 1688, in which he was recognized as the sole owner and proprietor in fee simple under the patent of 1669, and all the powers and privileges conferred by that charter were confirmed to him. The grant also was 'enlarged' by omitting a proviso contained in the previous charter requiring the lands to be 'possessed, inhabited, or planted at or by the means of procurement' of the patentees within the space of twenty-one years, and its boundaries were significantly defined as 'within *the first heads or springs* of the Rivers', instead of within their 'heads', as in previous charters. In this instrument the governor and council of Virginia and all minor colonial officials were charged 'not to intermeddle with the Disposal, or disturb the said Thomas Lord Culpeper in the full and quiet enjoyment of the aforementioned Tract and Territory, or any Part thereof, or of the hereby granted Escheats, Advowsons, Royalties and Premises, or any of them; but that they and every one of them in their respective Places and Stations be aiding and assisting to him'.[26]

In the twenty-five years that had elapsed since Charles II's renewal of the original Northern Neck charter in 1663, only two patents to land in the proprietary had been recorded. Of the agents during this period, Kirton had accomplished nothing beyond opening an office in Northumberland and commissioning a few surveyors, and in 1673 he was succeeded by William Aretkin, to whom fell the duty of registering the first Northern Neck grant, that of the Mt. Vernon tract to Nicholas Spencer and John Washington in March, 1675.[27] It was issued by Culpeper as managing partner and if it was meant as a test of public confidence in the validity of his charter, it failed, as the grantees applied for and obtained a confirmatory patent from the colonial council in 1677.[28]   The other grant made at this time was that of the Brent Town tract in 1687.[29]

Lord Culpeper died in London, January 27, 1689,[30] and his interest in the Northern Neck descended to his only daughter Catherine,[31] a minor, who, shortly after her father's death,[32] married Thomas, fifth Baron Fairfax of Cameron.[33]

It appeared that Culpeper in October, 1688, had settled his estate upon trustees for the benefit of two daughters by a Mrs. Willis, with whom he had been living for many years, and that by a will, dated January 17, 1689, he had confirmed the conveyance. His widow, Margaret, Lady Culpeper, in ignorance of the existence of such a will, had sued out letters of administration on his estate, only to find herself blocked by this settlement.   She then filed a claim in chancery alleging undue influence and fraud, and later had a bill introduced in the House of Lords to set aside her husband's will.   The latter failed, but eventually her son-in-law, Thomas, fifth Lord Fairfax, negotiated a compromise by which Leeds Cas-

tle and the estates in Kent together with Lord
Culpeper's interest in the Northern Neck, were
secured for her daughter. Fairfax subsequently
took an active part in the management of the proprietary and it was through his efforts that the
collection of quit-rents in Westmoreland became
possible and that Robert Carter was secured as
proprietary agent.[34]

Colonel Nicholas Spencer, who had succeeded
Aretkin as agent in 1677, died in 1689, a few months
after Lord Culpeper's death, and in 1690 Colonel
Phillip Ludwell, then Governor of North Carolina,
was appointed in his place.[35] Ludwell inaugurated
his agency by opening land books for the proprietary, the first entry in which is dated August 29,
1690.[36] These manuscript records, continued until
1781, were after the Revolution, transferred to the
Land Office at Richmond by order of the Assembly[37]
and today constitute one of the most important
source records of Virginia history. At this time,
too, the Stuart grant of 1688 was confirmed by
William and Mary. Virginia had again petitioned
the Crown to take over the Northern Neck, but
the Culpeper heirs with more confidence in their
influence at court than was anticipated, filed a
counter petition in which they asked that the
validity of their charter be investigated and if sustained that the charter be confirmed. The Privy
Council referred both petitions to the Attorney
General and on his report an order was entered
January 11, 1694: 'That the Pet[n] Margaret Lady
Culpeper, Thomas Lord Fairfax, Katherine his wife
and Alexander Culpeper, Esq[r] be permitted to enjoy
the said Letters Patents according to Law, so as
they keep strictly to the Tenor thereof, in Execu-

tion of the several powers and authorities thereby granted; of which all Persons whom it may concern are to take notice'.[38]

In the few patents issued by Ludwell, 1690-1692, Alexander Culpeper's interest in the proprietary is recited, the proprietors being described as 'ye Honorable Mistress Katherine Culpeper sole daughter and heire of ye sd. Thomas late Lord Culpeper & Allexr. Culpeper, Esq., who cometh in part Proprietor by lawfull conveyances from Thomas late Lord Culpeper and confirmed by ye sd. Mistress Katherine Culpeper, who are thereby now become ye lone and lawfull Proprietors of said tract or territory'.[39]

Alexander Culpeper's partnership had existed since the grant of 1669, under which he and Thomas 2nd Lord Culpeper, although not named in the charter, each held a one-sixth interest as heirs respectively of Thomas Culpeper and John Lord Culpeper. When Thomas 2nd Lord Culpeper purchased the other interests and nominally became sole proprietor in 1688, Alexander Culpeper evidently retained his original one-sixth, for in his will, proved January 5, 1695, in which he described himself as 'of Hollingborne in co. Kent, Esqr.', he bequeathed his 'one full sixth part' of the Northern Neck of Virginia to Margaret Lady Culpeper.[40] Lady Culpeper's name, however, first appears in Northern Neck patents as her husband's administratrix soon after the order of William and Mary was made confirming the Culpeper grant. Thomas 5th Lord Fairfax's name, as Catherine Culpeper's husband, was also added at this time, and from October 1, 1694, to July 2, 1709, patents were issued in the names of 'Marguritte Lady Culpeper, Thomas Lord Fairfax and Catharine his wife', Alexander Culpeper appearing as part proprietor until 1698,[41] although he died a few months after the first patent bearing Lady Culpeper's name was issued.[42]

Many of the Northern Neck grants, as in this case, were issued under a misunderstanding by the Virginia agents of the frequent changes in proprietorship, and to protect the grantees from defects in title arising from these and other irregularities in conveyancing, the Assembly, in 1736, passed an act providing that 'the grantees, their heirs and assigns, respectively, shall forever hereafter peaceably and quietly have, hold and enjoy the same granted premises, according to such granted estates, under the rents and services by the said grants reserved, notwithstanding the infancy, coverture or any misprision or mistake of the names, dignity or title of the said proprietors, or either of them.'[43]

During these transfers of title Colonel Ludwell, after a short term of office, had been succeeded by George Brent of Woodstock, one of the Brent Town proprietors, and William Fitzhugh of Bedford, extracts from whose voluminous correspondence with Nicholas Hayward, of London, have been cited in a previous chapter. Their agency was chiefly notable for the fact that in refusing Colonel Robert Carter the grant of some escheated lands they aroused his enmity, expressed later in an address to the Crown which he persuaded the House of Burgesses to adopt. In it he inveighed against the administration of the Northern Neck agents, stating that 'for lands lapsing for want of Seating, none such will happen, for in the Conveyances of

the sd. Lds. Agents there is not any Limitation upon
that accounte, and accordingly a man may hold
50,000 or more acres of land by a secure title, and
that without so much as actually seating or building
upon any part of it';[44] a practice of which he himself
later became the chief exponent.   His somewhat
splenetic attack in this instance failed, and his interests were soon after ranged with those of the
proprietors.

Brent, who seems to have controlled Fitzhugh in
their joint administration of the agency, died in
1699, and Fitzhugh who survived him by eighteen
months, did much in that time to smooth out the
local antagonisms which Brent's arbitrary methods
had created.   The land business of the proprietary
was now becoming established; the charter had recently been upheld by an important decision; land
books had been opened and, following the example
of the second Richard Lee who had paid a composition[45] on his own large holdings, other landlords
in Westmoreland were paying their fees to the proprietary agents.[46]   At this juncture Thomas 5th
Lord Fairfax, acting for his wife and Lady Culpeper, sought the advice of Micajah Perry, the leading Virginia merchant of his day in London, and
on his recommendation appointed Colonel Robert
Carter, 'one of the greatest freeholders in that
proprietary',[47] as agent in the spring of 1702.   The
wisdom of this appointment was soon apparent and
from it dates the success of the Culpeper enterprise,
although many controversies were still to be waged
and much litigation was to follow.[48]

Already a dispute had arisen which was terminated forty years later by the decision of the Privy
Council in the cause of *Virginia* v. *Fairfax*.   The

Northern Neck had been defined in the various charters as comprising the tract bounded within the
heads of the rivers Rappahannock and Potomac, the
courses of the rivers and Chesapeake bay, but as
both of these rivers forked above their falls, the
question arose as to which in each case was the
tributary and which the main stream. The first
attempt to obtain a decision in this prolonged controversy was made in 1706. On the colonial council
in November of that year granting a piece of land in
the forks of the Rappahannock to Henry Beverley,
Colonel Carter on behalf of the proprietors filed a
protest claiming that the south branch of the river,
afterwards known as the Rapidan, was the true
boundary of the Northern Neck, and that the land
granted by the Council was, therefore, within the
proprietary. The Council then issued an order sus-
pending further grants in this region, either by the
Crown or the proprietors, until both branches of the
river could be viewed and the main stream determined. The commissioners appointed for this
purpose, however, reported that both streams 'appeared to be of equal magnitude' and, no decision
being reached, grants by the Council were resumed.[49]

While these negotiations were pending further
changes in succession to the proprietary title occurred, with continued confusion in contemporary
conveyances. Thomas 5th Lord Fairfax died January 6, 1710,[50] and although Margaret Lady Culpeper
died May 10th of the same year,[51] grants were made
in the names of 'Marguritte Lady Culpeper and
Catherine Lady Fairfax' from July 20, 1710, to May
11, 1711, after which 'the Right Honorable Katherine Lady Fairfax, Dutchess Dowager[52] (*sic*) of

Cameron in Scotland, the only daughter and Heir of
Thomas, late Lord, and Marguritte, late Lady Culpeper, Decd.', appears as the 'sole and only Proprietor of the Northern Neck of Virginia.' This recital,
however, omits the mention of Alexander Culpeper's
one-sixth interest which Lady Culpeper had inherited from him and which in her will, proved June
19, 1710,[53] she left in fee to her grandson, Thomas
6th Lord Fairfax. Lady Fairfax, although described
as 'the sole and only proprietor,' represented, as a
matter of fact, only five shares in the proprietary,
the remaining one share being held by her son.

Left with an involved estate in England on her
hands and sadly in need of funds, Lady Fairfax now
turned her attention to her Virginia possessions, the
income from which seemed to her insufficient for so
extensive a property. Hints of mismanagement
also reached her and she was informed by one ad-
viser that 'Mr. Perry is a sharp man and I fear you
are but very indifferently dealt with by him and his
friend [Colonel Carter] in Virginia'.

On such reports and in ignorance of real conditions in the colony, she broke off relations with
Perry and his correspondent, and turned her affairs
over to Thomas Corbin, another prominent Virginia
merchant in London, who named as resident agents
his brother-in-law, Edmund Jennings, and his
nephew, Thomas Lee. Colonel Carter was thus
superseded, and Jennings being in England at the
time, a power of attorney was issued December 11
1711, to young Lee, who for four years remained
in sole charge in Virginia.[54] Lee signed his first
grant in 1713, and of those subsequently issued by

him were many to lands in the Elk Marsh, in what was afterwards Fauquier county. Jennings returned to Virginia in 1716 and took over the general management of the proprietary, leaving the books and estate office to Lee, but this arrangement proved unsatisfactory and on a change of title in 1719, both he and Lee were removed.[55]

[1] Reference is made to an article by the writer entitled 'Northern Neck Lands', published in Bulletin No. 1, of the Fauquier Historical Society, August, 1921.

[2] Bond, *The Quit-rent System in the American Colonies,* p. 17.

[3] This period was two years in the Northern Neck and three years in other parts of the colony.

[4] *Rev. Code,* 1819, II, p. 333.

[5] Kingsbury, *Records Va. Co.,* I, p. 22.

[6] *Rev. Code,* 1819, II, p. 333.

[7] Hening, II, p. 320.

[8] His succession was acknowledged in Virginia by an act of Assembly passed October 10, 1649, which provided, 'that what persons soever shall by words or speeches indeavor to insinuate any doubt, scruple or question of or concerning the undoubted and inherent right of his Majesty that now is to the colony of Virginia, and all other his majesties dominions and countryes as King and Supreame Gouvernour, such words and speeches shall be adjudged high treason'. (Hening, I, p. 358.)

[9] Quirriough was the name given on Smith's Map of 1612, to Aquia Creek, which was confused on later maps with the main stream of the Potomac. (*Old Prince William,* II, p. 602.)

[10] From recital of this charter in Cal. Am. & W. I., 1669-74, No. 63, p. 22. (*Ibid.,* II, pp. 604 and 646.)

[11] *Va. Magazine,* XII, p. 395.

[12] *Rev. Code,* 1819, I, p. 343.

The two Culpepers who appear as grantees under this charter were first cousins. Sir John Culpeper (1600-1660), first Baron Culpeper of Thoresway, was the son of Thomas Culpeper of Wigsell, co. Sussex, and described himself as of Hollingbourne, co. Kent. He matriculated at Oxford, in 1616, and was admitted to the Middle Temple in 1618. He was knighted by James I in 1622, and served in wars abroad for five years under Gustavus Adolphus. He was returned to the Short Parliament (1640) from Rye, and sat in the Long Parliament as Knight of the Shire for Kent. In 1642 under Charles I, Culpeper was sworn as a member of the Privy Council and appointed Chancellor of the Exchequer, which office he subsequently exchanged for Master of the Rolls. He fought gallantly under Prince Rupert at Edgehill and again distinguished himself at Newbury. For this service he was raised to the peerage in 1644. Under the Parliament his estates were forfeited, but he lived to take part in Charles II's entry into London and thereafter sat in the Privy Council and resumed his office as Master of the Rolls.

He m. 1st., 1628, Philippa, dau. of Sir Geo. Snelling, by whom he had a son and a dau.

He m. 2nd., 1631, Judith, dau. of Sir Thomas Culpeper, called "the elder", by whom he had three dau.'s; a son who d. in infancy, and Thomas (1635-1689) who succeeded as second Lord Culpeper. (*Proprietors of the Northern Neck,* hereafter cited as *Proprietors,* pp. 62-70.)

Thomas Culpeper (1602-1652), of the Middle Temple, was the son of John Culpeper of Feckenham, co. Worcester. He took part in the royalist plots in Kent, 1648, and in the defence of Colchester in June of that year. After the capitulation of that place he was liberated, probably at the cost of all he possessed, made his way to France and was present at St. Germain-en-Laye, when the first patent of the Northern Neck was issued.

He m., 1628, Katherine, dau. of Sir Warham St. Leger, of Ulcombe, co. Kent, and adopted dau. of Alexander Culpeper of Greenway Court, by whom he had several dau.'s including Frances, wife of Sir William Berkeley, and a son, Alexander (1631-1694), of Hollingbourne, co. Kent, who was Surveyor General of Va., 1671-1694, and who inherited from him his one-sixth interest in the Northern Neck. (*Proprietors,* pp. 90-103, 107-111).

[13] *Rev. Code,* 1819, I, p. 344.

[14] In the petition to the Commissioners of Foreign Plantations for a grant of land between the rivers Rappahannock and Potomac in 1639, the Somers Islands Company had asked that, if granted, the territory should be 'exempted from the jurisdiction of Virginia', and although the grant was never made, the idea of the Northern Neck as a separate political division was reflected in the grants of 1649 and 1669. (*Va. Mag.,* XII, pp. 395-6.)

[15] *Rev. Code,* 1819, p. 345.

[16] *W. & M. Quarterly,* VI, pp. 222-6.

[17] Hening, II, p. 569. It appears that Col. Henry Norwood of Gloucestershire, England, a staunch royalist, had received from Charles II, September 22, 1650, a commission as Treasurer of Virginia with a grant of all the quit-rents, and that after the Restoration these had been collected and paid to him by his deputies, Francis Moryson and Thomas Ludwell. As Arlington and Culpeper's charter conflicted with this grant, they deemed it expedient to make a compromise with Norwood by which he was to receive one-third of their profits. Culpeper subsequently bought Norwood's interest under this arrangement, as he did Arlington's. (*Va. Mag.,* XXXIII, p. 7.)

[18] Wertenbaker, *Va. Under the Stuarts,* p. 124.

[19] Burke, *History of Virginia,* II, App., p. liv. Anthony Trethewy was the brother and assignee of John Trethewy, who purchased Lord Hopton's original interest under the charter of 1649.

[20] *W. & M. Quarterly,* VI, pp. 222-6. Governor Berkeley had offered to lend the colony £1200 toward the purchase of the proprietors' interests. (*Virginia Land Grants,* p. 65.)

[21] Wertenbaker, *Va. Under the Stuarts,* p. 126.

[22] *Va. Land Grants,* pp. 68-69.

[23] Occasional 'headright' patents were issued for Northern Neck lands by the Colonial Council until the Restoration, when the charter of 1649 was recognized and the Crown issued orders to the colonial government to assist the proprietors in asserting their rights in this territory. These orders were locally resisted and the Council compromised by re-

fusing to authorize new head right patents, but continued the re-issue
of patents for entries which had already been made. It was this practice
that Lord Culpeper stopped on his accession to office as Governor of the
Colony. (*Old Prince William*, II, p. 677-8.)

[24] Wertenbaker, *Va. Under the Stuarts*, p. 239.

[25] *W. & M. Quarterly*, VI, pp. 222-6.

[26] *Grant of the Northern Neck in Virginia to Lord Culpeper*, from a
contemporary print in Harvard College Library.

[27] This was a tract of 5,000 acres 'lying upon the freshes of Potomack
river' surveyed by John Alexander, April 27, 1669, for 'Coll. Nicholas
Spencer and Lieut. Coll. John Washington' and granted to them March
1, 1674/5 by 'The Owners and proprietors of all that Tract and Terry-
tory of Land in Virginia in America mentioned in his Majty's Letters
patent under the Broad Seale of England bearing date the eighth day
of May in the one and twentieth year of his now Majesty's reign'.
(*Old Prince William*, I, p. 49). The original patent now hangs in the
hall at Mt. Vernon and is signed 'Tho. Culpeper, Antho. Trethewy',
and sealed with the common seal of the proprietors.

[28] *Old Prince William*, I, p. 50.

[29] *Ibid.*, I, p. 195.

[30] Thomas 2nd Lord Culpeper sat in the House of Lords, January
30, 1689, and his brother John, who succeeded to the title, occupied his
seat March 2, 1689.

[31] In a patent dated Aug. 29, 1690, she is also described as 'sole
daughter and heire to ye sd. Thomas late Lord Culpeper'. (*Northern
Neck Grants*, I, p. 1).

[32] Catherine Culpeper married Thomas 5th Lord Fairfax prior to
November 6, 1690. See letter of Lord Howard of Effingham to the
Council in Virginia under that date, in which he says, 'I have already
spoken to my Lord Fairfax who married Mrs. Culpeper', etc. (*Va.
Mag.*, IX, p. 32).

[33] This title dates from 1627 when Sir Thomas Fairfax, Knight (1560-
1640), of Denton, near Otley, Yorkshire, was created 1st Baron Fairfax
of Cameron in the peerage of Scotland. His son Ferdinando Fairfax
(1584-1648), the 2nd baron, represented Yorkshire in the Long Parliament of 1640, sitting in the House of Commons. He commanded
the Parliamentary forces in Yorkshire on the outbreak of the Civil
War in 1642. Unsuccessful at first he subsequently defended Hull and
was victorious at Selby in 1644. At Marston Moor he commanded the
infantry. He later held the position of Governor of York. His oldest
son Thomas succeeded him as 3rd baron. Charles, his second son, a
colonel of horse, was killed at Marston Moor.

Thomas Fairfax (1612-1671), the 3rd baron, first served under Charles
I as commander of a troop and was knighted by him in 1640. He was
opposed to the arbitrary prerogative of the Crown and when war broke
out was made lieutenant general of the horse under his father. At the
battle of Marston Moor, Sir Thomas bore himself with the greatest
gallantry and although severely wounded managed to join Cromwell
and the victorious cavalry on the other wing of the army. On the removal of Essex from supreme command he was selected as the new
lord general, with Cromwell as his lieutenant general and cavalry commander. This appointment was justified by his victory at Naseby, and
the subsequent reduction of the whole of the west of England. He

52   FAUQUIER DURING THE PROPRIETORSHIP

succeeded his father in the barony in 1648 and in the same year took
the field against the English royalists, his operations culminating in the
successful siege of Colchester. He was placed at the head of the judges
to try Charles I, but on being convinced that the King's death was intended, refused to act. When the Scots proclaimed Charles II in 1649
and it was planned to send an army against them, Fairfax resigned his
commission and was succeeded by Cromwell. He was then given a
pension of £5,000 a year and lived in retirement on his estates in Yorkshire until Cromwell's death. Convinced of the futility of the government under the Commonwealth he took arms in 1659 against Lambert's
army and his operations led to the restoration of the monarchy. Fairfax was made head of a commission to wait on Charles II and urge his
return, and later provided the horse on which the king rode at his
coronation. He died at Nunappleton, November 12, 1671. It is said of
him that 'as a soldier he was exact and methodical in planning, in the
heat of battle so highly transported that scarce anyone durst speak a
word to him, chivalrous and punctilious in his dealings with his own
men and the enemy. Honor and conscientiousness were equally characteristic of his private and public character'. (*Enc. Brit.* X, pp. 131-2).
He had issue, Elizabeth, who died in infancy, and Mary, who married
George Villiers, 2nd Duke of Buckingham and died without issue.

Henry Fairfax (1631-1688), the 4th baron, was a first cousin of his
predecessor. He was M. P. for Yorkshire in 1678-1685, and was
succeeded by his son.

Thomas Fairfax (1657-1709), the 5th Baron, was M. P. for York-
shire, 1688-1707; Lieut. Col. 3rd Horse Guards, 1688; promoted to
King's Own Reg't. of Horse, 1693, and made Brigadier General, 1701,
(*Burke's Peerage*, 1914, p. 754).

34 *Proprietors*, pp. 85-88.

35 *W. & M. Quarterly*, VI, pp. 222-6.

36 *N. N. Grants*, I, p. 1.

37 Act of Oct. 17, 1785 (*Rev. Code*, 1819, I, p. 350).

38 *Va. Land Grants*, p. 79.

39 *N. N. Grants*, I.

40 *Proprietors*, p. 111. A certificate was obtained by the Culpepers in
1675 from the grantees named in the charter of 1669, that 'Thomas
Lord Culpeper, and Alexander Culpeper, Esq., by collateral agreement
with us do hold two sixths part of the said Grant.' (*Ibid.*, p. 110.)

41 *N. N. Grants*, II and III.

42 Alexander Culpeper was buried Dec. 26, 1694. (*Proprietors*, p. 110).

43 *Rev. Code*, 1819, I, p. 349.

44 *Old Prince William*, I, p. 239.

45 A composition, theoretically, was a sum paid by the tenant for the
commutation of indefinite feudal services to the fixed service expressed
by the annual payment of a money rent. (*Marshall v. Conrad*, Call, V,
p. 398). The proprietors of the Northern Neck charged a composition
or 'fine', on each grant made by them, the amount at this time being
five shillings for every one hundred acres up to six hundred, and ten
shillings for every one hundred acres above six hundred, to be paid
within six months after the patent was signed and delivered. The composition money was payable in pounds sterling, in Spanish pieces of eigh'
at the rate of five shillings for each piece, or in good tobacco at the rate
of six shillings per one hundred pounds. (*Northern Neck Grants*, I).

[46] *W. & M. Quarterly*, VI, pp. 222-6.

[47] *Va. Land Grants*, p. 93.

[48] Thomas 5th Lord Fairfax had petitioned the Crown in 1708 to be vested with 'the lott and cope, and office of Bergmaster in the wapentake of Wicksworth, in the county of Derby, which was then worth £300 per annum, but on receiving a report from Colonel Carter that the income from the Northern Neck in 1708 had grown to £584, 13s. 2d., the petition was withdrawn.' (*Ibid.*, p. 96).

[49] *Hite* v. *Fairfax*, Call, IV, pp. 42 and 57.

[50] *Proprietors*, p. 122.

[51] Wykeham-Martin, *Leeds Castle*, p. 172.

[52] *N. N. Grants*, IV. In a grant April 11, 1712, this title is changed to "Baroness Dowager". (*Ibid.*, V).

[53] *Proprietors*, p. 83.

[54] *Old Prince William*, I, p. 146.

[55] *Ibid.*, p. 231.

CHAPTER IV

Lord Fairfax's Estate.

THE conditions under which the seating of Fauquier was effected and the boundaries of the proprietary carried across the Blue Ridge, can best be explained by further developing the history of the Northern Neck charter and by following the controversies which led to the final determination of the geographical limits of the grant and the assertion of the proprietor's rights within the boundaries eventually established. The discussion of this subject will also serve to introduce the Lord Fairfax in whom all traditions of the Northern Neck popularly center and to whom, in fact, its successful administration was ultimately due.

Catherine Lady Fairfax died at Leeds Castle in May, 1719,[1] leaving three sons and three daughters: Margaret (1692-1755), who married Dr. David Wilkins and died without issue; Thomas, sixth Baron Fairfax of Cameron; Henry Culpeper (1697-1734),[2] who died unmarried; Frances (1703-1791), who married Denny Martin of Salts, in Loose, county Kent, and had three sons, Denny Martin, Thomas Bryan Martin and Philip Martin, to whom title to the Culpeper estates in both England and America finally passed; Mary (1705-1739), who died unmarried; and Robert (1706-1793), who succeeded his brother Thomas, as seventh baron.[3]

Thomas 6th Lord Fairfax, who will hereafter be referred to as Lord Fairfax, was born at Leeds Castle in the county of Kent, October 22, 1693. He succeeded to the title on the death of his father in 1710, and matriculated at Oriel College, Oxford, January 21st of the same year. There he acquired some literary reputation and, according to Archdeacon Burnaby, became a contributor to the *Spectator*. Shortly after his coming of age, the final alienation of the Fairfax estates in Yorkshire occurred, the trustees under the fifth Lord Fairfax's will finding it necessary under its terms to sell Denton and Bilborough,[4] the remaining properties, to pay the testator's debts. In this transaction the young Lord Fairfax joined, feeling bound in honor, to give effect to his father's intention, but this disposition of his Fairfax patrimony reduced him at the time to the income derived from his grandmother Culpeper's legacy, which, in addition to her one-sixth interest in the Northern Neck, consisted of £4,000 in 'Mault Tickets'.[5]

When his mother died, Lord Fairfax was in his twenty-sixth year and, less straitened in circumstances, seems to have embarked on a public career, holding in 1721 the post of Treasurer of the Household under the Lord Chamberlain at the court of George I, and, in the military tradition of his family, a cornetcy in the Royal Horse Guards. This phase of his life, however, was a comparatively brief one, and whether it was that he lost his place at court on a change of administration or was discouraged by the failure of an ambitious matrimonial project, he shortly afterwards retired to Leeds Castle, which he had inherited from his mother, and there until 1733, led the life of a country gentleman and devoted himself to fox hunting and the breeding of hounds.[6]

Lady Fairfax had resented the extravagance
of her husband's family and the loss of the Fairfax
estates after his death, and her bitterness was reflected in the restrictions she placed on the inheritance of her property by her eldest son. By her will
she vested her manors in England and her interests
in Virginia, in trustees, to be held by them for the
payment of certain legacies and then for the benefit
of her son Thomas for life, and 'to his sons successively in tail male'. Failing issue by him, the property passed on similar terms to his brothers, and in
default, to the testatrix's daughters, 'in common in
tail'.[7]

In respect to the Northern Neck, therefore, Lord
Fairfax, on his mother's death, held her five-sixths
interest as tenant in tail, and of this interest he
could neither make conveyance nor testamentary
disposition. The one-sixth interest, on the other
hand, which he had inherited from his grandmother
Lady Culpeper, he held in fee, that is to say, he
had the right to sell or otherwise dispose of his
proprietary rights to the extent of that interest. In
both cases, however, he had power to grant the
lands held by him as proprietor to such persons as
made entry for them.

To understand correctly the land transactions of
the proprietors it must be borne in mind that out-
right sales of land were never made by them. With
the exception of the manors, in which land was held
on long terms of years or lives, the land was
granted in fee but subject to a reservation of rent
and whatever disposition a tenant might make of
it, his successors in title held under the proprietor
as in the case of the original grantee. After the
proprietor, on his part, had granted the land his

subsequent interest in it consisted of the right to collect the quit-rents or to resume possession should the quit-rents remain unpaid. In the case of lands already granted succession in proprietorship, therefore, included only the transfer of this right and did not disturb the tenant in his possession. Over the ungranted lands,[8] each proprietor could exercise the right under his charter of making original grants, and, as such lands were necessarily unproductive of revenue until settled, patents were issued for them as fast as tenants could be found.

Lord Fairfax at first appears to have taken no interest in the management of the Northern Neck property, leaving the business to Colonel William Cage, the trustee named in Lady Fairfax's will, who immediately upon her death took steps to place the local agency in competent hands. After some negotiation Colonel Robert Carter was induced to resume the office, but this time on the basis of a lease to him of the entire proprietary for a fixed yearly rent of £450.[9] Under this arrangement the land office was reopened at Corotoman, the first grant being issued December 1, 1722. In this and subsequent grants during Carter's second agency, the proprietors were recited as:

'The Right Honourable Thomas Lord Fairfax of Leeds Castle in The County of Kent and Baron of Cameron in Scotland, and William Cage of Millgate in the parish of Bearstead in the County of Kent, Esqr., devisee in trust and sole executor of the last will and testament of the Right Honourable Catherine Lady Fairfax deceased, Proprietors of the Northern Neck of Virginia.'[10]

The new agent, in addition to actively promoting immigration, now put into effect certain feudal

privileges granted to the proprietors in the charter
of 1688. Among these was the collection of deodands
and forfeitures for crime, which under the charter
of 1669 appertained to the jurisdiction of a court-leet
held within a duly constituted manor, as that institution was known in England. The application
of the manorial principle to conditions in America,
however, having proved impracticable under Lord
Baltimore's government in Maryland, Lord Culpeper in his last charter had the forfeitures adjudged by the county courts made collectible by the
proprietors, and in the exercise of this privilege
Carter added materially to the profits of his lease.[11]

During Colonel Carter's second agency questions
of the boundaries of the Northern Neck grant were
constantly arising. The settlements in this territory had been progressing steadily towards the
mountains and for convenience of administration
more definite limits were being assigned to its political divisions.[12] Old Rappahannock county had
been divided into Richmond and Essex in 1692, and
from Richmond, King George had been formed in
1721, while Spotsylvania, from whose territory the
Northern Neck counties of Culpeper and Madison
were taken at a later date, had been created from
Essex in the same year. The lands in these counties
were taken up by new settlers, and by small farmers
from the tidewater region who were attracted by
the more productive Piedmont soils. Beyond these
settlements an advance guard of pioneers was pushing forward and before 1728 had crossed the mountains,[13] while great landholders of the tidewater
counties were also turning their attention to the

new country west of the Blue Ridge. A much more
numerous migration into this part of the Northern
Neck, however, had set in from another source, and
to these people the colonial council was making
concessions either in ignorance of the limits of Lord
Fairfax's grant or with little regard to his proprietary rights. The immigrants were of German and
Scotch-Irish origin from Pennsylvania and other
northern colonies, who had learned of the fertile
Shenandoah lands from the Indian traders returning from their expeditions through the valleys between the Blue Ridge and the Alleghany mountains.

To promote colonization on the new frontier, the
governor and council, exercising the general powers
of the Crown, had adopted the practice of issuing
orders giving the applicant permission to take up
lands located by him, and if settled with one family
to every one thousand acres within the space of two
years, to issue patents 'to him & them for the same
in Such Several Tracts & Dividends as they shall
think Fit, & in the meantime that the same be reserved Free from the entry of any other p'son'.[14]
The land when granted was to be held by them
'under the same Condicons of Cultivation & planting
and paym't of Quit Rents as the lands held of his
Majesty within this Dominion'.[15]

Colonel Carter had in such cases protested that
lands on the Shenandoah were within the proprietary, but had been unable to obtain a suspension
of the orders. An order, however, of such magnitude was now issued as to demand vigorous action
by the Proprietor himself. Two land speculators
from Pennsylvania, Jost Hite and Robert McKay,
had petitioned the Council, October 21, 1731, alleging 'that they and divers other families to the

number of one hundred are desirous to remove from thence and Seat themselves on the back of the Great Mountains within this Colony, & praying that one hundred thousand acres of Land' be assigned to them between the lands granted John Van Meter, Jacob Stover and others, and the residue upon and including the several branches of the 'Sherundo'.[16] On securing an order giving them leave to locate this tract, Hite, McKay and their following, including Robert Green and William Duff who were later taken into partnership, moved from Pennsylvania, 'cutting their road from York, and crossing the Cohongoruton about two miles above Harper's Ferry'. Their party, consisting of fifteen families, reached the Shenandoah Valley and effected a settlement in 1732.[17] By 1734, Hite and his associates, however, had succeeded in procuring only forty families, and the Council then extended the time allowed them for complying with the conditions of the order, to Christmas, 1735.[18] At that date fifty-four families all told had been established and the partners having filed their surveys, became entitled under the council order to patents for 54,000 acres of land. In the meantime, however, Lord Fairfax had taken steps to halt these encroachments until his boundaries could be finally determined.[19]

The colonial authorities, also, were pressing for a decision definitely fixing the limits of the Northern Neck grant. Lieutenant-Governor William Gooch in June, 1729, had addressed a communication to the Lords of Trade and Plantations, in which he called their attention to the ambiguity of the proprietor's charter arising from the fact that both the Rappahannock and Potomac rivers branched several times above their falls and that it was impossible

to distinguish which were the branches and which
the main stream. He had further expressed his
intention to 'refuse the suspension of granting of
patents, notwithstanding the remonstrances of the
proprietor's agent, until the case should be fairly
stated and determined according to the genuine construction of the proprietor's charter'. His letter was
followed by a petition to the King in Council, concurred in by the House of Burgesses, in June, 1730,
which stated 'that the head springs of the Rappahannock and Potomac are not yet known to any of
your Majesty's subjects; but much inconvenience
has resulted to grantees therefrom', and prayed, 'the
adoption of such measures as might lead to their
ascertainment to the satisfaction of all interested'.[20]

When this petition finally reached England in
1732, the report of Hite's application for land in
the valley had been received by Lord Fairfax, soon
to be followed by the news of Colonel Carter's
death. Aroused by the emergency, he now took
matters into his own hands and for the first time
asserted his individual authority as proprietor. In
July, 1733, he filed a counter petition with the
Crown, in which he set forth 'that the Governor
and council of Virginia had, from time to time, actually taken upon them to issue grants for several
parcels of land, part of the petitioner's said tract;
and had actually run out surveys of several other
parcels of land, though the same, as the petitioner
apprehends, were clearly within the bounds of the
lands so granted from the Crown as aforesaid,
under which the petitioner claims. The petition
therefore prayed, that your majesty would be
pleased to order a commission to issue for running
out, marking and ascertaining the bounds of the pe-

titioner's said tract', and in the meantime that no more patents be issued for lands in the disputed territory. Agreeably to this petition a Privy Council order was issued November 29, 1733, restraining the governor and council from perfecting such grants and directing them to appoint commissioners to ascertain the true boundaries of the proprietary.[21] These instructions, however, were not delivered until Lord Fairfax reached Virginia in May, 1735.[22]

On his arrival the Proprietor repaired to Williamsburg and after presenting letters of introduction to the Governor and exchanging ceremonial visits, seems at first to have applied himself to the task of establishing a friendly footing at the capital and settling some of the contentions that had arisen between the proprietary office and the landholders of the Northern Neck. Before taking up the survey of his boundaries he effected an agreement with the colonial authorities resulting in the act of 1736, referred to in the last chapter. The bill was expeditiously put through. It was introduced September 13th and in ten days, during which Lord Fairfax was the guest of Governor Gooch and publicly expressed his acquiescence, it was enacted and received the governor's approval.[23] In addition to smoothing out irregularities in conveyancing by successive Northern Neck agents, the act acknowledged Lord Fairfax as the sole owner of the proprietary and eliminated Lady Fairfax's trustee, the recital of proprietary interest in all subsequent grants reading:

'The Right Honourable Thomas Lord Fairfax, Baron of Cameron in that part of Great Britain called Scotland, Proprietor of the Northern Neck of Virginia'.[24]

When this matter was well under way Gooch in compliance with the Order in Council of November, 1733, appointed William Byrd, John Robinson and John Grymes, to act for the Crown, and Lord Fairfax having named William Beverley, William Fairfax and Charles Carter, the commissioners met at Fredericksburg, September 26, 1736. The specific object of the investigation was to ascertain by 'actual examination and survey, the true fountains of the Rappahannock and Potomac Rivers', and to this end the commissioners were given full authority to obtain such evidence as they required. Their 'journey of observation and survey', which began October 12, 1736, was completed December 14th of the same year[25] and separate reports were made, the Crown commissioners reporting August 10, 1737, and those representing Lord Fairfax, August 11th.[26] It appeared from this survey that the greater part of the contested lands lay within the limits of the proprietary, and numerous protests were received, the hearing of which caused much delay. The colonial government, however, on Lord Fairfax's promise to issue patents for lands granted by the crown in the disputed territory, issued an order, December 21, 1738,[27] approving the survey, and a report covering the whole matter was then forwarded to the Lords of Trade. The finding of that board, reported July 27, 1739,[28] was confirmed by the King in Council, April 11, 1745. The decree, after setting forth the facts in the controversy in a preliminary recital and stating that the maps and

reports of the commissioners had been examined
and counsel on behalf of the Crown and Lord Fairfax had been heard, adjudged:

"It is hereby Declared and Ordered, that within the words
and meaning of the Letters Patent granted by King James the
Second, bearing date the 27th. day of September in the Fourth
Year of his Reign, the Boundary of the Petitioners Land doth
begin at the first Spring of the South Branch of the River
Rappahannock now called Rappidan, which first Spring is the
Spring of that part of the said River called Rappidan as is
called in the Plans returned, by the name of Conway River,
And that the said Boundary be from thence drawn in a Strait
Line North West to the place in the Alagany Mountains where
that part of the River Patawomeck alias Potowmack which is
now called Cohongoroota alias Cohongoronton first arises; the
other Boundarys being the said Rivers themselves as they run
from their said respective Heads till they fall into Chesapeyock
alias Chesapeak Bay.

"And that the said Governor or Commander in Chief do
not make any Grants of Lands within the said Boundarys, nor
Molest or Disturb the Petitioner in the quiet possession and
Enjoyment of the Lands contained therein, but the said Lands
to be Subject to the Grants made of any parts thereof by His
Majesty or any of his Royal Predecessors, and so as the said
Lord Fairfax do Comply with his proposal mentioned in the
aforegoing Report.

"And His Majesty doth hereby likewise Signify His Royal
Pleasure, that the Lord Fairfax shall for the future be intitled
to all the Advantages, Profits and Emoluments whatsoever to
arise from Grants, made by the Crown, of Lands within his
Boundarys, which the Crown would or might have been intitled to by the Terms, or in consequence of the said Grants;
and where, upon such Grants, Quit Rents are reserved, that
he the said Lord Fairfax shall be intitled to demand and receive the same from the Grantees to his own use and benefit
from the time that this Order shall be made known to the said
Governor and to his Majestys Receiver General of the Quit
Rents in that Province."[29]

The Cohongarooton was the name given by the Iroquois to the Potomac river above the confluence of the Shenandoah, and the Conway was the main stream of the south branch of the Rappahanock (Rapidan) above its forks. By this decree, therefore, Lord Fairfax had fully established Col. Carter's contention as to the true boundaries of the Northern Neck, and his inheritance, as now defined, comprised 5,282,000 acres of land including the present counties in Virginia and West Virginia, of Northumberland, Lancaster, Westmoreland, Richmond, Stafford, Warren, King George, Prince William, Fairfax, Loudoun, Fauquier, Rappahannock, Culpeper, Madison, Clarke, Page, Shenandoah, Hardy, Hampshire, Morgan, Berkeley, Jefferson and Frederick.[30] Truly a princely estate.

To end a controversy which had begun in 1706, it remained only to run the 'back line', or western boundary, of the proprietary and for that purpose Gov. Gooch appointed Joshua Fry, Lunsford Lomax, and Peter Hedgman, while Lord Fairfax reappointed William Fairfax and William Beverley. The commissioners met September 15, 1746, and starting at the source of the Conway in the Blue Ridge, ran out their line to that point in the Alleghany mountains which William Mayo, surveyor for the Crown, had marked as the head spring of the Potomac in 1736. Here the 'Fairfax Stone' was set up October 23, 1746, and the party returning to the head waters of the Conway, planted a similar monument on November 13th of the same year.[31] 'The Fairfax line' so established was about eighty miles long and crossed the Valley of Virginia two

miles south of the present town of Newmarket, in
Shenandoah county.[32]

In the original survey of the Northern Neck
boundaries, separate maps had been prepared by the
commissioners for the Crown and Lord Fairfax, and
forwarded with their respective reports. That for
Lord Fairfax was drawn by John Warner but had
been reduced in size by the proprietor's orders, and
engraved before being submitted. It bore the
legend:

'The Courses of the Rivers

RAPPAHANNOCK and PATOWMACK

in

VIRGINIA

*as surveyed according to Order
in the Years 1736 & 1737'*

When the survey of 1746 was registered, Lord
Fairfax had the second 'printed' state of this map
prepared in London on which the new boundary line
was displayed, and between that line and the Blue
Ridge he stamped his coat of arms as if to seal his
possession of the new territory. He also caused his
Manor of Leeds, in what was later Fauquier, to be
shown, as well as Belvoir, on the Potomac, where
the proprietary office was then established. Above
the legend on the first state of the map, which was
left undisturbed, he placed another as follows:

'A survey of the Northern Neck of Virginia, being the lands belonging to the Rt. Honourable
Thomas Lord Fairfax, Baron Cameron, bounded by
and within the Bay of Chesapoyocke and between
the Rivers Rappahanock and Potowmack, with' etc.

The final confirmation by the colonial government
of the boundary settlement was recorded by an act
of 1748, in which the interests of Jost Hite and his
partners were apparently protected and on the passage of which they withdrew the surveys, twenty-
seven in all, which they had originally filed with the
secretary of the colony, and lodged them with the
proprietor in order to obtain their patents from
him.[33] The act confirming the settlement after
reciting that 'Lord Fairfax hath consented, before
the king, in council, that the several grants and
patents made by the crown, of the lands included in
the boundary aforesaid, should be confirmed to the
several grantees, their heirs, and assigns, to be held
nevertheless of the said Lord Fairfax, under the like
rents, services, profits, and emoluments, as should
be paid, done and arise, by and from the said grants
made by the crown', ordered, 'that all grants and
patents whatsoever, under the seal of this colony, for
lands situate and lying within the limits and boundaries of the letters patent granted to the ancestors of
the said Lord Fairfax, as the same are now settled
and determined, heretofore made and granted by
the crown, shall be held, deemed and taken to be
valid and effectual; and the adventurers and planters to whom the same were granted, their heirs and
assigns, shall forever hereafter peaceably and quietly have, hold and enjoy the said granted premises,
respectively, according to such granted estates,
under the rents and services in the said grants reserved, to be paid and performed to the said Thomas
Lord Fairfax, his heirs and assigns, forever, any
misrecital or defect in the said grants notwithstanding'.[34] The latter clause, it will be seen, renewed
also the guarantees contained in the act of 1736.

On the death of Col. Carter in 1732, Lord Fairfax had placed the management of the Northern Neck property in the hands of his cousin William Fairfax,[35] at that time Collector of Customs at the port of Salem in Massachusetts, securing for him at the same time the office of Collector for the South Potomac. In the Northern Neck appointment, Lord Fairfax by a special power of attorney dated February 21, 1734, gave his kinsman authority to collect quit-rents and transact the routine business of the proprietary pending his own arrival in the colony.[36] The new agent had sailed from Salem, June 18th, and on reaching Virginia had opened an office in Westmoreland where in the following summer he was joined by Lord Fairfax who was his guest there, and later at Falmouth on the Rappahannock, until his return to England in September, 1737. After the legislation of 1736, the Proprietor, in confirmation of that agreement, issued a few patents from the Westmoreland office over his own signature, the first being dated July 21, 1736; later in the same year, however, patents were signed 'By Order of his Lordship, W. Fairfax, Agent'.[37]

During the survey of his boundaries, Lord Fairfax had ridden over the northern counties of the proprietary and selected certain tracts which he ordered to be surveyed for his own use and, among them, those which afterwards constituted the Manor of Leeds. What he then saw of his vast possessions seems to have decided him to return to Virginia and, as Burnaby says, 'to settle and cultivate that beautiful and immense tract of country, of which he was the proprietor'.[38]

With this object apparently in view he entered into a family compact while in England awaiting the decision of the Privy Council. The Lords of Trade had examined the data furnished by the boundary commissioners and reported to the Privy Council in 1739, as previously stated, but owing to adverse political influences at Court the matter had been held up and it was not until Walpole's fall in 1742, that Lord Fairfax had obtained his decree. The family agreement made during this period broke the trust created by his mother's will, the remainder interests conceding his assumption of authority as sole proprietor of the Northern Neck in consideration of his making over 'Leeds Castle and the estates in Kent to his brother Robert, to be held by him in tail'.[39]

After the order of April 11, 1745, had been entered, Lord Fairfax in the summer of 1747, sailed again for Virginia to secure from the colonial Assembly a ratification of his convention with the Crown. On this occasion also he was his cousin's guest; William Fairfax during his absence having built 'Belvoir' on a neck of the Potomac below Mt. Vernon, in what was then Prince William, and removed the land office to that county in 1741.[40] Lord Fairfax remained at Belvoir for one or two years, gradually assuming the full management of the proprietary and thence-forward from July 21, 1747, he personally signed all Northern Necks grants.[41] It was at Belvoir, too, that he met George Washington, who, as a lad of sixteen, he employed in 1748 to make surveys of his lands beyond the Blue Ridge.

Lord Fairfax in 1749, opened a new land office in Frederick 'for the county', but retained the main office at Belvoir under the management of George

William Fairfax, who had succeeded his father, William Fairfax, as agent in 1747. The Proprietor's intention had been to build a manor house for himself on a western spur of the Blue Ridge in Leeds Manor, for which he had brought furniture from England, but this plan he never carried out. He had, however, established a 'quarter' on another tract of 8840 acres lying on the north bank of the Shenandoah and on the branches of Opeckon, adjoining Jost Hite's and Robert McKay's tracts. It was on the latter property that his branch office for Frederick was located and there he took up his residence, probably in the same year. He was, at all events, living on this tract, which he afterwards named the 'Manor of Greenway Court', when his young nephew, Thomas Bryan Martin, joined him in 1751.[42] The young man apparently at once gained his uncle's confidence for when he came of age in the following year, Lord Fairfax granted this property to him 'in consideration of the natural affection I have and bear unto the said Thomas Bryan Martin as my nephew and for the annual rent hereafter reserved.' This consisted of the payment at Michaelmas each year of 'one good buck and doe, over and above the usual accustom'd Rent'.[43]

The Greenway Court manor was eventually laid out in farms which were leased to tenants, Lord Fairfax and his nephew reserving the farm on which the dwelling house stood. The house was not a very pretentious affair being built of timber one story high with a half story under the roof, and covered with clapboards. The roof was shingled and projected down over an ample porch running the full front of the building, while dormer windows gave light to the half story or attic. The land about the house was heavily timbered and only a sufficient space was cleared for the principal buildings, which, in addition to the dwelling house, consisted of a house for the bailiff, or overseer, and a small stone building which served at first as the local, and afterwards as the proprietary land office.[44] The slaves, about one hundred and fifty in number, were quartered in log cabins scattered about in the woods. There were stables and other buildings on the estate, to which Lord Fairfax had planned extensive additions, but these he never completed.[45] The farm was stocked with cattle, sheep and horses, and the land was doubtless cultivated in such crops as Indian corn, wheat, oats, flax and tobacco. It was on this property that Lord Fairfax for thirty years lived out his long life.

Burnaby writing contemporaneously thus describes his way of living:[46]

"He kept many servants, white and black; several hunters; a plentiful but plain table, entirely in English fashion; and his mansion was the mansion of hospitality. His dress corresponded with his mode of life, and, notwithstanding he had every year new suits of clothes, of the most fashionable and expensive kind, sent out to him from England, which he never put on, was plain in the extreme. His manners were humble, modest and unaffected; not tinctured in the smallest degree with arrogance, pride or self-conceit. He was free from selfish passions, and liberal almost to excess. The produce of his farms, after the deduction of what was necessary for the consumption of his own family was distributed and given away to the poor planters and settlers in his neighborhood. To these he frequently advanced money, to enable them to go on with their improvements; to clear away the woods, and cultivate the ground; and where the lands proved unfavourable, and not likely to answer the labour and expectation of the planter or husbandman, he usually indemnified him for the expense he had been at in the attempt, and gratuitously granted him fresh

lands of a more favourable and promising nature. He was
a friend and father to all who held and lived under him; and
as the great object of his ambition was the peopling and cultivating of that fine and beautiful country, of which he was the
proprietor, he sacrificed every other pursuit, and made every
other consideration subordinate, to this great point. * * *
He presided at the county courts held at Winchester, where
during the sessions he always kept open table; and acted as
surveyor and overseer of the highways and public roads. His
chief, if not sole amusement was hunting; and in pursuit of
this exercise he frequently carried his hounds to distant parts
of the country; and entertained every gentleman of good character and decent appearance, who attended him in the field, at
the inn or ordinary, where he took up his residence for the
hunting season."[47]

He had, by order of the colonial council, October
30, 1749, been empowered to act as Justice of the
Peace in all counties of the Northern Neck and, on
Governor Dinwiddie's solicitation, he assumed in
1754, the active duty of County Lieutenant of Frederick.[48] He was intensely interested in the settlement of the western country and seems to have
adapted himself to the existing conditions in the
locality in which he chose to reside. The incon-
gruity of the great manor house which he had
planned must soon have become evident to him and
one can hardly picture him presiding at a backwoods
court in clothes of the latest London mode. The
people among whom he lived were frontiersmen, and
Winchester, his county seat, at that time was
merely a military base in a territory greatly disturbed by the depredations incidental to the French
and Indian wars.[49] In these surroundings his life
was necessarily a simple one. His selection of a
place of abode so remote from the centers of social
and political life in the colony, was doubtless gov-

erned by the fact that it placed him in the heart of the region in which the active business of the proprietary was then being conducted and where he could best safeguard his own interests and most effectively promote the colonization of the new territory. In this he was himself a pioneer and the incentive to the important part he played in the settlement of that portion of Virginia, is overlooked in the generally accepted theory of his desire for solitude.

He did not, as a matter of fact, altogether deny himself the pleasures of tidewater society. He made occasional visits to Williamsburg and was present at the reception given by Governor Fauquier on that official's arrival in Virginia. He also maintained affectionate relations with his cousin's family and frequently visited Belvoir prior to William Fairfax's death in 1757. After that event the son, George William Fairfax, was continued as agent until 1760, when he asked to be relieved that he might return to England to take possession of an inheritance in Yorkshire. Even then the main office of the proprietary was not removed from Belvoir until 1762, when George William Fairfax, writing to his counsin Robert, alluded to the transfer and to Thomas Bryan Martin's part in effecting it. He said, 'Mr. M. has carried his long laboured point of getting the management of the office into his own hands, and removing it *with them* to Frederick'.[50]

The regulations under which lands were granted in the Northern Neck were prescribed and published by the proprietors without regard to the land laws in force elsewhere in the colony.[51] The system of

the head right as the basis of the patent was un-
known in the proprietary where the extent of the
grant was not limited and a payment, or composition, was required when the patent was issued. In
the case of lands granted in fee, the applicant made
entry for the tract he wished to acquire and secured
a warrant from the proprietary land office under
which the survey was made at his cost, and on its
return and the payment of the office fees and composition, the deed, or patent, was issued.[52] The consideration expressed in the patent was the composition, usually at the rate of thirteen shillings and four
pence for each one hundred acres,[53] and the reserved
fee rent of one shilling sterling for every fifty acres
to be paid annually at Michaelmas. If this rent remained unpaid for two years, the grantor had the
right to re-enter and hold the land as if the grant
had never passed. The patent also reserved to the
Crown its rights in all mines, and to the proprietor
a third part of all lead, copper, tin, coal and iron
ores.

In addition to the lands granted in fee, Lord Fairfax, during his proprietorship, followed the practice
established by his agents and reserved for his own
use and for the benefit of his heirs, certain large
tracts of land to which he retained title and which
he leased to settlers on long terms of lives. These
tracts, known as 'manors', were divided by the
Proprietor's surveyors into lots or farms, and, in all
the manors, leases were granted under more or less
similar terms and conditions. The duration of the
lease was almost uniformly that of three lives, that
is, the life of the lessee and of any other two persons
he chose to name; in some cases the wife and one
child being named, in others, two children, and in

others again, a child and a grandchild. The lease
was renewable at the expiration of the term on the
payment of a fine of one year's rent. The rent was
at the rate of twenty shillings for every one hundred
acres, payable yearly at Christmas, or in some cases
Michaelmas, with the right of re-entry in default of
payment within twenty days. The lessee was also
required to pay all taxes levied by the Assembly and
to comply with certain conditions, such as building
a house on the land, if one was not found there;
planting an orchard of one hundred and fifty apple
trees 'at fifty feet distance', and generally con-
serving the resources of the farm. After Lord Fairfax's death, however, the terms and conditions
under which the manor lands were leased, varied
widely. In the Manor of Leeds, for instance, leases
for certain lots were made for twenty-one years at
the yearly rental of one shilling, the lessee being
required to have the lot surveyed, build a house
twenty feet long by sixteen wide, with a stone or
brick chimney, and plant an orchard of one hundred
apple trees thirty feet apart. In other cases, leases
for three lives were made but at yearly rents con-
siderably higher than those charged during Lord
Fairfax's life, the conditions in respect to the survey
and improvement of the farm being the same.[54]

The Manor of Leeds, the largest and most important of the manors, consisted originally of a tract
of 119,927 acres of land described in the grant of
1767 as lying in the counties of Fauquier, Loudoun
and Frederick, 'on the north branch of the Rappahannock, formerly called the Hedgman river, on the
upper side of Carter's run, on the branches of Goose
creek, and on the lower side of the Shenandoah river
below Happy creek, including the Blue Ridge be-

tween Happy Creek Gap (now Chester's Gap) and
Ashby's Gap'. This tract was surveyed for Lord
Fairfax by John Warner, November 15, 1736, and is
shown on the 'Map of the Courses of the Rivers
Rappahannock and Potowmack, 1736-7', as occupy-
ing the eastern slope of the Blue Ridge, in what is
now Fauquier. Its boundaries in that county, in
which by far the greater portion of the land lay,
may be roughly given as running from Ashby's gap,
along the top of the Blue Ridge to Chester's gap at
the headwaters of the Rappahannock river, from
thence with that river to its confluence with Carter's
run at Waterloo, thence with Carter's run to where
the run crosses the Fredericksburg-Winchester
road near Marshall, and thence along that road from
Marshall to Ashby's gap. The land contained in
the original survey was granted by Lord Fairfax to
Thomas Bryan Martin and re-conveyed to him by
Martin, August 21, 1767.[55] Another tract, afterwards included in the Manor of Leeds, was surveyed
for Lord Fairfax, also by John Warner, November
29, 1736. It consisted of 26,535 acres of land and
is described in the patent by which it was granted
to Thomas Bryan Martin and re-conveyed by him,
August 21, 1767,[56] as being in the counties of Fauquier, Loudoun and Frederick, and lying on the
southern bank of the Shenandoah river, including
the Blue Ridge between Ashby's gap and Williams'
gap, now known as Snicker's gap. A third tract
held with the Manor of Leeds, containing 13,920
acres, was surveyed by William Green, March 10,
1748. It was granted by Lord Fairfax to Thomas
Bryan Martin and re-conveyed by him, November
1, 1777,[57] and is described in the conveyances which
then passed as lying between Goony run and Happy

creek in the counties of Frederick and Dunmore. This tract was known as the Goony Run Manor,[58] and with the two tracts first described, completed the 160,382 acres of land which eventually came to be known as the Manor of Leeds. The South Branch Manor, next in importance to the Manor of Leeds, contained 54,596 acres. It was surveyed by James Genn, March 31, 1747, and in Thomas Bryan Martin's patent, August 21, 1767,[59] is described as lying on the Wappacomo, or the Great South Fork of the Potomac river, in Hampshire county. It is shown on the north bank of that river on Fry and Jefferson's map of 1751 under the name of 'Fairfax Manor'. Other smaller tracts[60] were laid off and granted to Thomas Bryan Martin in the same way, and on the proprietor's death the manor lands, exclusive of the Manor of Greenway Court to which he only retained the seignorial title, aggregated 219,341 acres.[61]

The method of conveyance and re-conveyance in fee[62] secured to Lord Fairfax private property in these lands irrespective of his seignorial title and proved an effective barrier to confiscation in the final dissolution of the proprietary.[63]

[1] Her will, in which she described herself as 'Catherine Lady Fairfax, Baroness Dowager of Cameron, in the Kingdom of Scotland,' was dated April 21, 1719, and proved June 23, 1719. She was buried in Bromfield Church, June 1, 1719. (*Proprietors*, p. 119).

[2] Henry Culpeper Fairfax matriculated at Oriel College, Oxford, Jan. 29, 1714, and graduated B. A., Oct. 15, 1716. He was Captain-Lieutenant in Sybourg's Horse (Seventh Dragoon Guards), Feb. 24, 1719, and commanded a company in Brigadier Edward Fielding's Regiment of Invalids, Aug., 1730. He was made a Fellow of the Royal Society, Jan. 11, 1727. (*Ibid.*, p. 123).

[3] *Ibid.*, pp. 123-5.

[4] These estates had been held in the Fairfax family since 1518, when Sir William Fairfax married Isabel, dau. and heir of Thomas Thwaites, of Denton Castle, Yorkshire. The property was inherited by her son,

Sir Thomas Fairfax, father of Thomas, 1st Lord Fairfax. (*Burke's Peerage*, 1914, p. 754).

[5] Lord Fairfax, writing from Oriel College to a kinsman, July 7, 1710, says, 'My father's debts were near two and twenty thousand pounds and all I have during my mother's life is what my Grandmother Culpeper left me'. (F. H. S. *Bulletin*, No. 1, p. 23).

[6] *Proprietors*, pp. 125-6.

[7] See text of Lady Fairfax's will, in *Proprietors*, p. 119.

[8] Such lands were described as 'waste' lands or 'unappropriated' lands, in the Acts of Assembly relating to them. (*Rev. Code*, 1819, II, p. 333).

[9] *Proprietors*, pp. 101-102. Robert Carter reported to the fifth Lord Fairfax that the income from the Northern Neck in 1708, was £584, 13s., 2d. (*Ibid.*, p. 96), and in July, 1730, Gov. Gooch reported to the Lords of Trade that 'the Northern Neck is now farmed by the Proprietors at £450 per annum and it is supposed to be worth £700 beside that 'tis still increasing by new Settlements'. (*Ibid.*, p. 161).

[10] *N. N. Grants*, A, p. 1.

[11] *Proprietors*, pp. 161-2.

[12] Counties in the Northern Neck, as in other parts of Virginia, were created by act of Assembly, the proprietors in this respect not claiming the privileges of their charter.

[13] *Va. Magazine*, XIII, p. 114.

[14] *Ibid.*, p. 119.

[15] *Ibid.*, p. 133.

[16] *Ibid.*, XIII, pp. 133-4.

[17] Kercheval, *Hist. of the Valley*, 1902, pp. 45 and 156-7.

[18] *Va. Magazine*, XIII, pp. 354-6.

[19] *Hite* v. *Fairfax*, Call, IV, p. 147. Lord Fairfax entered a general *caveat* in 1734 against all Orders of Council, deeds, patents, entries, etc., issuing from the Crown for lands within the proprietary.

[20] Faulkner's Report, 1832, in Kercheval, *Hist. of the Valley*, 1902, pp. 163-4.

[21] *Hite* v. *Fairfax*, Call, IV, pp. 45-6 and 50-1.

[22] *Proprietors*, p. 127.

[23] *Va. Land Grants*, p. 106.

[24] *N. N. Grants*, E, p. 1.

[25] Faulkner's Report, 1832, in Kercheval, *Hist. of the Valley*, 1902, p. 164.

[26] C. O., 5: 1324, pp. 137 and 199.

[27] *Hite* v. *Fairfax*, Call, IV, p. 46.

[28] *A. P. C. Col.*, 1720-1745, p. 281.

[29] *Va. Land Grants*, p. 112.

[30] Howe, *Historical Collections of Va.*, 1852, p. 236.

[31] *Old Prince William*, II, p. 624.

[32] *Va. Magazine*, XIII, p. 115.

[33] *Hite* v. *Fairfax*, Call, IV, p. 46. When Hite's claims were presented at the Frederick county office of the proprietary, the surveys were found to include only bottom lands, isolating the adjacent upland and

rendering it inaccessible to future seating. Lord Fairfax accordingly refused to issue patents until new surveys had been made. This re-opened
the controversy. Hite entered a *caveat* against other warrants issuing
for these lands from the proprietary office, and filed a bill in chancery
in the General Court, Oct. 10, 1749, against Lord Fairfax, claiming
that the latter had refused to make the grants to himself and partners
as provided in the act of 1748, and also that he had conveyed a portion
of the land contained in their surveys to other persons. (*Ibid.*, p. 42
et seq.). This case was not heard until after the death of Hite and his
first partner, McKay, but finally an interlocutory decree was entered,
Oct. 13, 1769, in favor of the plaintiffs, declaring that they were entitled
to such lands as had been actually surveyed under orders of the Council
before Christmas, 1735. This decree was confirmed Oct. 15, 1771, and the
court then ordered that Lord Fairfax should execute deeds to the plaintiffs for such lands, within the 54,000 acres included in their surveys, as
were not possessed by any other person when the suit was brought;
such deeds to be subject to the usual quit rents but not to the payment
of composition money. From this decision Lord Fairfax appealed to the
Privy Council, but the Revolution intervened and the appeal was not
prosecuted. The Hite interests, however, were not yet satisfied, and
Isaac Hite and John Green, then representing the company, took the case
to the Court of Appeals. It was heard in May, 1768, after Lord Fairfax's death, Hite appealing from such parts of the decree of the General
Court as confirmed the grants made by Lord Fairfax to other parties
before the commencement of the suit. The decree in this case, when it
was reached, was in favor of the plaintiffs and reversed the decree of
the lower court, thus ending a controversy which had agitated the
western settlements for over fifty years and had out lived all the
original parties to it. (*Ibid.*)

[34] *Rev. Code*, 1819, I, p. 349.

[35] William Fairfax (1691-1757), was the son of Henry Fairfax, of
Tolston, Yorkshire, the younger brother of the fifth Lord Fairfax.
He served in the navy during the war of the Spanish Succession and,
in 1718, in the Bahamas under Capt. Woodes Rogers, the first royal
governor of the islands. In 1729 he received the appointment of Collector
at Salem. In Virginia, he served as burgess for Prince William and
Fairfax until, in 1743, he became a member of the Council. (*Va. Land
Grants*, p. 162.)

[36] When Lord Fairfax found that in the prosecution of his claims
he might be detained in England for several years, he sent William
Fairfax, January 24, 1739, a power 'to grant to any person or persons
of ability any part of the lands tenements or hereditaments heretofore
and now in the possession of or anyways belonging to me, the said
Thomas, Lord Fairfax, in Virginia, in such manner and for such con-
siderations as to my said attorney shall seem fitting, and grants thereof
in due form in my name to execute'. (*Ibid.*, p. 110.)

[37] *N. N. Grants*, E.

[38] Burnaby, *Travels through the Middle Settlements*, 1798, App. 4.

[39] *Va. Land Grants*, p. 108.

[40] *Proprietors*, p. 128.

[41] *N. N. Grants*, F, *et seq.*

[42] *Proprietors*, p. 128.

[43] *N. N. Grants*, H, p. 179.

[44] This building is still standing but the original manor house was destroyed in 1834.

[45] Howe, *Hist. Coll. of Va.*, 1852, p. 236. Lord Fairfax planted a white post one mile from his house as a guide to travelers approaching through the woods. The present village of White Post took its name from this landmark which has been carefully preserved. (*Ibid.*, p. 235.)

[46] During Archdeacon Burnaby's travels in America, 1759-1760, he visited Greenway Court and although Lord Fairfax was not at home at the time, he met him personally at the 'Palace' in Williamsburg, at a reception held by Gov. Fauquier. Burnaby also had opportunities to converse with prominent men in the colony to whom Lord Fairfax was well known, and his narrative in spite of certain inaccuracies, must, on the whole, be taken as an authentic account of the details of Lord Fairfax's life in Virginia.

[47] Burnaby, *Travels, etc.*, 1798, App. 4.

[48] *Proprietors*, p. 128. The following entry is found in the Frederick county records: 'At a council of war, held for regulating the militia of Frederick county, in order to take such steps as shall be thought most expedient in the present critical conjuncture, the 14th. day of April, 1756; present, the Rt. Hon. the Lord Fairfax, county lieutenant; John Hite, major; John Lindsey, Isaac Parkins, Richard Morgan, Samuel Odell, Edward Rogers, Jeremiah Smith, Thomas Caton, Paul Long, captains.

'Proposals having been sent to the several captains of the militia, signed by the commanding officer of the said militia, and dated the 7th day of April, 1756, to get what volunteers they could encourage to go in search of the Indian enemy who are daily ravaging our frontiers and committing their accustomed cruelties on the inhabitants; and the aforesaid officers being met together, and finding the number of men insufficient to go against the enemy, it is considered that the men be discharged, being only fifteen. Fairfax.' (Kercheval, *Hist. of the Valley* 1902, p. 158.)

[49] In 1756 it was judged necessary by the Assembly to erect a for within the town 'for the protection of the adjacent inhabitants agains the barbarities daily committed by the French and their Indian allies' and the sum of £1000 was appropriated by the Assembly for the pur pose. (Hening, VII, p. 33.)

[50] *Va. Land Grants*, p. 117.

[51] *Rev. Code*, 1819, II, p. 344.

[52] *Hite* v. *Fairfax*, Call, IV, p. 50.

[53] For the composition exacted in 1690, see foot note to Chapter II. *supra*.

[54] See *Fauquier D. B.'s*, 1 to 13.

[55] *N. N. Grants*, O, p. 76.

[56] *Ibid.*, O, p. 80.

[57] *Ibid.*, Q, p. 215.

[58] Kercheval, *Hist. of the Valley*, 1902, p. 158.

[59] *N. N. Grants*, O, p. 72.

[60] One of these was a tract of 931 acres surveyed by John Warne Oct. 30, 1739. It lay in Fauquier on the upper side of Cedar Run, ac joining the Brent Town tract.

[61] From a statement by the Register of the Land Office, April 4, 1921, of grants to Thomas Bryan Martin between the years 1751 and 1781. In *Hunter* v. *Fairfax's Devisee,* Munford I, p. 221, the case agreed stated 'that Thomas Lord Fairfax died seised in fee of sundry tracts of land in the County of Frederick, and other counties in the Northern Neck, containing altogether 300,000 acres, which had been granted and conveyed by him to Thomas Bryan Martin, in fee, upon the same terms, etc., which lands were soon thereafter re-conveyed by the said Thomas Bryan Martin unto him in fee'. Also, in *Marshall* v. *Conrad,* Call, V, p. 392, Judge Roane, in his opinion, stated that the 'renunciation [of the vacant lands under the act of 1796] is also founded upon a full and valuable consideration; upon the grant by the Commonwealth of Virginia, of at least 300,000 acres of land claimed by Mr. Fairfax as his private property'. These figures, however, are not confirmed by the records of the Land Office.

[62] *Hunter* v. *Fairfax's Devisee,* Munford, I, p. 221.

[63] See Chapter X, *infra.*

CHAPTER V

The Seating of Fauquier.

FOR twenty years after the establishment of Hayward and Brent's block house 'overlooking the Indian road', fear of the 'Senecas' had kept the future territory of Fauquier closed to settlement and left it to the Indian and the backwoods hunter. Now the Iroquois, although still frequenting the region, had been compelled to abandon the original 'plain path' of the Susquehannocks and to avoid observation from the Brent Town outpost, had changed their route through Fauquier to a trail which crossed Broad run below its forks and giving the block house a wide berth, passed the sites of Auburn and Germantown, leaving the territory of the future county by Norman's ford of Rappahannock river. Soon pressure drove them further west and when the Long House, by the Treaty of Albany in 1722, relinquished the Piedmont to Virginia, they transferred their southern path to the Shenandoah Valley.

With the Indian menace thus removed and the business management of the proprietary in the able hands of Colonel Carter, the permanent development of the region began.

Colonel Carter himself gave an impetus to the movement and we find him taking grants in the name of James Innes as early as 1704. The first three patents covered an aggregate of 2,227 acres (3:21, 22, 29)[1] immediately above the falls of Rappahannock where the town of Falmouth was to be laid out in 1728. Another grant soon followed, to Innes

also, of 11,158 acres 'in Richmond and Stafford
counties in the forrest above the falls of Rappahannock river, upon the branches of the run called
Potowmack run falling into Potowmack creek and
upon the run called Deep Run, falling into Rappahannock river about ten miles above the falls thereof' (3:34). This was the 'Richland' tract and upon
it Colonel Carter later established the quarter
known as 'Stanstead', which is shown on Fry and
Jefferson's map of 1755. Edward Mountjoy and
Thomas Walter then took 931 acres at the mouth
of Richland run, which was the first grant on the
North Branch of the Rappahannock (3:19), and
upon it they built in 1705, the first tobacco house
above the falls.[2] Hancock Lee's surveyors were
also at work and he began about this time his investment in river lands with three grants in 1704
and 1705, of 1,353 acres, 1,110 acres and 470 acres
respectively, on Rocky Pen run adjoining Mountjoy
(3:33, 96, 101). Deep run was reached by Andrew
Jackson July 29, 1704, in a grant of 1,238 acres
(3:35) of land beginning at its mouth, and Joseph
Belfield took 555 acres (3:87) in this locality in the
same year. In 1706 John and Augustine Higgins
also had a grant of 110 acres at the mouth of Deep
run, and Thomas Tibbit entered Fauquier, March 6,
1709, with a grant of 242 acres 'on the side of the
Northern Branch of Rappahannock river about four
or five miles above Deep run' (3:258). In the
same month Colonel Carter, advancing further into
the territory of the future county, took in the
name of his son Charles, who was then two years
old, a grant of 1,100 acres on Rocky run and one
of 77 acres on Summerduck (4:255, 257), and passing him in June, Philip Ludwell took two grants on

Persimmon aggregating 5,860 acres (4:219, 221).
William Allen and John Brown continued the up-
river movement by taking 713 acres, September 25,
1710, 'on a run known by the name of the Marsh
run between the Great Marsh and the river' (4:5),
to the eastern branch of which Brown subsequently
gave his name. Brown and Allen took another
grant of 427 acres adjoining the first tract, January
1, 1711 (4:21), and Allen's name appears in many
subsequent grants.

The next large entry for land was made by Innis
Hooper, January 22, 1715, the tract consisting of
2,060 acres 'on the branches of the Great Marsh
run', but the deed lapsed and the land was regranted
to George Eskridge in 1715 (5:61, 171). It passed
to Philip Ludwell before 1727,[8] and with 2,658 acres
'on the western branches of the Elk Marsh & also
on Tinpot run' originally taken by William Thornton in 1715 (5:91), constituted the property known
as 'Ludwell Park', which Charles Carter of Cleve
devised to his son, Landon Carter, and which he
describes in his will as 'that tract or parcel of land
called Ludwell Park, situate, lying and being in the
County of Fauquier (which I bought of Philip
Ludwell)'.[4]

In 1715 Nathaniel Hedgman took a grant of 750
acres 'on the north side of Rappahanock river about
35 miles above the falls thereof', and his sons, Peter
and Nathaniel, Jr., in August, 1724, increased the
family holdings to 4,800 acres by each taking grants
of 2,025 acres, described as 'on the north side of
Rappahannock river opposite to the little fork' and
'adjoining the land of Nathaniel Hedgman dec'd.'
(A: 61, 62). The Hedgman acquisitions proved
more important historically than any yet made, as

the North Fork of the Rappahannock was soon to
become known by Hedgman's name and the quarter
established by his sons between Tin Pot run and
the river below the mouth of Great run, survived as
a landmark far into the century.

Most of these grants were in the nature of frontier land speculations by tidewater landholders who
had no intention at the time of becoming residents of the new country, nor, in many cases, of
establishing quarters. The terms of their patents
made no requirements in this respect, but the properties were usually developed as tobacco plantations,
the owners erecting buildings and establishing an
overseer with slaves under him to cultivate the land.
The equipment of such a plantation, a little later, is
explained in Charles Carter's will. In it he declares
his desire 'that there be built on every plantation
settled with ten hands of slaves * * * an overseer's
house, a quarter, a Cow house and two Tobo. houses,
according to the common method of building in
Virginia'.[5]

Such properties were in the end broken up into
smaller parcels and sold to settlers who perma-
nently established themselves on the land, but
although the return in quit-rents to the proprietors
was the same, the system of large grants to non-
resident landholders obviously retarded colonization. The policy, however, was favored in Virginia
by the Privy Council at the time and the argument
in support of it was stated by Governor Gooch.
'Without taking up these large tracts,' he said to
the Lords of Trade in a despatch of November 8,
1729, 'upon which great improvements were necessary to be made, these Counties would not have
been settled so speedily as they have been, and

much of that land which has been seated in small
Parcells would in all probability have remained to
this day desolate; as may be seen in the County of
Brunswick which having but few great Tracts of
Land taken up in it by men of Substance, hath advanced very little in the number of its inhabitants
in proportion to the other County, Spotsilvania,
where the greatest Tracts have been granted &
possessed and thereby given encouragement to the
meaner sort of People to seat themselves as it were
under the shade and Protection of the Creator'.[6]

Grants in 1715, 1716 and 1717 advanced the river
front holdings in Fauquier to the mouth of Great
run, John Jackson taking 576 acres December 14,
1715, 'on a Great run issuing out of Rappahannock
river about four miles above the second or little
fork of the said river' (5:107). Its original designation of 'Broad' or 'Golden' is given to this run in
the next grant to Joseph Chambers of 200 acres,
May 8, 1716 (5:162), and in that to Colonel Edward
Barrow, November 10, 1717, of 300 acres, 'upon
both sides of a run called the North run being some
low grounds between the mouth of the Golden or
Broad run and a poison field whereon an Indian
Town formerly stood' (5:177). The 'Indian Town'
was the Tanxnitania village of John Smith's map
of 1612, to which reference has already been made,
and the small run emptying into the river above that
point was named for Colonel Barrow.

Working back from the river, two important
grants on the headwaters of Great (Broad or
Golden) run were recorded in 1718. In June of
that year Captain John Hooe, of Barnsfield on the
Potomac, and his brother, Rice Hooe, took up a
tract of 2,900 acres, which they called 'North Wales'

and on which the descendants of John Hooe built
a large stone dwelling house in 1773. The other
grant, above the Hooes, occurred in November and
included the hill on which the town of Warrenton
stands. The survey was made by Thomas Hooper
for Thomas Lee, then in charge of the Northern
Neck land books, and on its return a warrant issued
for 4,200 acres 'situate, lying and being upon the
heads of a Run issuing out of the North Branch of
Rappahannock river, commonly known by the name
of the Great Run, falling into the said River above
the Second Great Fork thereof, and upon the heads
of Severall branches issuing out of the Main South
West Branch of Occaquon River, commonly known
by the names of Cedar Run, Turkey Run and Licking Run, and near the foots of the broken hills or
small mountains in the County of Richmond.' The
patent was signed by Edmund Jennings, managing
agent of the proprietary, and in this he reciprocated
for two grants on the North Marsh, aggregating
2,575 acres, received by him in 1716 (5: 231, 233),
the deed for which had been signed by Lee during
his term as sole agent. Such transactions afford
evidence of the consistent practice of the agents
from Nicholas Spencer to George William Fairfax,
of appropriating for their own account large tracts
of 'waste' lands, as the ungranted lands of the proprietary were termed. The rule, however, was that
such grants were never made directly, the agents
as individuals, regarding themselves, perhaps, as
not competent to take from themselves in their
official capacity. This principle was explained to
Bryan Fairfax by his brother, George William Fairfax, writing from England in 1783. He said: 'I
hope you'l second my intention of deputing you to

act as the present Lord's agent, for it strikes me
more forcible now to urge and intreat you to act in
that capacity; and I make no scruple in saying was
I in Virginia, I would undoubtedly avail myself in
making the best provision I could for our Family,
which has suffered so much by alienating so many
good estates in Yorkshire. Don't suppose, Sir, that
I mean by any unjustifiable ways for I dare say you
would scorn any act of that sort as much as myself
or any Person living; but I should now acquit my
conscience in looking over all the Surveyors returns
in the Office and where I found any vacant Lands,
etc., would make out the Deeds to your eldest son
or a friend you can trust, that would reconvey to
him or any of them, for you know that you cannot
make the Deeds to yourself'.[7]

While the larger grants were being recorded the
influx of small land hunters into the rich lowlands
of the upper Rappahannock drainage, continued.
These men were for the most part pioneers of
sturdy English stock who pushed into the wilderness in search of new homes or more fertile lands
and their migration is recorded by fifty or more
entries in the Northern Neck land books between
the years 1712 and 1719, after which the proprietary
office was temporarily closed by the death of Lady
Fairfax. The region in which they settled is va-
riously described in the grants as 'the Rappahannock Marsh', 'the Great North Marsh' and 'the Elk
Marsh', and there they founded the first community
in Fauquier, and in doing so opposed a bulwark to
the 'Senecas' behind which the Potomac river movement, halted at Brent Town in 1687, could advance

Among these Elk Marsh settlers were such names
as that of Captain William Russell, the backwoods

hunter and ranger, who had two grants in 1712,
one, on July 2nd, of 316 acres on the Horsepen
branch of the Marsh run, and the other of 214 acres,
described as 'on both sides of the Elk Marsh run'
(4: 100, 102), and who in 1715 was recited as
living there (5: 80):[8] John Marr, Jr., and John Hopper, who took a partnership grant of 588 acres, June
30, 1712 (4: 94), on the Horsepen branch, which
soon took Marr's name, while the lower, or Brown's
branch of Marsh run, is today known as Hopper's:
Jeffrey Johnson, who July 20th of the same year
took 232 acres on the upper branch of the Marsh
run (4: 101) which a few years later became 'commonly known as Jeffrey Johnson's Marsh': Mark
Hardin who had two grants in 1716, one of 122½
acres, June 4th, and one of 94 acres December 13th,
adjoining William Russell (5: 93, 153), and later,
July 31, 1724, another of 232 acres on 'Dutchman's'
(Horsepen, or Marr's) run (A:56), where his son,
Martin Hardin, afterward kept his ordinary on the
Falmouth road: Robert Duncan, who took 258 acres
on the Rappahannock, July 27, 1715 (5: 81), and
who increased this tract by a grant, October 14,
1726, of 500 acres 'round and adjacent to it,' on the
east side of Summerduck run (B: 19): Morgan
Darnel, who began his family's holdings in Fauquier
with a grant of 427 acres, August 2, 1715 (5: 90),
and John Smith, a tanner, who took 313 acres September 20th of the same year.

The more important holdings in this neighborhood comprised those of the Rev. Alexander Scott,
then minister of Overwharton parish and a shrewd
speculator in frontier lands, who took 450 acres on
the Horsepen, or Marr's, branch of Marsh run, January 21, 1715 (5: 122): James Berryman, who took

663 acres 'near a place called the Marsh', March 5, 1717 (5: 83), and William Skrein, who took 833 acres, January 10, 1719, 'on the east side of a branch falling into the southwest branch of Deep run' adjoining John Hopper's land (5: 224). William Allen, whose earlier grants have already been cited, took, February, 1719, 1,490 acres on both sides of Marsh run 'beginning at a place commonly known by the name of Peter Pocum's pulpit' (5: 193). This landmark is recognized today as a very large rock surrounded by smaller rocks, which stands on the east side of the Marsh run about one and a quarter miles above the junction of Brown's, or Hopper's, run and, according to local tradition, is a point at which certain Indians at one time conducted their religious ceremonies. It is known also as the 'Indian Pulpit'. Another grant in this year was that to Alexander Beach, December 15th, of 606 acres 'upon the head branches of a run issuing out of the east side of the Marsh run formerly known by the name of the Horsepen Branch and now called Marr's run' (5: 230).

The Elk Marsh settlement was included in Hanover parish, and the records of the vestry attest that in 1714, when that parish was organized and purchased its glebe, 'there were hardly Twenty Tithables in that Part of Hanover Parish which is now taken into the Parish of Hambleton, and the greatest part of them at the Time of purchasing the said Glebe and making the Improvement upon the same had not sufficient to pay their levies; but are now [1734] increased to near Two Hundred and fifteen'. Adopting the method employed by the colonial government of reckoning population by tith ables, under which to the total tithables was added three times the number of white tithables, the total population of the Elk Marsh community was only eighty souls in 1714, but in 1734 it had grown to eight hundred and sixty.[9]

In 1710 the long delayed Potomac river movement reached Fauquier. Colonel Carter, as on the Rappahannock, had inaugurated it in 1707 by two grants to his infant son, Robert Carter, Jr., of 902 acres and 10 acres 'on the north side of Occoquan river a little below the falls thereof' (3: 164, 165), which had been immediately followed by a grant to Hancock Lee of 460 acres adjoining Carter (3: 176). Thomas Harrison had taken 294 acres 'in the fork of Chappawamsick Main Run', October 16, 1707 (3: 170), and thereafter the surveyors followed the western tributaries of the Potomac until, October 13, 1710, we find Thomas Harrison again, and Thomas Whitledge, taking a grant of 938 acres 'on the south side of the branch of Occoquan called Cedar run and on the east side of Dorril's run' 4: 8), in the southeast corner of Fauquier. One-fourth of this tract was transferred by Thomas Harrison in 1740 to his son, Colonel Thomas Harrison, who on his death in 1744 bequeathed 'to my son Benjamin the Old Plantation, mill and land belonging, which I purchased of my father on Cedar Run below the mouth of Dorrell's Run, and the land I purchased of John Orear adjoining the aforesaid land'.[10] John and Daniel Orear had taken, August 30, 1711, 400 acres on Dorrell's run adjoining the Harrison and Whitledge grant (3: 49). John Catlett followed with a grant of 358 acres 'on both sides of the Brent Town road and on the easterly side of a run commonly called and known by the name of

Darells run' (5:97). This land was taken up November 7, 1715, and on Bertrand Ewell's survey of the Fauquier-Prince William line, John Catlett appears as seated on it in 1759. James Withers, passing these tracts, December 10, 1715, boldly pushed westward and nearly gained contact with the Rappahannock settlers in the Elk Marsh by a grant of 1,300 acres 'on the north side of the head branches of Licking run which said Licking run issues out of the main South West Branch [Cedar run] of Occaquon River' (5:99), and Thomas Garner took a grant of 1,400 acres in the same locality (5:100). Edward Ryley took 600 acres December 14, 1715, on the north side of Cedar 'opposite the lands of Captain Thomas Harrison and Thomas Whitledge (5:104), and in 1719 we encounter William Allen again, who March 14th of that year took 841 acres on the head of Elk run (5:94), while on the same day a grant to Mrs. Mary Mauzy is recorded on the south side of Elk (5:196).

Simultaneously with these grants on Cedar and its tributaries, the future boundary of Fauquier was being approached by Broad run and its lower branches, Kettle and Slaty, and passing its upper fork, the land hunters were, in the next decade, to enter the county by its great north door in the thoroughfare of the Bull Run mountains. Clement Chevalle and Samuel Duchiminia, waifs probably from the Huguenot settlement at Manakin Town, took grants in August, 1711, of 968 acres and 202 acres, respectively, on Occoquan near the mouth of Broad run (4:43, 51): February 3, 1715, Thomas Hooper had 355 acres on Broad adjoining Chevalle and his partner, Lewis Reno (5:59): Daniel Tebbs, December 14, 1715, took 116 acres on the north side

of Broad (5: 103), and we find Patrick Fisher and
Maurice Bivings on Slaty with a grant of 320 acres,
February 7th (5: 63), and Valentine Peyton with
770 acres on Kettle, November 15th, of the same
year (5: 211).

The second stage in the settlement of Fauquier
began with the resumption of the Northern Neck
agency by Colonel Carter in 1723. This may be
termed the period of the manors during which huge
tracts were taken by individuals for their private
accounts and an attempt was made to seat them
under a system of leaseholds. When the land books,
after being closed for three years, were reopened,
the office was at first occupied with an accumulated
demand for moderate holdings by settlers and
smaller operators, and among them grants were
issued during the year 1723 to William McBee for
342 acres on both sides of Marr's run (A: 8): Joseph
Waugh for 840 acres 'beginning on the north side
of a branch of the north Marsh run' (A: 9): Christopher Marr for 266 acres on a branch of the Marsh
run (A: 11): Mark Hardin for 642 acres on the
west branches of Elk run (A: 12): William Allen
for 313 acres on Elk run adjoining an earlier grant
to him (A: 13): Thomas Furr for 1,072 acres 'upon
the head of the southernmost branch of Elk run'
(A: 17): William Hackney and John Allen for 1,013
acres 'upon the head of Town run' (A: 18), and
another grant to Hackney for 247 acres adjoining
the first grant (A: 20): John Johnson for 1,348
acres 'on both sides of Elk run adjoining Mary
Mauzy' (A: 22): William Triplett for 300 acres on
Dorrell's run (A: 25), and Dennis Connyers for 840

acres on the head branches of Licking, adjoining
James Withers and Rice Hooe (A: 27).

In 1724 Colonel Carter's manorial grants began,
none of which, however, were taken in his own
name. Following the Germantown grant on Licking run August 22nd, he granted to George Turberville, August 25th, 10,227 acres 'lying along and
east of Licking run above Germantown and across
Owl and Turkey runs to what was then supposed
to be the boundary of the Brent Town tract'
(A: 64).[11] Colonel Carter in his will calls this tract
'The Lodge', although it is generally known as the
Licking run tract.

His next grant was to his son-in-law, Mann Page,
August 28th, of 10,610 acres on Turkey run immediately above the Turberville tract. This land was
subsequently purchased by Colonel Armistead
Churchill, and on his death, prior to 1765, passed
to his sons, William, John and Armistead. It is
referred to in the Fauquier county deed books as
'Pageland' (A: 65).

Adjoining the above tract he granted to his son,
Charles Carter, October 13th, 6,166 acres 'on Kettle run and the branches thereof Beginning on the
north side of said run about two pole below Kettle run Lick, commonly called Adam Horsepen'
(A: 91). Charles Carter described this tract in his
will as 'situate, lying and being in the county of
Fauquier and Prince William'.[12]

Crossing the future boundary of Fauquier, Colonel Carter continued his appropriation of proprietary lands by a grant September 18th, to his
sons, John and Charles Carter, of 12,285 acres 'beginning in the forks of Broad run, running thence
up the North Branch' (A: 70). This was known

as the Broad run tract and extended from the fork
of Broad run to Thoroughfare gap, lying mainly in
Prince William. Charles Carter, who inherited his
brother's interest, bequeathed this tract to his son,
Landon Carter.[18]

Another grant was made on the following day
to Lewis Burwell, Mann Page and Carter Page, of
41,660 acres, lying above the Broad run tract and
across the upper waters of Bull run (A: 71), which
became known as the Bull run tract.

The Lower Bull run tract was made up of 6,030
acres taken in the name of Robert Carter, Jr., October 12, 1724 (A: 90), and 2,823 acres taken in the
name of Landon Carter, January 15, 1726 (C: 7).
Altogether Colonel Carter had carved out for his
own use and that of his children and grandchildren,
89,800 acres, lying above the lands already seated
in the lower part of the county and stretching from
Licking run across the head of Cedar to Broad, and
from thence to the Bull Run mountains.

His purpose was to administer these properties as
manors, in the application of that term to such
estates in Virginia. In the Northern Neck the characteristic manor was an entailed estate in which the
proprietor retained his title in fee and rented his
lands to leasehold tenants. None of the jurisdic-
tional rights conferred by the successive Northern
Neck charters were exercised or claimed, and the
name implied nothing more than the system under
which certain tracts of land were operated. The
proprietor, and his successors in title, held under
the proprietors of the Northern Neck and were
responsible for the payment of the quit-rents, as in
the case of all other freeholders, but instead of
taking their profits by sales and reconveyances in

fee, they divided their holdings into small farms which they settled under long leases, usually of three lives. The tenants paid a fixed annual rent of so many shillings an acre to their landlord and assumed the payment of the quit-rents,[14] which in this case could only be regarded as an addition to the land rent and not as a feudal, or quasi-feudal, obligation.

Colonel Carter had conceived the idea of seating his manors with Scotch-Irish immigrants who had come out to the colony as indentured servants and who having served out the terms of their indentures were seeking permanent homes. To many of these he had, as agent of the proprietors, already made small grants of land south of Brent Town and, in some cases, in Fauquier. He proposed now to divert future outcrops from the lower plantations and, through the attractions offered by his agents, to seat them as tenants on his newly created manors. An opportunity was soon presented to test the feasibility of the plan when in 1726 a fresh lot of ex-indenture men arrived in Stafford, but in spite of the inducements offered, they passed his lands by, electing to take title themselves and be no man's tenants, doubtless in assertion of their newly gained independence. The failure of this and similar attempts resulted in Colonel Carter's manors in Fauquier remaining practically unseated until they were finally sold as freeholds, which in the case of the Turkey run tract, for instance, did not occur until it had passed into the hands of the Churchills.

In the meantime the land lay in the dead hand and the contrast it offered to the cultivated plantations of the individual freeholders was thus de-

scribed by a foreign observer who traveled the
Carolina road much later in the century:

"Along the road", he said, "it was matter of no little astonishment to see so much waste or new cleared land, having
just come from the very well settled and cultivated regions of
Pennsylvania and Maryland. The reason does not lie in any
worse quality of the land, which is scarcely inferior to that
beyond the Potowmack, but in the fact that individuals own
great and extensive tracts of land of which they will sell none
so as to leave their families the more. All of them are very
much disposed to let land in parcels, they retaining possession
and seeing their land as much as possible worked and settled
by tenants; but tenants are not easily to be had so long as it is
anywhere possible to buy land. This policy which will certainly be advantageous to the posterity of such rich and important families, has in the neighborhood of New York and
elsewhere stood much in the way of cultivation and settlement;
whereas the back part of Pennsylvania, Maryland and even
a portion of Virginia have been more rapidly settled, poor
families being able to get title to small tracts of land. The
smallest possession has for every man more charm than the
most imposing leasehold."[15]

The system of indenture under which men and
women were imported as so-called 'servants' from
England and the north of Ireland, enabled emigrants from those countries who wished to make
a start in the New World and who had not the
wherewithal to pay their passage, to enter into a
contract under bond to work four or five years after
their arrival for the landholder who had advanced
the necessary money to bring them out. The new-
comers worked in the fields and were uniformly
treated as members of their masters' families.
There was nothing servile in their duties, and after
the period of their indenture had expired they took
up lands of their own and themselves became re-

sponsible planters. Necessarily, however, they lacked capital and in cultivating their small holdings they sought the cheapest form of labor available. This unfortunately was supplied by the convicts 'cast for transportation' to 'the plantations' under the Act of Parliament of 1718. Their services could be bought by the planters much more cheaply than slaves could be acquired, and to this class many of the small landholders of the Northern Neck resorted. Beverley says in 1722, 'as for malefactors condemned to transportation, tho' the greedy planters will always buy them, yet, it is to be feared they will be very injurious to the country, which has already suffered many murders and robberies, the effect of that new law in England'.[16]

It seems likely that this element was involved in the Prince William 'insurrection' of 1732, under the leadership of turbulent planters in revolt against the tobacco laws. Of those whose names appear in this uprising Thomas Furr had had a comparatively large holding in the neighborhood of Elk Run Church since 1723, and James Bland and Henry Filkins were seated on the Occoquan in 1715. The record of the mutiny is set forth in the minutes of the colonial council as follows:

"1732, March 26. Whereas the Governor was this day pleased to communicate to the members of his Majys. Council now present, a letter sent him by express from Coll. Thomas Harrison, of the County of Prince William, advising that a number of the meaner sort of people of that county, consisting of fifty men, were got together in arms, designing, as they gave out, to destroy the public warehouses in that and the adjacent counties, expecting to be joyned by other malcontents from the neighboring counties in the Northern Neck: It is the opinion of this Board that for the more effectual suppressing the said insurrection it is necessary that orders be forthwith issued to the

commanding officers of the militia in the Northern Neck to
call together the several troops and companies under their
respective commands, and cause to be read to them an Act
of Assembly for establishing the Militia, and to acquaint them
that this is such an insurrection as they are bound by that act
to suppress under the penalties therein mentioned; and in case
the mutineers in Prince William County should presume to continue in arms, that they then march against, and endeavor to
suppress them; And that the like orders be issued to the commanding officers of the militia on this side Rappahannock River
to take all necessary measures for preserving the peace of their
counties and for obstructing the passage of any number of men
from the Northern Neck who shall attempt to cross that river,
and in like manner to seize and secure all such as they shall find
going about to stir up the people to mutiny or disobedience to
the laws, sending from time to time to the Govr. accounts of
their proceedings, to the end that they may receive his further
directions therein.

"May 2. On reading the petition of James Bland, John
Shuemack, Thomas Furr, and others concerned in the late
insurrection in Prince William County, humbly acknowledging
their offence and praying pardon for the same: It is the
opinion of the Council that before the petrs. be received into
the benefit of his Majesties pardon, they ought to appear before
this Board to answer such matters as they shall be interro-
gated on touching the design of their tumultous and unlawfull
meeting wherein they were engaged. And it is accordingly ordered that the sheriff of Prince William County summon the
said James Bland, Thomas Furr, and Thomas Furr the younger,
together with Henry Filkins of the said county, to attend this
Board at the next court of Oyer and Terminer, held the second
Tuesday in June, and that all the other persons concerned in
the said insurrection, upon their giving security for their future good behavior for one twelve month and one day, before
the court of the said County of Prince William, be discharged
from all further prosecution for their aforesaid offence; And
the Justices of the said County of Prince William to notify
the same and to take recognizance accordingly."[17]

In 1724 the settlements on the Rappahannock had reached the mouth of Carter's run and back from the river, they had advanced by 1727 to the Watry mountain and to both sides of the Pignut, while new seatings in the lower end were recorded. Of the more important of these grants were those to Captain John Crump, afterwards sheriff of Prince William, July 14, 1724, of 472 acres on Elk run (A: 41): Captain Thomas Carter, of Lancaster, a valued friend of Colonel Robert Carter's but not related to him, of 304 acres, July 21st, at the mouth of the stream that afterwards took his name (A: 47): George Crosby, Sr., July 22nd, of 453 acres 'on the branches of Town Run' (A: 48): Alexander Clements, July 30th, of 354 acres on the north side of Elk run (A: 55): John Coppedge, September 15th, of 1,354 acres 'in King George and Stafford counties, adjoining William Allen, Thomas Evans and Alexander Clements' (A: 67): Waugh Darnell, September 16th, of 1,205 acres on 'Indian Cabin Branch' (A: 68): Thomas Berry, September 17th, of 926 acres 'on small runs of the Town run and Elk run' (A: 69): Thomas Stone, September 22nd, of 611 acres, 'corner to the land of Waugh Darnell' (A: 73): Henry Chalfee, September 24th, of 696 acres 'adjoining Colonel Carter's land' (A: 75): Charles Morgan, September 26th, of 425 acres on the north side of Great run (A: 77): Richard Gibbs, September 28th, 400 acres on the lower side of Deep run (A: 78): James Hackley, September 30th, 740 acres, 'beginning at Robert Carter's corner on the lower side of the said land and on the westernmost side of Summer Duck run' (A: 80), and the Rev. John Bell, October 14th, 2,470 acres, north of Warrenton, 'on the Great Branch of Occoquon river called Ceader run and on the headbranches of said run, adjoining Thos. Lee' (A: 92).

Captain Samuel Skinker, who was seated on the lower Rappahannock prior to 1722 and later sat as a justice of the King George County Court, took two grants in 1725, one of 542 acres, January 7th, 'on the south side of the Great Marsh and adjoining the land of Philip Ludwell and William Allen' (A: 101), and another, November 12th, of 672 acres 'on the branches of the Broad run of Occoquon and on the south side of the Pignut Ridge' (A: 174). The latter tract, known as 'Huntley,' has been held continuously by Captain Skinker's descendants under the proprietary patent until the present day and is one of the very few properties in Fauquier, title to which has persisted in one family since the original grant. In November, 1725, also, William Russell and James Warren, pioneers of the Elk Marsh, began the westward movement from that community and advancing along the route of the future Falmouth-Winchester road took up tracts of 643 acres and 630 acres, respectively, on the west side of the Pignut (A: 178, 179). Joseph Wright followed, January 26, 1727, with 121 acres 'on the south side of the Watry mountain' (B: 39), and John Blower, April 9th, took 453 acres, afterwards known as 'Clifton', 'on the Great run of the North Branch of Rappahannock river and on the upper side of the Watry Mountain' (B: 73), while John Corbin, June 10, 1728, took 298 acres 'on the Great run of Watry Mountain' (B: 126), and Thomas Jackman received 419 acres, June 28th (B: 132), both of these tracts adjoining Blower's. John Hudnall, an original Elk Marsh settler, in May of this year had taken 412 acres 'on the branches of Ceader run at the Thoroughfare of the Rappahannock Mountain' (B: 123) where Joseph Neavil kept an ordinary a few years later.

This nucleus of a settlement on the future Winchester road was, at the time, the extreme verge of Virginia civilization and toward it the Rev. Alexander Scott now made his way by another route. Entering the county by the thoroughfare of Broad run in the Bull run mountains, he took, August 10, 1726, 781 acres 'on the branches of Broad run above the Thoroughfair' (A: 213), and July 10, 1727, 2,823 acres 'on a branch of Rappahannock river called Carter's run in King George County and on the head of a branch of the Broad run of Occoquan river in Stafford County' (B: 85). The latter grant was on the western side of Pignut and included the site of the present town of Marshall. The tract was subsequently found to contain 3,533 acres,[18] and on it the Scott estate of 'Gordonsdale' was afterwards created. Walter Anderson in the following year took two grants in this locality, one, June 15th, of 395 acres 'on the northwest side of Watry Mountain on Great run adjoining John Hudnall's land' (B: 127), and the other, June 19, of 818 acres 'on Carter's run on the west side of the Rappahannock mountain adjoining the land of Parson Scott' (B: 128).

Behind the new frontier thus established, settlers were still pushing into the 'lower end.' Grants in 1725 were made to John Dinwiddie, February 8th, of 549 acres, 'on the Elk Marsh run' (A: 121), afterwards transferred to James Carter: Innis Hooper, on the same date, of 783 acres, 'beginning by Brent Town run adjoining John Johnson' (A: 122), and

Thomas Barber, of 1,956 acres on Kettle run
(A: 124). Five grants were made on February 9th;
to Travers Downman of 1,271 acres on Kettle, adjoining Colonel Carter (A: 126): Michael Meldrum,
of 635 acres on Great run (A: 127): Peter Lehew,
of 972 acres on 'Ceader run, beginning at Mann
Page's corner' (A: 128): John Coppedge, of 879
acres on Brent Town run (A: 129), and William
Russell, of 545 acres adjoining Mann Page (A: 130).
Thomas Gardner took 625 acres on Tinpot and Licking, May 10th (A: 144): Elizabeth White, 800
acres on Persimmon run on the same day (A: 146):
William Duff, 774 acres on the south run of Broad
'at the foot of the Broken Hills [Pond Mountain]',
May 12th (A: 149): Nathaniel Hillings, 434 acres
'between the branches of Turkey run and Ceader
Run adjoining John Bell and William Russell', May
20th (A: 154): Colonel Charles Barber, 1,542 acres
'on the branches of Occoquan run adjoining John
Bell and Peter Lehew', June 1st (A: 156): John
Flowrence, 434 acres 'on some branches issuing out
of the north side of Occoquan, adjoining Maurice
Biven', August 20th (A: 167): Alexander Bell, 1,110
acres 'on the branches of Cedar run and adjoining
land lately surveyed for the Rev. John Bell', his
father, November 16th (A: 177), and 'Mr.' William
Mones, 1,880 acres on the branches of Town run,
Elk run and Deep run, November 20th (A: 182).

In 1726 Owin Greenin took 467 acres, February
5th, on the branches of Summerduck (A: 190):
Waugh Darnall, 916 acres, February 7th, on the
north branches of Cedar run, south of Pignut
(A: 192): William Hackney, 1,343 acres, August
11th, on the branches of Cedar adjoining Thomas
Barber, Colonel Carter's, &c. (A: 215): Captain

Augustine Washington, 4,360 acres, August 13th, 'on the branches of Deep run in King George County and on a branch of Acquia in Stafford County' (A: 220): Edward Twentymen, 733 acres, October 13th, 'on the north side of Rappahannock river adjoining the land of Philip Ludwell' (B: 16): Lazarus Dameron, 838 acres, October 18th, on the branches of Deep run and Rocky run (B: 23): John Edy, 497 acres, October 19th, 'on the branches of Deep run adjoining Charles Carter' (B: 24), and January 22, 1727, Peter Rout took 714 acres 'on both sides of the Great run on the north side of Rappahannock river adjoining Nathaniel Hedgman' (B: 31), where his name survives in 'Rout's Hill,' a small settlement shown on modern maps near the mouth of Great run.

The year 1727 found most of the lands in the southern end of the county taken up and the 'western' movement toward the Pignut and beyond, well under way. Before following the pioneers again, however, a few grants from 1727 to 1730 must be noted. January 24, 1727, Leonard Helme took 152 acres on the upper side of Dorrell's run (B: 35) and on the 25th, another grant of 673 acres 'on a branch of Ceader run commonly called Lucky run' (B: 37), and Thomas Helme on the same day took 283 acres 'on Dorrell's run adjoining John Catlett' (B: 36). March 4, 1727, John and Peter Kemper took 264 acres 'on the branches of the Great run beginning at and corner to the land of John Hooe and Col. Thomas Lee' (B: 50). This property, on the road from the river and about two and a half miles below Warrenton, was and is still known as 'Cedar Grove.' William Strother took 266 acres, May 26, 1727, 'adjoining Christopher Marr and on the head of a branch that falls into the Marsh run' (B: 83), and Laurence Debutts, in October, 1727, took 3,928 acres in two parcels, 'adjoining Robert Carter and William Duff' (B: 99, 100). Captain John Williams took May 28, 1728, 85 acres 'on Marr's run adjoining William McBee, John Bradford &c' (B: 121): November 21, 1729, another tract of 1,500 acres adjoining Morgan Darnel, William Thornton, &c. (C: 2); November 22nd, 19 acres adjoining Timothy Reading (C: 3), and August 7, 1730, 460 acres 'about three miles from the Great Marsh of Rappahannock, adjoining the lands of McBee, Coppedge, Mercer and others' (C: 64). Catesby Cocke, February 8, 1730, had a grant of 420 acres 'on the branches of Deep run', and another, February 16th, of 481 acres 'on the branches of Elk Marsh run and Tinpot run adjoining Hooe's land and the land of John Kemper' (C: 99, 126), while Hancock Lee, February 13, 1729, took 595 acres 'adjoining his own and Knight's land' (C: 23). This was an addition to Lee's other Rappahannock river holdings, on one of which the Fauquier White Sulphur spring was subsequently discovered.

Among the early settlers above the Pignut were some of the more adventurous spirits from the German community on Licking run. Jacob Holtzclaw, February 9, 1725, had taken a grant of 496 acres on the south side of Broad run (A: 125), and John Fishback, pushing forward to the Rappahannock, February 27, 1729, took 280 acres about four miles above the mouth of Great run (B: 190). Another venture, in 1731, brought them together between the headwaters of Broad run and Little river and gave Fishback's name to a spur of the Bull Run mountains. The grant to Fishback was for 1,028

acres 'at the head fork of two branches of the Broad
run of Occoquan', June 12th (C: 158), and to Holtzclaw, 362 acres, July 9th, 'adjoining a small branch
of Goose Creek and on the Broad Run Mountains,
adjoining land of John Fischback' (C: 198). Tilman
Weaver also made an investment of land in this locality in 1741, taking, on March 26th of that year,
539 acres 'on some of the branches of Crummey's
run adjoining Ball's land' (E: 240). He, however,
never lived on this tract and the property eventually
passed to John Rector, another descendant of Germantown, who, as will appear, laid off upon it the
village now known as Rectortown.[19]

In 1727, John Blowers took a grant of 402 acres,
January 26th, 'on the head of the north branch of
Ceadar run' (B: 38), and John Macquire took 282
acres, January 21st, on the south side of the Pignut.
'On the Middle Grounds' between Broad run and
Bull run, Valentine Barton, July 10th, took 377
acres (B: 86), and Thomas Stribblin on the follow-
ing day took 1,050 acres in the same locality
(B: 87).

John Glascock in 1728 had 633 acres, April 10th,
above the thoroughfare of Broad run and at the
foot of Mother Leathercoat mountain (C: 119):
Samuel and William Nelmes, June 5th, 1,126 acres
'on the south side of the Broad run of Occoquon at
a point of the Pignut Ridge' (B: 125): Bryan
Obanan, June 26th, 635 acres on the north side of
Pignut (B: 129): James Henderson, August 28th,
299 acres 'in Stafford and King George counties, at
the Watry Mountains' (B: 140), and Dennis Connyers, October 16th, took 605 acres on the north side
of Pignut (B: 149). In 1729 John Blowers increased
his holdings by grants, February 13th and 14th, of

405 acres 'on some of the small branches of Ceadar
run, adjoining Coll. Carter, Coll. Tarpely and Parson Scott' (B: 173), and 159 acres 'on the branches
of Ceadar Run on the south side of Pignut Ridge
adjoining the land of Waugh Darnall' (B: 174), and
Hugh Lambert, February 14th, had 699 acres at the
head of the South run of Broad (B: 176).

'At the Pignut Ridge on the east side of Mr.
Skinker's and Parson Scott's lines', Joseph Gibson
took a grant of 693 acres, December 3, 1730 (C: 80):
Peter Byrum, March 1, 1731, took 450 acres 'on the
Pignut Ridge adjoining the land of John Maquire'
(C: 115): John Mercer, March 20th, of the same
year reached Goose creek from the south and took
1,000 acres 'near the Coblers Mountain' (C: 128),
and Alexander Bell, June 1st, took 1,435 acres 'between and upon the branches of Broad run of Occoquan and Cedar run adjoining land of Waugh
Darnell, John MacGuire, Samuel Skinker and John
Blower' (C: 147).

When the settlements on the Potomac had passed
Difficult run and were approaching Goose creek, Colonel Carter turned his attention to the new frontier
and made another cut into the proprietary lands.
Of the 52,000 acres which he now appropriated to
the use of his family, the Goose creek tract of
25,909 acres was accumulated between the years
1728 and 1731 and was extended westward into the
northwest corner of Fauquier by a grant to Landon
Carter, June 30, 1731, of 4,197 acres 'on the upper
side of Goose creek adjoining said creek and on the
upper side of Ashby's Bent Branch and adjoining
to the next branch [Crooked run] above the same'
(C: 175). At the same time, June 29, 1731, he took

another grant, not included in the Goose creek tract, in the name of his son, George Carter, of 3,312 acres 'at the upper Thoroughfare of the Blue Ridge known by the name of Ashby's Bent, including the same' (C: 174).

In 1731 also, two other great tracts were surveyed and patented in the foothills of the Blue Ridge. Colonel Charles Burgess, of Lancaster county, extended his land speculations on the west side of the Rappahannock by crossing that stream and taking up 24,000 acres in five parcels, reaching from the mouth of Thumb run to the head springs of Goose creek in Manassas gap or, as it was then called, Calmes gap. His grants were: June 15th, 13,879 acres 'on the east side of Goose Creek' (C: 162); 3,230 acres 'beginning at the south end of the mountains known by the name of Coblers adjoining Blowers land' (C: 163), and 3,056 acres 'beginning at the mouth of a small branch of Rappahanock river and the Main North run thereof' (C: 164); June 17th, 1,176 acres 'beginning on the east side of Goose creek' (C: 167), and September 13th, 2,927 acres 'beginning near the head of Goose Creek' (D: 64).

Captain James Ball, of Bewdley, July 1, 1731, took 7,883 acres 'beginning by Ashby's Bent run corner to Landon Carter.' This land lay between the Blue Ridge and Crooked run and extended south to Goose creek (C: 179). Another grant, May 5, 1732, was for 2,003 acres 'on the head of the Piney Branch of the Broad run of Occoquan by the Horsepen and branches of Goose Creek' (D: 87), and still another on the following day of 871 acres 'on some of the head branches of the North River of Rappahannock' (D: 88).

Two other grants were recorded in 1731 in this locality, one to Lewis Elzey, September 12th, of 1,004 acres 'on the head of a small branch of Carter's run by the side of a Small Mountain and adjoining three others called the Coblers' (D: 60), and another to Rawleigh Chinn, December 7th, of 3,300 acres 'adjoining land of Charles Burgess & William Stamp and near Goose Creek' (D: 73).

These great tracts and the Manor of Leeds, which Lord Fairfax was to create a few years later, left little ungranted land in the highlands of Fauquier and formed an effectual barrier against small freehold settlements. The lands in most cases being held as manors, remained intact and practically undeveloped until after the Revolution, and although a few seatings were effected along the line of the Winchester road, that future highway of Fauquier after 1730 saw only an ever lengthening line of travel to the Shenandoah Valley where opportunity still beckoned to the seekers of freehold homes. The region immediately north of the Pignut had been penetrated, as we have seen, by a handful of pioneers, and although after Colonel Carter's death and during William Fairfax's agency a demand for grants from the Potomac set in, it does not appear that the lands then taken up were occupied until a much later period.

The invasion by the Potomac river element is recorded between the years 1737 and 1747, when William Fairfax, September 20, 1737, took from Lord Fairfax 1,015 acres 'between the Short Hills and the Blue Ridge' (E: 18). After he himself became agent he granted to his son, Bryan Fairfax,

November 1, 1740, 3,400 acres 'adjoining land
of McCarty, Sample, Chinn, on Goose Creek'
(E: 177); June 18, 1741, 236 acres 'beginning on
Little river by some called Hunger run of Goose
Creek, adjoining Chinn and Stamp' (E: 281), and
November 28th of the same year, 102 acres, 'on the
south side of Goose Creek' (E: 381). He granted
to his son, William Henry Fairfax, November 14,
1741, 680 acres 'adjoining Ball, Weaver, Burgess
Thornton &c, on the branches of Crummie run of
Goose Creek' (E: 361), and August 4, 1742, 600
acres 'on Chattin's run and Goose Creek' (E: 495).
To his wife's brother, John Clarke, July 5, 1740,
2,448 acres in the vicinity of Rectortown and east
of William Henry Fairfax's land (E: 158), and to
Edward Washington, for his own account, an
escheat of 614 acres, December 12, 1739, on the
Pignut ridge (E: 115). Miss Ann Fairfax received,
June 17, 1741, a grant of 1,400 acres 'on the branches
of Bull run and Broad run of Potomac' (E: 277):
John Peyton, June 25, 1741, 186 acres 'between the
lands of Debutts, Flitter and Mercer' (E: 292), May
28, 1745, 287 acres 'on the north west side of Pignut' (F: 222), and September 10th, of the same
year, 1,299 acres adjoining Dennis Connyers, John
Fishback and Bryan Obanon (F: 236): Captain
Charles Ewell, of Dettingen parish, July 10, 1741,
1,184 acres 'adjoining the land of Tayloe, Gregg and
Walker' (E: 302), and September 4th, 270 acres
'on the upper side of Leathercoat Mountain and on
the north side of the Broad run of Occoquan'
(E: 236). George Byrn, December 14, 1743, had
210 acres 'beginning by a branch of Little River &c'
(F: 145), a property still known as 'Byrnley', and
Nathaniel Chapman, June 1, 1749, had 699 acres 'on

the north side of the Pignut ridge adjoining William Fairfax, William Johnson &c' (G: 151).

Other grants in the upper end of the county about this time were those to Harry Turner, of King George, November 18, 1740, of 1,700 acres 'near a mountain called the North Cobler, adjoining land of James Ball also the Manor of Leeds' (E: 198): to Lewis Elzey, December 12, 1740, of 1,611 acres 'between the lands of Honbl. Thomas Lee &c upon the branches of the Broad run of Potomac' (E: 227): to John Grant and John Graham, May 23, 1741, of 1,175 acres 'on the south side of Goose Creek adjoining William Fairfax, Hewes and Chinn' (E: 256), and in the Upperville region in 1741, to Francis Triplett, August 29th, of 505 acres 'on both sides of Goose Creek, beginning in the fork between Painters Skin Cabbin Branch and Goose Creek' (E: 314): to William Nichols, August 31st, of 405 acres 'on the South Fork of Goose Creek, adjoining Triplett' (E: 315), and to James Wiatt, September 1st, of 318 acres 'beginning on a fork of Beaverdam adjoining Nichols and Tripletts' (E: 318).

With the smaller grants which have not been recited, the territory of Fauquier had practically been partitioned by 1750 and its social and economic development now demanded its erection into a separate political division, which, as we shall see, was effected a few years later.

---

[1] The references included in the text are to volume and folio of the *Northern Neck Land Grants*, a MS. record preserved in the Land Office at Richmond.

[2] Mountjoy in partnership with Thomas Brooks took, Sept. 1, 1709, another grant of 800 acres 'on the North West Branch of Deep Run' (4: 224), both tracts eventually passing to Col. Carter. (*Old Prince William*, I, p. 202.)

[3] *Ibid.*, p. 203.

[4] *Va. Magazine*, XXXI, p. 53.

[5] *Ibid.*, p. 67.

[6] *Old Prince William*, I, p. 242.

[7] *Ibid.*, p. 251.

[8] William Russell took a grant of 645 acres on Turkey run, February 9, 1725 (A: 130), and recited himself as living there in 1741. It was on a dividend of this tract which had descended to his granddaughter, Elizabeth Holtzclaw, wife of John Duncan, that the court for Fauquier County was held June 28, 1759 (*Ibid.*, p. 204.)

[9] *Ibid.*, p. 201.

[10] F. H. S. *Bulletin*, No. 4, pp. 375 and 484.

[11] *Old Prince William*, I, p. 242.

[12] *Va. Magazine*, XXXI, p. 52.

[13] *Ibid.*, p. 55.

[14] Bond, *The Quit-Rent System in the U. S.*, p. 18.

[15] *Old Prince William*, I, p. 247.

[16] *Ibid.*, p. 159.

[17] *Ibid.*, pp. 235-7, from Council Journal in C. O., 5: 1420, pp. 79, 85.

[18] *Ibid.*, p. 258.

[19] See Chapter IX, *infra*.

CHAPTER VI

Germantown[1]

THE task common to American communities
of assimilating an alien race, confronted the
people of Fauquier very early in the history
of that territory.

The first projected settlement with French
Huguenots at Brent Town had failed and normal
colonization by English pioneers was under way,
when a small band of Germans, migrating from
their original location on the Rapidan, crossed the
North Branch and established a settlement on
Licking run from which they spread, taking up
lands in other parts of the county and founding
families which by inter-marriage and association
have become merged with the English speaking
population of today.

These people had been iron miners in the Sieg
valley and subjects of the Catholic Counts of
Nassau-Siegen. As Protestants they had been
subjected to religious persecution and although this
had been abated at the time of their emigration,
the disturbances it created had left behind an industrial disorganization and depression from which
the district continued to suffer. When Christopher
de Graffenried, therefore, offered them employment in the new world, they were glad to accept
the opportunity to better their fortunes and incidentally to insure their religious freedom.

Graffenried and Franz Louis Michel, both natives
of Switzerland, had been active in establishing Ger-

man and Swiss Protestants in the colonies, and although the New Berne settlement in North Carolina was Graffenried's most important enterprise, among his other plans was that of founding a frontier colony in Virginia. With this end in view he employed Michel to explore the lower valley of the Shenandoah and on the latter reporting the discovery of a silver mine in the Massanutten mountain, he took a grant in that locality in 1709. Before the attack on New Berne by the Tuscaroras in 1711 and Graffenried's escape, he had written to Germany to obtain skilled miners for his Virginia project. The result was that a party consisting of J. Justiss Albrecht, the head miner, and forty others, was eventually organized and leaving Siegen in 1713, travelled to London where Graffenried met them, but he being at that time without funds was unable to carry out his original purpose. He writes in his autobiography:[2]

"On my arrival in London I was extremely surprised to learn that the master miner had arrived with 40 other miners. This caused me much trouble, care, concern and expense, since these people came so inconsiderately, without orders, in the opinion of finding everything necessary for their maintenance as well as work in the mines, but there was nothing for them to do, and my purse was so empty that it was with difficulty that I could supply my most urgent necessities, having used all my money in America, and being as yet without a bill of exchange from Berne. Thus it was impossible to assist so large a number, and the reader can easily conjecture what care and embarrassment all this caused me, since these people were persuaded that according to the agreement, I was compelled to assist them. This would have been so, had they come at my order. I theretofore wrote them several letters from America, in German, of which they received some, in which I had ad-

vised that the master miner should not come until new orders
were received and saying that there was nothing for them
to do as yet by reason of the unexpected Indian war in Carolina, and that M. [Michel] had not yet indicated the place,
but that if the master miner nevertheless wished to come alone
or in company with one or two he could do so but merely to
see the place. But without paying attention to what I had
just written him he made preparations and came to London
with his company and all their baggage.

"But what was there to do here? I could not give them
better advice than to return home. This displeased them very
much, so much so that they preferred to serve for four years
as servants in America. However, there was no vessel ready
to sail for America and it was therefore necessary for them
to remain in London all winter, but where to obtain subsistence? This gave me an inconceivable amount of trouble, so
that finally I was moved to apply to several Lords for work
and bread for these people. They were then employed to make
or repair a large dyke (or dam) but a heavy rain set in and
all was overturned. This made it necessary to devise new ex-
pedients for their subsistence. I found a place for one party
but not for all. In the meantime I was anxious to hurry home,
fearing to travel in winter, and already feeling an attack of
gout, which could ill accomodate itself to the cold.

"Finally I found two wealthy merchants doing business in
Virginia to whom I stated and recommended this affair as best
I could. With that I also consulted a noted Lord, to whom I
was honestly recommended by the Governor of Virginia, concerning the miners, to the end that he was able to serve me
and render for me his good offices at court. We concluded
that these people should put their money together, taking account of the same proportionately, and that one of the above
mentioned merchants should procure the remainder necessary
for the transportation and maintenance of the miners, and that
the Governor of Virginia should receive and care for them on
their arrival at Williamsburg, and pay the captain of the vessel,
who in turn should return to the merchants of London the
money advanced by them. On this subject I wrote a long letter
to Gov. Spotswood, to whom I represented as best I could
both affairs, saying that if the mines did not turn out as de-

sired, these good people should be sent as a colony to the land, which we con-jointly own in Virginia, situated not far from the place where we found raw minerals (by which we presumed we had silver mines there) where they would be able to locate through the good offices and care of the Governor, but in case there was not sufficient indications to show silver mines, to look elsewhere. And since there are no iron or copper forges in Virginia, although there are quantities of such minerals, one will be able to trade in these, for which no royal patents are needed, as in the case with those of silver. In the hope that this will succeed I recommended these good people to the Almighty, wishing them also a happy voyage. Thus they departed in the beginning of the year 1714."

The merchant referred to by Graffenried as the financier of the expedition, was Micajah Perry, who acted in the belief that Governor Spotswood would welcome the importation and reimburse him for the money advanced. In this he was not disappointed and Spotswood at a meeting of the Council, April 28, 1714, reported the arrival of 'sundry Germans * * * invited hither by the Baron de Graffenried', and obtained permission to establish them above the falls of the Rappahannock with the status of Rangers in respect to exemption from parish levies and an allowance for their support equivalent to rangers' pay. There is no evidence, however, that they performed any active military service.

Governor Spotswood with characteristic energy, promptly set about the business of locating the new outpost and temporarily providing for the Germans. On May 17th he started on 'a fortnight's expedition to Reconnoitre the Norward Frontier' for this purpose, and on his return he reported to the Lords of Trade, July 21, 1714.

"In order", he said, "to supply that part which was to have been covered by the Tuscaroras I have placed here a number of Protestant Germans, built them a Fort and furnished it with 2 pieces of Cannon and some Ammunition which will awe the stragling partys of Northern Indians and be a good Barrier for all that part of the Country. These Germans were invited over some years ago by the Baron de Graffinried who has her Majesty's Letter to the Governor of Virginia to furnish them with Land upon their arrival. They are generally such as have been employed in their own country as Miners and say they are satisfyed there are divers kinds of minerals and even a good appearance of Silver Oar, but that tis impossible for any man to know whether those Mines will turn to account without digging some depth in the earth, a liberty I shall not give them until I receive an Answer to what I represented to your Lo'ps concerning yo'r Ascertaining her Majesty's Share."[3]

The site selected by Spotswood for the settlement which became known as Germanna, was on the banks of the Rapidan and is thus described by Colonel William Byrd in 1732 in his 'History of the Dividing Line': 'The river winds in the form of a horseshoe about Germanna, making it a peninsula containing about 400 acres. Rappahannock forks about 14 miles below this place'. (Byrd, II, p. 64). Here the German miners were placed to subsist as best they might on the rangers' pay and by hunting, while Spotswood sought to obtain a royal license to develop the silver mines in the Shenandoah Valley. In writing to the Lords of Trade, January 27, 1715, he claims credit for their support during this period. He says,

"The act for exempting certain German protestants from ye payment of levys, and is made in favor of several families of that nation, who upon the encouragement of the Baron de Graffenried came over hither in hopes to find out mines, but the

Baron's misfortunes obliged him to leave the country before
their arrival. They have been settled in ye frontiers of Rappa,
and subsisted since chiefly at my charge and the contributions
of some gentlemen that have a prospect of being reimbursed
by their labor, whenever His Majesty shall be pleased, by ascertaining his share, to give encouragement for working these
mines, and I hope the kind reception they have found here will
invite more of the same nation to transport themselves to this
colony."[4]

The act exempting them from levies was based
on the Huguenot legislation of 1700, and was
passed at Spotswood's instigation, December 24,
1714. It was entitled 'An Act to exempt certain
German Protestants from the payment of levies
for seven years and for erecting the Parish of St.
George', and provided that,

"Whereas certain German protestants, to the number of
forty-two persons or thereabouts, have been settled above the
falls of the River Rappahannock, on the southern branch of
the said river, called Rapidan, at a place named Germanna,
in the county of Essex and have there begun to build and
make improvements for their cohabitation, to the great advantage of this colony and the security of the frontiers in those
parts from the intrusions of the Indians; for the encouragement therefor of the said Germans in their infant settlement, be
it enacted by the Lieutenant Governor, council and burgesses
of this present General Assembly, and it is hereby enacted by
the authority of the same, that all and every of the Germans
now seated at Germanna, shall be and are hereby declared to
be free and discharged from the payment of all and all manner
of public or county levies or assessments whatsoever, for and
during the term of seven years from and after the end of this
session of assembly; and if any other German or other foreign
protestants shall within said term of seven years settle themselves at Germanna aforesaid, such German and Germans and
other foreign protestants shall be free and discharged from
the payment of all such levies for the term of seven years

from the time of their settling at Germanna respectively, provided such Germans or foreigners, who now are, or who, within the said term of seven years, shall be and continue for so long time to cohabit at Germanna. And if any of the said Germans or others shall depart from the said settlement at Germanna and inhabit any other part of this colony, such German and Germans and other foreign protestants leaving the said settlement, shall be assessed and pay all such levies and taxes as his Majesty's subjects of this dominion shall and do pay.

"And be it further enacted by the authority aforesaid, that the place called Germanna, together with a precinct of land thereunto next adjoining, extending five miles on each side of the said town or settlement of Germanna, is and shall be from henceforth a distinct parish of itself, and shall be called by the name of the Parish of St. George, and is and shall be divided and exempt from the parish of St. Mary, in said county of Essex, and from all dependencies, offices, charges and contributions, for and in respect thereof, and from the cure of the minister of said parish of St. Mary, and his successors, and also is and shall be discharged of all levies, oblations, obventions and all other parochial duties whatsoever, relating to the said parish of St. Mary.

"Provided always that the parishioners of St. George shall not be obliged to pay any minister or ministers of their said parish the salary allowed by law to the ministers of other parishes of this colony, until such time as there shall be the number of 400 tithable persons in the said parish of St. George; but the said parishioners are and shall be at liberty in the meantime to agree with their minister and ministers to serve the cure of their said parish upon such terms as by the Lieutenant Governor or the Governor or Commander in Chief of this Dominion for the time being with the advice of council shall be thought reasonable, any law, statute or custom to the contrary thereof in any wise notwithstanding."[5]

The Germanna colonists in the first year of their residence on the Rapidan were put to work build-

ing a blockhouse, a road and a bridge, but it does
not appear that they were engaged at first in any
organized industry, indeed Spotswood answering a
political charge that he was exploiting them, testifies February 7, 1716,[6] that 'the terms upon which
the Germans are settled will not appear very like
oppression, seeing they have lived for two years
upon this land, without paying any rent at all, and
that all which is demanded of them for the future
is no more than twelve days' work a year for each
household, which is not so much as rent of their
houses, without any land, would have cost in any
other part of the country'.

A description of their village over a year after its
establishment, is found in John Fontaine's diary.[7]
His entry under date of June, 1715, is as follows:

"About five we crossed a bridge that was made by the
Germans and about six we arrived at the German settlement.
We went immediately to the minister's house. We found
nothing to eat, but lived on our small provisions, and lay upon
good straw. We passed the night very indifferently.

"Our beds not being very easy, as soon as it was day we
got up. It rained hard, but notwithstanding, we walked
about the town, which is palisaded with stakes stuck in the
ground, and laid close the one to the other, and of substance
to bear out a musket shot. There are but nine families, and
they have nine houses, built all in a line, and before every
house, about twenty feet distant from it, they have small sheds
built for their hogs and hens, so that the hog sties and houses
make a street. The place that is poled is a pentagon, very
regularly laid out: and in the very centre there is a blockhouse,
made with five sides, which answer to the five sides of the
great inclosure: there are loop holes through it from which
you may see all the inside of the inclosure. This was intended for a retreat for the people, in case they were not able
to defend the palisades, if attacked by the Indians.

"They make use of this blockhouse for divine service. They

go to prayer constantly once a day, and have two sermons on Sunday. We went to hear them perform their service, which was done in their own language, which we did not understand: but they seemed to be very devout and sang the psalms well.

"This town or settlement lies upon Rappahanoc River thirty miles above the Falls and thirty miles from any inhabitants. The Germans live very miserably. We would tarry here some time, but for want of provisions we were obliged to go. We got from the minister a bit of smoked beef and cabbage which were very ordinary and dirtily drest. We made a collection between us three of about thirty shillings for the minister and about twelve of the clock we took our leave."

In 1716, Governor Spotswood, tired of waiting for a special license to mine silver and convinced perhaps by his 'transmontane' expedition that the valley was not a safe place to plant a colony, turned his attention to the prospect of iron mining in the vicinity of Germanna. The Germans had reported on their arrival that they saw indications of iron and Spotswood now accepted this possibility as a means of recompensing himself for their transportation and support. He accordingly took title, October 31, 1716, to 3,229 acres (*Patents* 10:290) including the site of Germanna, about ten miles east of which he subsequently built his famous furnace.

The commencement of industrial activity, however, developed a disagreement between Spotswood and his miners over the terms of their employment. The arrangement at the time of their importation was that they should work out in wages the money advanced for their transportation, instead of serving under the customary terms of indenture, and in this they were liberally treated. But now they asked for title in themselves to the ore lands subject only to the payment of their debt,

a demand that Spotswood flatly refused. Religious
differences may also have arisen between the original miners from Siegen, who belonged to the
Reformed Church, and a second supply of twenty
families from Alsace and the Palatinate imported
in 1717, who were Lutherans. At any rate, the
Siegenians, dissatisfied with Spotswood's terms,
cast about for an opportunity to establish themselves independently. In this frame of mind they
were approached by an agent of the proprietors of
the Northern Neck and induced to make entry for
a tract of land east of the new Elk Marsh settlement in what was afterward Fauquier, but was
then Stafford county. A warrant was issued in the
summer of 1718 for 1,805 acres lying on both sides
of Licking run, to 'Jacob Holtzclaw, John Hoffman,
John Fishback, Peter Hitt, Harman Fishback, Tilman Weaver, John Spillman and several other
Germans.' Of the latter were John Kemper, John
Joseph Martin, Joseph Coons and Jacob Rector.[8]
These men and one other, whose identity is not
established, moved with their families from Germanna and traveling the old Iroquois trail occupied
the Licking run tract in 1720, although owing to
the death of Catherine Lady Fairfax, the proprietary land office was closed at that time and the
patent was not issued until August 22, 1724 (*N. N.
Grants*, Book A., p. 63). The conveyance was made
by Colonel Carter during his second agency and re-
cites that 'Whereas, Capt. Thos. Hooper, late surveyor, formerly made a survey of a tract of land
at the instance and request of the Germans settled
upon Licking run, one of ye branches of Occaquan,
In Stafford county, and whereas the said Germans
having returned a platt of the said survey under the

hand of Thos. Barber, surveyor, making the said
survey to contain eighteen hundred and five acres
and one hundred and eight perch of land, and the
said Germans now moving to have our grant for the
said land to be passed in the name of three of their
number that are naturalized, to-witt: John Fishback, John Hoffman and Jacob Holtzclaw, of Stafford county, know Yee therefore, etc.'

The bill filed in the Fauquier County Court, September 27, 1759, in *Spillman* v. *Gent* (*Minutes*,
1759-63) states that the twelve Germans entered
into an agreement with each other that each should
bear equally the expense of acquiring title to this
tract; that the land should be divided into twelve
parts of 150 acres each, which should be distributed
by lot; that Hoffman, Fishback and Holtzclaw, acting as their trustees, should make leases for 99
years to the others for their allotments, and that the
leases should be renewable at the expiration of their
terms.

The Rev. James Kemper, a son of John Peter
Kemper and a grandson of John Kemper, throws
further light on the organization of the Germantown community. He says in his 'Life's Review',
an autobiography written 1830-1834, that each of
the twelve shares in the Germantown grant was
surveyed 'in an oblong square, the run or creek passing through the middle of each tract'.[9] He also
testifies that in their trek to Germantown the colonists packed all their provisions on their heads
and thereafter 'raised their first crop with hoes, in
both of which their women bore a part'. He continues, 'my grandfather invented the first shovel
plow, and in a few years they had large stocks of
tame and very large cattle'.

The Siegen miners had been joined soon after their arrival at Germanna by a pastor of their own Evangelical Reformed Church, the Rev. Henry Haeger, and he subsequently followed them to Germantown. Born at Anthausen, near Siegen, about 1644, he had taught Latin in schools in that town, and afterwards had served as pastor to various congregations in the district. A petition laid before 'The Society for the Propagation of the Gospel in Foreign Parts', of London, in October, 1719, describes his ministrations at Germanna:

"The case of thirty-two protestant German families settled in Virginia humbly showeth; that twelve protestant German families, consisting of about fifty persons, arrived April 1714 in Virginia, and were therein settled near the Rappahannock River. That in 1717, seventeen Protestant German families, consisting of about four score persons came and set down near their countrymen, and many more both German and Swiss families, are likely to come there and settle likewise. That for the enjoyment of the ministries of religion there will be the necessity of building a small church in the place of their settlement, and of maintaining a minister who shall catechise, read and perform divine offices among them in the German tongue, which is the only language they do yet understand. That there went indeed with the first twelve German families, one minister named Henry Haeger, a very sober, honest man, of about 75 years of age, but he being likely to be past service in a short time, they have empowered Mr. Jacob Christopher Zollicoffer, of St. Gall, in Switzerland, to go into Europe, and there obtain, if possible, some contributions from pious and charitable christians, towards the building of their church and bringing over with him a young German minister, to assist the said Mr. Haeger in the ministry of religion, and to succeed him when he shall die; to get him ordained in England by the Rt. Rev. Lord Bishop of London; and to bring over with him the liturgy of the Church of England, translated into high Dutch, which they are desirous to use in their public worship. But the new settlement consisting of but mean persons, being utterly unable of themselves to build a church, and to make up a salary sufficient to maintain such assisting minister, they humbly implore the countenance and encouragement of the Lord Bishop of London and others, the Lords and Bishops, and also the venerable society for the propagation of the Gospel in foreign parts; that they would take their case under their pious consideration, and grant their usual allowance, for the support of a minister, and if it may be, to contribute something towards the building of their church. And they shall ever pray that God may reward their beneficence both here and hereafter."[10]

The society considered this appeal, but decided that Virginia was not included in its field of activity and that it could not send out a missionary. Through this agency, however, twenty-five copies of the book of common prayer, printed in German, were eventually received by the colonists.

Meantime Zollicoffer had gone to Germany and June 15, 1720, inserted an advertisement in a newspaper published at Frankfort-on-the-Main, in which Germanna and Germantown appear to have been confused. It read:

"It will be well remembered by everybody how some years ago several thousand people, of both sexes and different religions, emigrated from the Palatinate and neighboring places, to be transported to America. Although a part of this people died and a part returned to Germany, yet 700 persons were sent to Carolina, and 300 families to New York. But 72 families came to Virginia, the largest part of them, however, had to pay the passage, according to the custom of the country, with several years of servitude among the Englishmen there. The rest, being free, consist of thirty-two families, of whom twelve are Evangelical Reformed and twenty are Evangelical Lutherans. They, together with an old Reformed minister, Henry

Haeger, 76 years of age, have established a colony in the year 1714 in the said Virginia, called Germantown, on the Brapenhenck [Rappahannock]. Here at a well situated place, under the sovereignty of Great Britain, they support themselves in all quietness by agriculture and the raising of cattle, hoping that they will increase and prosper more and more, especially when within the next year the remaining German families, scattered through their servitude, will obtain their freedom and settle at Germantown and thus strengthen the colony."[11]

An appeal was then made for contributions for a church and school house 'which is served by the above named minister in common', and the advertisement ended with the statement that Zollicoffer's credentials had been signed by Henry Haeger, 'minister of the Germans in Virginia; John Jost Merdten [Martin] and John Jacob Rechtor [Rector], elders of the congregation'.

The exemption from taxes obtained by Governor Spotswood for his German tenants in 1714 had been extended by the act organizing Spotsylvania, November 20, 1720 (Hening IV, p. 299), which provided that, 'because foreign Protestants may not understand English readily, if any such shall entertain a minister of their own, they and their tithables shall be free for ten years from said first day of May, 1721'. Before the expiration of this period, the Germantown settlers prayed for a further extention which was granted in an act of 1731, 'to exempt certain German Protestants in the Colony of Stafford from the payment of Parish levies'.[12]

Henry Haeger died in the spring of 1738 at the advanced age of 94 years, and it does not appear that the Germantown congregation ever again had a resident minister of their own faith, nor that further exemption from taxation was accorded them. A Moravian missionary passing through Germantown in 1743, testifies that the congregation at that time had only a lay reader whose name was 'Holtzklo,' and that for the services of a minister they were dependent on annual visits from John Bartholomew Rieger, pastor of the Reformed church at Lancaster, Pennsylvania. That they eventually acquired a church and school house, however, appears from an entry in the diary of the Rev. Matthew G. Gottschalk who traveled through Maryland and Virginia in 1748:

'[April] ninth, Germantown, Virginia.

'It is like a village in Germany where the houses are far apart. It is situated along a little creek, Lucken [Licking] Run. They are from the Siegen District and are all Reformed people. They live about ten miles from the Little Fork of the Rippehanning [Rappahannock]. They have as their lay reader the old Mr. Holtzklo [Jacob Holtzclaw] who receives from each family thirty pounds of tobacco as salary. There is a church and a school house'.[13]

Later in the same year the place was visited by Bishop Spangenberg, another Moravian, who says:

'Toward evening we came to Licken Run, or Germantown. We stayed with an old friend by the name of Holtzklo. The village is occupied by Reformer miners from Nassau Siegen. They live very quietly together and are nice people'.[14]

Again, in 1748, the Rev. Michael Schlatter, a missionary of the German Reformed Synod organized in Philadelphia in 1747, visited Germantown and records in his journal:

'On the 12th of May we continued our journey

toward the southwest, not without weariness and
danger from wild beasts, 42 miles further to New
Germantown. Here I preached on the 13th and
spoke with the good congregation, promising them
that by the help of God, I would visit them again
and remain longer with them'.[15]

The German miners prospered in their new en-
vironment and soon supplemented their earlier ven-
tures in cattle and corn by the cultivation of tobacco,
to market which they opened a road that joined the
Shenandoah Hunting Path at the future site of
Elk Run Church and formed a link in what afterwards became the Fredericksburg-Winchester road.
This road was first described in grants of land adjacent to it, as the 'German Path' (N. N. Grants, F.,
p. 39), and later in a deed of 1746 (*Prince William
D. B.* 1, p. 127), it is referred to as the 'German rol-
ing road'. Over it the colonists transported their tobacco to Falmouth and with the profits of this trade
embarked in the speculative competition for new
lands so characteristic of that period. Indeed, soon
after the Germantown settlement had been made
transactions of this nature are recorded. Jacob
Holtzclaw, for instance, in 1725, took a grant on
Broad Run; John and Peter Kemper in 1727, acquired the 'Cedar Grove' property, and in 1729, John
Fishback took 280 acres above the mouth of Great
run (see Chapter V, *supra*).
The occupation of these lands and the dispersal of
the settlers to individual holdings in Fauquier and
Culpeper had probably begun in 1746, when a portion of the original Germantown patent was sold to
the church wardens of Hamilton Parish to be used

as a glebe (*Prince William D. B.* 1, p. 158), and at the time of the Revolution, Germantown as a settlement had ceased to exist.[16] Tilman Weaver seems to have been the only one of the founders whose family continued on the land originally allotted to him, and Mr. Willis M. Kemper, writing in 1899, says:

"At the present time there are descendants of but one of the twelve families living on the Germantown tract. A Miss Weaver and her brother still own about 130 acres of this tract, and it is evidently a part of the tract that was originally set off to Tillman Weaver. The original Weaver house, built of logs, now weatherboarded with poplar, still stands.[17] It was built in 1721, as a poplar board over the door with this date carved on it shows * * * The present members of the Weaver family say that their ancestor Tillman or his immediate descendants gradually acquired the larger part of the land covered by the patent, and they say that certain parts of it have always been known as the Hitt tract, the Utterbach tract, etc., and that remains of the old houses are occasionally plowed up in the fields to this day."

Germantown is shown on the Fry and Jefferson map of 1755, and on Thomas Jefferson's map of 1787, but does not again appear except as a place of historic interest on recent local maps.

---

[1] For the matter contained in this chapter general reference is made to the following works: Kemper, *The Genealogy of the Kemper Family in the U. S., Landmarks of Old Prince William,* and an article by Chas. E. Kemper in F. H. S. *Bulletin,* No. 2.

[2] From a MS. copy in the Public Library of Berne, Switzerland. (Kemper, *Genealogy of the Kemper Family,* p. 11.)

[3] *Spotswood's Letters,* II, p. 70.

[4] *Ibid.,* p. 95.

[5] Kemper, *Genealogy, etc.,* pp. 21-2.

[6] *Spotswood's Letters,* II, p. 193.

[7] *Memoirs of a Huguenot Family,* Putnam's reprint, p. 268.

[8] Rev. James Kemper, gives, in addition to these names, those of Utterback, Wayman and Handback (Kemper, *Genealogy, etc.,* p. 40), one of whom may have been the M. Brumback, included in Mr. Chas. E. Kemper's list in F. H. S. *Bulletin,* No. 2, p. 127. Mr. Willis M.

Kemper in *The Fishback Family*, p. 36, is of the opinion that Utterback, Wayman and Handback did not belong to the original Germantown colony.

9 The Germantown tract was a parallelogram the sides of which were 2 1/3 miles long and the ends 1 1/16 miles long. Licking run bisected it lengthwise.

10 Perry, *Church Papers, Virginia*, I, p. 247.

11 Kemper, *Genealogy, etc.*, p. 24.

12 Hening, IV, p. 306.

13 *Va. Magazine*, XI, p. 233.

14 *Journal, Presbyterian Hist. Society*, II, p. 98.

15 Kemper, *Genealogy, etc.*, p. 42.

16 Wills of the founders of Germantown were proved as follows: John Fishback, March 19, 1734; Jacob Holtzclaw, February 29, 1760; Tilman Weaver, March 27, 1760; Peter Hitt, July 27, 1772; John Hoffman, Aug. 17, 1772; and John Rector (son of Jacob), March 22, 1773 (Kemper, *Genealogy, etc.*, p. 52 and F. H. S. *Bulletin*, No. 4, p. 483.)

17 The Weaver house stood until the summer of 1924 when the owner of the property at that time tore it down and in that act of vandalism destroyed probably the oldest house in Fauquier. Mr. Henry I. Hutton, who viewed it just before it was demolished, furnishes the following description of its construction: The original house was a two story frame building 16 ft. by 26 ft. in plan, the lower floor being divided by a partition into two rooms, under one of which was a cellar containing a spring of water. The sills of the house were of hewn oak 10½ in. by 9 in., mortised at the ends and secured by 1 in. oak pins. The studding consisted of 4 in. x 7 in. oak, mortised and pinned to the sills and plates, and dressed and beaded at the door and window openings to serve as frames. The house was weatherboarded outside with boards of heart yellow poplar 10 in. by 1 in., rabbited and laid on flat with ⅜ in. bead. The walls inside were made by plastering a composition of small stones in a red clay and straw mortar between the studding, the surface being trowelled smooth and white washed. The rafters were 4 in. x 4 in. oak and the roof covering consisted of boards 4 ft. long, 7 in. wide and ⅜ in. thick, overlapping like shingles. The joists were 4 in. x 7 in. oak and the floor was laid with 10 in. x 1 in. dressed boards nailed down with hand made 20 d. nails. At the north end of the house there was a chimney 10½ ft. wide, with two fireplaces, side by side, on the first floor, and one on the second; another chimney at the south end was 8½ ft. wide with one fireplace on the first floor and one on the second. The entrance door was on the west side under the eaves with a projection of the wall of the house to one side of it in which there was a port hole overlooking the door. Wings 10 x 26 ft. were later added to each side of the house, the whole being covered by a shingle roof running from the eaves of the wings to the peak of the original roof. All hardware, nails, hinges and latches were of hand wrought iron.

CHAPTER VII

The Parishes and Their Churches.[1]

BEFORE discussing the organization of Fauquier as a separate political unit, it is necessary to examine the system under which the parishes were created and to describe the influence of that system on the civil and ecclesiastical development of the community.

The parish in Virginia was a survival of a primary local division in England through which taxation was imposed and the cost of religious administration, the relief of the poor and the conservation of the moral health of the inhabitants provided for.[2] The early practice in the colony had been to create counties by act of Assembly and to require the justices of the court for the new county to divide it into parishes as local convenience might dictate. At the beginning of the 18th century, however, the colonization of the frontier counties by a class untried in the responsibility of self government, gave rise to the policy of establishing parochial administration in a new territory before its organization as a county was authorized. Under this system the vestry in its civil jurisdiction became a training school for the future justices of the county court, and not until a certain measure of political capacity had been demonstrated by them, was the district entrusted with the full responsibility of county government.

In its ecclesiastical functions the parish was an administrative unit of the English church, supported by parochial taxation and governed by the local

vestry under laws enacted by the Assembly. There
was no diocesan organization in the colony and the
clergy were without direct episcopal control,[3] although a general spiritual oversight was exercised
by the Bishop of London and no minister was allowed to officiate who had not been certified to him
as 'conformable to the Doctrine and Discipline of the
Church of England'.[4] The authority of the London
See was represented by a Commissary, an official
who sat as a member of the colonial council, presided at the very infrequent conventions of the
clergy,[5] made visitations and had other ecclesiastical
duties in the performance of which he appears to
have been constantly engaged in controversies with
the Council.[6]

The vestry of a parish consisted of twelve men,
usually influential land holders,[7] who were elected
by the freeholders for an indefinite term. It was
the only representative body in the parish, or the
county indeed, and on it fell the important duty of
laying the parish levy out of which poor relief was
provided for; the salaries of the minister, clerk and
sexton, paid; glebe lands purchased and buildings
erected; churches and chapels built and repaired,
and other parochial expenses defrayed.[8] In addition
to choosing a minister, its other duties included
judicial inquiry into and presentation for immoral
practices, the apprenticing of bastards and the discipline of vagrants. The vestry was also made responsible for dividing the parish into precincts and
appointing 'procession masters', under whose supervision the business of processioning the boundaries
of every free-holder's property was conducted. Most
of these services, such as collecting and disbursing
the tithes,[9] presenting persons to the court for im-

moral practices,[10] etc., were performed through the two churchwardens, officials selected by the vestry from its own number and re-elected each year.[11]

In the election of the vestries the suffrage qualification at first extended to all freeholders, but by an act of Assembly in 1736 it was restricted to those owning 100 acres of unimproved land or 25 acres of land with a house and plantation.[12] The qualification was even then very broad and in a local government which was practically aristocratic, it soon became the custom for the vestries to retain office without submitting to periodical re-election and to fill vacancies by their own choice. The prolonged term of office which this practice insured together with the arbitrary authority held by the vestry, engendered an autocratic spirit in its members which often brought the body into disfavor with the people and in some cases led to its dissolution by the Assembly.

In its relations with the clergy, an early act of Assembly (1643) conferred on the vestries the power to present for induction a minister of their own choosing. The right of induction was vested in the Governor, who also had authority to induct of his own motion a clergyman whom the vestry had failed to present. This power, however, was rarely exercised and when the system grew up in most of the parishes of retaining ministers from year to year without presentation, the Church bitterly complained of the Governor's failure, in such cases, to present and induct *jure devoluto.* A clergyman regularly inducted acquired a permanent legal claim to his living and became quite independent of the favor or disfavor of his vestry. An unworthy incumbent also, after induction, could only be removed by act of Assembly,[13] and in this relation to their ministers, the vestries, with some justice, were unwilling to be placed.

The salary of a minister, fixed by law, was 16,000 pounds of tobacco,[14] in addition to which he was provided with a glebe consisting usually of about 200 acres of fertile land[15] on which the parish was required to erect a parsonage. Buildings for tenants and livestock completed the equipment and when thus improved and ably managed the glebe added materially to the clergyman's income. That this happy condition seems rarely to have existed, however, was due on the one hand to the vestries' frequent failure to supply adequate accommodations for the minister or to keep the buildings, when provided, in repair;[16] and on the other, to the indifference or ignorance of practical management displayed by the clergy. This, added to the fact that the system of cultivation prevailing during the 17th century at its best had a tendency to rapidly exhaust the land, rendered the glebes in many cases so unproductive that they had to be sold and new land purchased by the vestries or, when this was not done, the ministers often ceased altogether to cultivate their holdings and let them out for such insignificant sums as twenty to forty shillings a year.[17] Often, too, the glebes were so inconveniently situated that the ministers found it necessary to provide residences for themselves nearer to their churches.

Much of the remissness on the part of the clergy in keeping up their glebes was ascribed by the Church to the failure of the vestries to present for induction, it being held that the uncertainty of a minister's tenure deprived him of any interest or incentive in the care of the parish property.[18] Of

twenty-nine answers to queries by the Bishop of
London in 1724, three ministers reported that their
parishes had no glebes; seven reported that there
were no houses on their glebes; five reported that
the houses were untenantable and the glebes rented
out; one that he operated the glebe successfully,
but did not live on it; and thirteen that they lived on
their glebes.[19]

The descent of Hamilton, the parish in which the
county of Fauquier was included, is traced through
the Potomac river line of Northern Neck parishes.
When Stafford was taken from Westmoreland in
1664, it was divided into two parishes separated by
Potomac creek, which were at first generally described as the 'upper' and 'lower' parishes. The
'upper' parish, from which Hamilton was derived,
was referred to in early county records as 'Potomack' parish but prior to 1702 it became known as
Overwharton, while the 'lower' parish took the
name of Chotanck and subsequently that of St.
Paul's, and under the latter designation it survives
today as a parish of King George.[20]

Overwharton parish originally embraced what are
now the counties of Stafford, Prince William, Fairfax, Loudoun, Arlington and the eastern watershed
of Fauquier, or perhaps a more accurate statement
would be that this vast territory was yet to be sub-
divided into the parishes which it afterwards comprised. As a matter of fact parochial jurisdiction
in Overwharton shortly after its formation was confined to a comparatively small strip of land along the
Potomac about eighty miles in length and from
three to twenty miles in width. The Rev. Alex-

ander Scott,[21] minister of Overwharton from 1711
until his death in 1738, states in a report to the
Bishop of London in 1724, that there were 650
families in his parish, 80 to 100 communicants, one
church and several chapels.[22]

When in 1730, the Assembly undertook to create
the parishes as it had the counties, the policy
adopted, as we have seen, was to precede the organization of the new county by the formation of a
parish covering the proposed territory. The first
parish thus created was Hamilton,[23] in May of the
year in which the system was inaugurated. It preceded the formation of Prince William county and
was taken from Overwharton by a line from the
Potomac, following the course of Chipawansick
creek 'and a southwest line to be made from the
head of the north branch of the said creek to the
Parish of Hanover'.[24] Hanover, formed from St.
Mary's in 1712,[25] lay on the Rappahannock river in
what was then Richmond county (afterwards King
George), and was bounded on the east by Deep run.
When Prince William was cut off from Stafford and
King George in March, 1731,[26] it included 'all the
lands on the heads of the said counties above Chipawansick creek, on Potomac river, and Deep run, on
Rappahannock river, and a southwest line to be
made, from the head of the north branch of the said
creek to the head of the said Deep run'. Its territory thus overlapped the northern end of Hanover
and exceeded that of Hamilton, its pre-established
parish. This condition, however, was corrected a
year later when that part of Hanover which lay
north and west of Deep run was added to Hamil-

ton,[27] the latter parish after this accession claiming
all the territory between the rivers from Chipawansick creek and Deep run north to the Blue Ridge
mountains.

Of the places at which services were originally
held in Overwharton, the Stafford court record testifies, April 3rd, 1667, that 'The Court does order that
the minister preach at three particular places in this
county—viz.: At the southeast side of Aquia and at
the Court House, and Chotanck, at a house belonging to Robert Townshend; to officiate every Sabbath Day in one of these places, successively until
further Order.' And later, October 8th, 'Whereas,
There is no certain place in the upper precincts of
this county for the reading of Divine Service, the
court doth order that John Withers, Church Warden
for these precincts, agree for a house to read at the
most convenient place'.[28] The first of these entries
seems to indicate that the original parish church of
Overwharton was on, or near, the site of the old
Aquia Church built in 1751. In Hamilton, the first
parish church was situated 'above Occaquan ferry'
and was originally a chapel of Overwharton. There,
on the creation of Hamilton, the 'freeholders and
housekeepers' were ordered to meet and select a
vestry,[29] while the vestry of Overwharton was required to raise a levy of 10,000 pounds of tobacco
toward the purchase of a glebe for the new parish.[30]

When Truro parish was taken from Hamilton in
1732 the church at Occoquan was assigned to Truro[31]
and Hamilton was directed to pay 'a moiety' of the
ten thousand pounds of tobacco received from Overwharton to be applied by Truro to lessening its

levy.[82]   The creation of Truro preceded the erection
of Fairfax county which was taken from Prince William ten years later.   Truro was formed by dividing
Prince William into two parishes 'by the river Occoquan, and Bull run (a branch thereof) and a course
from thence to the Indian Thoroughfare of the Blue
Ridge Mountains' (Ashby's gap).[88]   This division
stripped Hamilton of the territory included in the
present counties of Fairfax, Arlington and Loudoun,
but left to it that now contained in Prince William
and Fauquier: a still vast area served by a single
church situated on the Quantico near the site of
the future town of Dumfries, which Hamilton took
over as its parish church on the separation of Truro.
Of this church Bishop Meade says that at the time
of the division, 'an old and indifferent church' stood
near Dumfries which in 1752, was sold 'for fifteen
hundred weight of tobacco' to make way for a brick
church.[84]

In the 'back country' of what remained of Hamilton, the settlements had already covered the lands
of the upper Rappahannock drainage and had passed
beyond the Pignut ridge, while the movement from
the Potomac below the Pignut had followed the
Occoquan and its tributaries to meet the earlier
spread from the western waterway. The population
of this territory, a few years after the creation of
Truro, set up its claim to separate local government
and, in anticipation of the formation of Fauquier
from Prince William, the second division of Hamilton parish was made in 1744. In this case the newly
created parish retained the original name while that
part of the old parish which remained in Prince William was given the new name of Dettingen. The act

(September, 1744) creating Dettingen[35] provided, 'that from and after the twenty-fifth day of April next, the said parish of Hamilton shall be divided by a line to be run from the dividing line of Stafford and Prince William counties, a straight course to the head of Dorrell's run; thence down the said run to Cedar run; thence to the fork of Broad run, near the lower line of Col. Carter's tract, called Broad Run tract; thence to the mouth of Bull Lick run, opposite to Jacob Smith's in Fairfax county; and all that part of the said parish, scituate below the said line, to be erected into one distinct parish and called by the name of Dettingen, and all that other part thereof, scituate above the said line, to be erected into one other distinct parish and retain the name of Hamilton'.

The boundary lines described in this act formed an angle at the mouth of the stream that is now known as the North Fork of Broad run, cutting out the southeastern corner of Hamilton to form Dettingen, but leaving the territory of the former intact to the north and west of the new parish.[36] A fact that must also be noted in connection with the delimitation of Dettingen is that its western boundary did not coincide with the line that later became the eastern boundary of the lower part of Fauquier, a discrepancy that has since caused some confusion.

In the formation of Dettingen the act provided that the glebe of Hamilton 'as it now stands' should be sold 'after September, 1746', and the proceeds divided between the two parishes for the purchase of new glebes more convenient to each, but in the meantime that the old glebe and the parsonage house belonging to it, should be occupied by the minister of Hamilton.[37] In conformity, therefore,

to the provisions of the act, John Wright and Joseph
Blackwell, churchwardens of Hamilton, and Valen
tine Peyton and William Butler, acting in the same
capacity for Dettingen, duly advertised its sale in
the *Virginia Gazette*, August 21, 1746.   The property
offered consisted of '300 acres of land conveniently
situated, with a very good dwelling house and other
good houses thereon', but no sale at the time was
effected and it was not until the glebe had again
been advertised that it was finally sold in December,
1748.[38]   In the meantime the vestry of Hamilton
had, in 1746, purchased a new glebe of 258 acres in
two parcels,[39] being part of the original Germantown tract and lying on the Falmouth-Winchester
road, and on it they built a parsonage.[40]   It was
necessary also to provide a new parish church as the
Quantico church was situated in Dettingen and had
been taken over by that parish.   The site selected
was at Elk run about eight and a half miles south
of the parsonage where an Overwharton chapel
probably stood and where a handsome brick church
was built prior to 1759.   Bishop Meade says of the
latter: 'Elk Run church was about fifteen miles, I
think below Fauquier Court House, on the road to
Fredericksburg, upon a small stream from which it
took its name.   It was a substantial brick church—
cruciform, I believe.   I am not certain that the roof
was on it when I first saw it, in 1811.   Its walls
continued for many years after this and I saw them
gradually disappear during my annual visits to the
convention'.[41]   Another church was built in 1755 to
serve the growing cross-roads settlement soon to
be known as Fauquier Court House.   This was St.
Mary's, commonly called the Turkey Run church, a
large frame building situated on the Dumfries-Rap-

pahannock road about one and a quarter miles south of the Court House. Being more conveniently placed than the brick church it eventually super-seded it, and was used long after the latter had been abandoned and allowed to fall into decay.

Of the vestry of Hamilton at this time, other than the churchwardens, the only clue is found in a leaf bound in at the front of the Dettingen Parish Reg-ister containing signatures of vestrymen subscribing to the 'test' in the years 1748 and 1749. The sheet seems to have been used indiscriminately by the vestries of both Hamilton and Dettingen, but the appearance on the list of the names of John Crump, John Frogg, William Eustace, John Bell and William Blackwell, is significant, as all of them figured later as Justices of the first court for Fauquier, and from that and the fact that they were not members of the contemporaneous vestry of Dettingen,[42] it may be inferred that they served on the first vestry of Hamilton after its second division.[43]

The first minister of Hamilton was the Rev. James Keith, of Peterhead, Scotland.[44] A younger son of a distinguished family, he had been destined for the Church, but attracted to the cause of the Pretender, he fought in the Jacobite uprising of 1715 and on its suppression fled to Virginia. Mr. Keith then definitely decided to enter the ministry and later returned to England for Orders. He be-came rector of Henrico Parish prior to 1730, and is found presiding at a meeting of its vestry held at Curles Church, October 28th of that year. He re-signed this charge October 12, 1733,[45] and appears subsequently to have removed to Maryland.[46] On his return to Virginia he was made minister of Hamilton and preached at Quantico until that church was transferred to the new parish of Dettingen in 1745. On the division Mr. Keith's services were retained by Hamilton, where he officiated until his death in 1751. Bishop Meade says, 'from all that I can learn of him he was a worthy man'.[47]

In the choice of Mr. Keith's successor the vestry of Hamilton was less fortunate, as the next incumbent, the Rev. John Brunskill, Jr.,[48] became notorious for evil living and brought open reproach on the Church throughout the colony. He assumed his charge of the parish before July, 1753,[49] and seems almost immediately to have given rein to his dissolute propensities, for on the vestry preferring written charges against him in 1757, Commissary Dawson in a report to the Bishop of London, said, 'The Rev⁴ Mr. John Brunskill, Junʳ, Minister of Hamilton Parish, Prince William, *after having rec⁴ reproof, advice & exhortation,* continued to persist in a most abominable course of life to the great scandal of his Profession & evil example of all good Christians: till at length the church-wardens & gentlemen of the Vestry, in justice to themselves & in Pity to the unhappy Parishioners drew up a Complaint', etc.

In this complaint the vestry charged their minister with 'divers immoralities such as profane Swearing, Drunkenness & immodest actions.' A hearing was then ordered and Mr. Brunskill appeared before a council held May 19, 1757, at which were present, the Governor [Dinwiddie], Wm. Fairfax, John Blair, Wm. Nelson, Thos. Nelson, Philip Grymes, Peter Randolph, Richard Corbin, Philip Ludwell, Mr. Commissary [Dawson] and

Philip Ludwell Lee. The unanimous opinion of this board was 'that every fact he [the defendant] was charged with had been fully proved; that he was a scandal to his profession & ought to be disqualified from ever exercising the office of a clergyman'. At a session held the following day, the members in the meantime having satisfied themselves of the Governor's authority in the case, the council advised that 'his Honor would remove and deprive him, the s⁴ Brunskill, from officiating as a Minister in any church within this Dominion'.

The Governor accordingly issued an order to the vestry of Hamilton to exclude him from their churches, but on Brunskill's being notified of this action he defied the Governor's authority and posted notices in his own handwriting 'at his churches and other public places', citing the 122nd canon (no sentence of deprivation, etc.), and appending the following statement: '(N. B.) According to the above mentioned Canon, I look upon the letter of deprivation, brought up, or said to be brought up, from our Gov' by Mr. Josp⁴ Blackwell to be a *forgery* otherwise a *nullity*. Notwithstanding the late proceedings, I am still lawful Minister of Hamilton Parish & shall continue to officiate as formerly. Given under my hand this 18th day of June, 1757. Jn° Brunskill, Jun''.

This behavior greatly incensed the Governor who, however, believed, as he said, that it had been taken by the advice of others 'as the unhappy man is almost constantly drunk'. Writing to the Bishop of London, September 12, he declares: 'This trial and sentence is much resented by two or three hot headed, inconsiderate clergymen who have endeavored to exasperate others & have with ill manners, thrown out many reflections on the Counci and myself in a private manner'.[50] Of Brunskill he says, 'he was almost guilty of every sin except murder & this last he had very near perpetrated or his own wife'.[51]

As can readily be imagined this deplorable epi sode profoundly disturbed the parish and brought about the dissolution of the vestry, which at that time consisted of John Wright, John James, William Blackwell, Joseph Hudnall, Richard Hampton, Wharton Ransdell, William Rousau, George Neavill, Joseph Blackwell, Elias Edmonds, Benjamin Bullitt and George Crumpe.[52] The preamble to the act of Assembly (September, 1758) by which the dissolution was effected, recited that 'several vestrymen of the Parish of Hamilton, in the county of Prince William, have resigned their seats in the Vestry of the said parish and others who have been elected in their room have refused to act'. The freeholders were then ordered to meet 'at some convenient time and place' to be appointed by the sheriff 'before the 20th of November next' and 'there and then' elect a new vestry. This vestry was to be self-perpetuating, the act providing that 'upon the death, removal or resignation of any of the said vestrymen, so to be elected, the remaining vestrymen shall be, and they are hereby empowered to chuse and elect another vestryman in the room of such vestryman so dying, removing or resigning'.[53]

The minister chosen by the new vestry to succeed the unworthy Brunskill was the Rev. James Craig, who received the King's bounty for Virginia, October 11, 1758.[54] He was in charge in 1774, but probably retired before his death, which occurred in

1801. He was by that time evidently a man of substance, for by his will proved in Fauquier, June 22nd of the year in which he died, he freed all his slaves and left a considerable property to his brother and sister. An item in the account filed by his executor is, 'paid Mr. Iredell for funeral sermon £3'. This Mr. Iredell is referred to by Bishop Meade as one of Mr. Craig's successors in Hamilton. He says, 'I hear of the Rev. Mr. Kennor from Hanover parish, King George, and the Rev. Mr. Iredell, from Culpeper, as living in the parish and preaching, neither of whom was very creditable to the church'.[55]

The first Hamilton parish register, after being taken from the careless hands of a subsequent minister, was placed in the clerk's office of the county court for supposed safekeeping but was there 'torn up, page by page, by the clerks and others, for the purpose of lighting cigars or pipes'.[56] At least this is Bishop Meade's testimony, but its destruction, however it occurred, forces us to turn to the court records for such fragments of parish history as they supply. Thus an order of the court was entered, July 26, 1759, a few months after Fauquier became a county, which directed the vestry to divide the parish into as many precincts as it, the vestry, might consider convenient 'for processioning every particular persons land in the said parish', and to appoint two freeholders in each precinct to see that the processioning was properly performed and to make returns thereof to the vestry.[57] Again we find John Bell and William Eustace mentioned as church wardens in 1760 and 1761.[58] Minor activities at this time are also of record, such as penalties imposed by the court on certain persons 'for not

frequenting their parish church within two months'
These delinquencies were punished by fines of five
shillings, or fifty pounds of tobacco, to be paid to
the church wardens.[59] Fines were also levied for
'profane swearing' and that, in this matter at least
the law was no respecter of persons is shown by
the fact that at a court held November 27, 1760
Colonel John Churchill and his brother, Armistead,
were presented by the grand jury for this offense.[60]

The requirements of the increasing population of
Fauquier made a further division of Hamilton parish
necessary in 1769, and under date of May 10th of
that year, the following entry occurs in the Journal
of the House of Burgesses:[61]

"A Petition of the Minister and sundry inhabitants of the
Parish of Hamilton whose Names are thereunto subscribed
was presented to the House and read; setting forth that from
the large Extent of the Parish it is not in the Minister's Power
to perform his Duty as a Preacher to the whole Parish in so
regular a Manner as is necessary: and many of the Inhabitants reside so far from their Parish Churches that they
can but seldom attend Public Worship: from which causes
Dissenters have opportunity and Encouragement to propagate
their pernicious Doctrines: and that there being now in the
said Parish two thousand eight hundred and twenty-four Tithables, which Number is expected to increase, the said Parish
will admit of a Division, without being very burthensome to the
Inhabitants thereof; and therefore praying that the said Parish
may be divided into two Parishes by a straight Line to begin
at the North Fork of Broad Run at an Angle made by the
Line that divided the said Parish of Hamilton from the Parish
of Dettingen and to end at two red Oaks on the Bank of the
North Fork of Rappahannock River in the plantation of Jesse
Williams, which Line would divide the said Parish into nearly

equal parts, leaving a small Majority of Tithables in the lower Part."

This petition was granted and the division was made by an act passed in December, 1769, which established the line defined in the petition, as the dividing line between the two parishes and provided that the upper parish should be known as the Parish of Leeds[62] and that the lower should retain the name of Hamilton.[63]

The position of the angle in the Dettingen line has already been described and the new Leeds-Hamilton boundary passed westward from that point through the lower end of the settlement then known as Fauquier Court House[64] and terminated at a point on the north bank of the Rappahannock river opposite the mouth of Negro run.[65] Although not stated in the act, the territory of Leeds also included all that portion of Prince William lying north of Dettingen parish and west of Bull run, while its northern and western boundaries were identical with those of Fauquier county. Hamilton, after the separation of Leeds, included the southern half of Fauquier and a narrow triangle in Prince William between the boundary line of those counties and the western boundary of Dettingen parish.

The act creating Leeds further provided for the sale of the Hamilton glebe and the division of the proceeds between the two parishes in proportion to the number of tithables, after deducting the original contribution of Leeds toward building the Elk Run church. This distribution was, however, objected to and at the ensuing session another act was passed (January, 1770)[66] providing that the proportion to each parish should be on the basis of the tithables only, at the time of the division.

The original act, also, for the second time in the history of Hamilton, dissolved its vestry and ordered that the freeholders of each parish should meet 'at least one month before the first day of July next ensuing' (1770), and elect new vestries for their respective parishes.

The new vestry of Hamilton inaugurated its activities by a petition to the Assembly in 1771[67] alleging that before the division from Leeds there had been an agreement that a majority of one hundred tithables should remain in Hamilton, but that there proved to be instead a majority of sixty in Leeds, and that this condition should be corrected by a rectification of the boundary, the new line to begin at the same place as the former one but to run 'from thence in a direct Course to the Mouth of Carter's Run, which will include such a number of Tithables as the Petitioners think themselves entitled to by the said Agreement'.

The vestry of Leeds answered this appeal by presenting a memorial in 1772[68] denying that any such agreement had been made and stating that as a matter of fact there were at that time more tithables in Hamilton than in Leeds. The memorial further set forth that before the two parishes were divided 'two large Churches, one of Brick and the other of Wood, were built, both of which are in the present Parish of Hamilton, and that the Petitioners have been obliged to build four Churches in their own Parish at a very considerable Expence and therefore praying that the said Petition for another Division of the said Parishes may be rejected, and that the Parishioners of Hamilton may be obliged to refund to those of Leeds a reasonable proportion of the Tobacco paid for building the said Brick Church'.

The result of these proceedings was that Hamilton's claim was rejected and the Assembly passed an act appointing Elias Edmonds, James Bell, William Waite, Charles Chilton, Charles Morehead, William Jones, Linaugh Helm and William Alexander, to appraise the value of the Elk Run Church and ordering Hamilton to levy one-half the valuation so established, to be paid to the vestry of Leeds 'to and for the use of the said parish'.[69]

In the meantime the Hamilton glebe had been sold to Martin Pickett for £200, 5s. and the conveyance was made November 26, 1770,[70] by the churchwardens, Jeremiah Darnall and John Blackwell, representing the Hamilton vestry elected after the separation of Leeds, the other members of which were, Landon Carter, William Grant, William Blackwell, Daniel Bradford, James Wright, Jonathan Gibson, Zachary Lewis, William Eustace, Nicholas George and Armisted Churchill. This vestry then purchased of Robert Knox, June 30, 1773, a new glebe for Hamilton consisting of 345 acres of land on the Marsh road between the present villages of Liberty and Bealton,[71] a position not so convenient to the two churches of the parish as that of the former glebe.

The first vestry of Leeds, several of whose members lived in the Court House village, consisted of Martin Pickett, John O'Bannon, James Scott, Henry Peyton, William Edmonds, Humphrey Brooke, Samuel Grigsby, William Pickett, Charles Chinn, Thomas Marshall, John Moffett and John Chilton.[72] They lost no time in providing conveniences for public worship as appears from their address to the Assembly in 1772. The four wooden churches which they had built by that time were, Taylor's Church at Bethel near Warrenton, Goose Creek Church at Salem (afterwards Marshall), old Bull Run Church in Prince William and Pipers Church in Leeds Manor.[73]

A glebe of 220 acres was secured for Leeds in 1773 by the purchase of three adjoining tracts on Little river. In May, 25 acres were purchased from Thomas Bartlett for £31, 5s.,[74] and 83 acres from John Fishback for £ 145, 5s., the vestry being described in the deed to the latter property as 'gentlemen and vestrymen of the Parish of Leeds in the counties of Fauquier and Prince William'.[75] The third tract was added in October, when 112 acres were purchased from John Glascock for £ 67, 4s.[76]

The first minister of Leeds was the Rev. James Thomson, a young Scotchman, who was born near Glasgow in 1739.[77] He came to Virginia in 1763 and lived at first in the family of Thomas Marshall at 'The Hollow', near the present village of Markham, where he taught the elder children. In 1765 he went to England to receive orders[78] and returned about 1768. He was chosen minister of Leeds in 1769, and in the same year married Mary Ann Farrow, sister of Nimrod Farrow. He lived on the glebe, which was provided a few years later. and there conducted a school in addition to his parochial duties, which were heavy as the churches of his parish were widely separated, and Bishop Meade testifies to his 'punctuality' in preaching at all four of them. The latter says of his ability as

a preacher, 'from an examination of some of his
sermons, or parts of sermons, I should say that
they were marked by more taste or talent than
most of those which have been submitted to my
perusal'. That they did not lack force, and that
Mr. Thomson as a minister of the Church of England dared in the cause of liberty, to preach treason, is shown by an extract from one of his ful-
minations in the stirring days of 1775:

"You have all heard before now," he said, "of the measures taken by the British Parliament to deprive his Majesty's
subjects of these Colonies of their just and legal rights, by imposing several taxes upon them destructive of their liberties
as British subjects. And to inforce those acts they have for
some time blocked up the harbour of the city of Boston with
ships-of-war, and overawed the inhabitants by British troops.
By which illegal steps, the people in general have endured great
hardships by being deprived of their trade, and the poor reduced to great want. It is therefore incumbent upon every
one of us, as men and Christians, cheerfully to contribute according to our ability toward their relief. And as we know
not how soon their case may be our own, I would likewise
recommend to you to contribute something toward supplying
the country with arms and ammunition, that if we be attacked
we may be in a posture of defence. And I make no doubt
that what you bestow in this manner will be employed in the
use you intend it for. If you want to be better informed with
respect to the Acts which have passed with a view to impose
illegal taxes upon us and deprive us of our liberties, I shall
refer you to the gentlemen of the committee for this county,
who will satisfy you on that head."[79]

Mr. Thomson officiated as minister of Leeds
until his death in 1812, and saw the decline of the
Church in the dark years that followed the Revolution.

The first measure leading to the disestablishment of the Church in Virginia was adopted soon
after the colonies proclaimed their independence.
The announcement of the principle of religious
liberty contained in the Bill of Righs of June, 1776,
was followed by an act of Assembly passed in
October of the same year, declaring null and void
all acts of Parliament which limited the freedom of
religious opinion or restricted the form of worship.
Dissenters were exempted by this act from the
payment of parish levies and that these levies
should not fall too heavily on persons still adhering
to the Church, the act suspended their payment for
one year.[80]   The Church was thus deprived without warning of its only source of revenue and a
condition created which it was totally unprepared
to meet.   The glebes, to be sure, were reserved to
the parishes, but from them alone the clergy could
at best obtain but a meagre living and the idea of
free-will offerings by the people for the support of
the Church, had as yet not been conceived.   The
trend of opinion at the time favored a general
assessment, the tax in the case of each individual
being applied to the purposes of such religious de-
nomination as he should designate, and a bill tc
this effect was introduced in 1784, but was eventually defeated.[81]   In 1786, Thomas Jefferson's
'Statute of Religious Freedom', introduced in 1779
was enacted, and under its provisions the vestries
lost their taxing power and were deprived of their
civil jurisdiction.[82]   This was practically the end o
the characteristic colonial parish, although the fina
disestablishment of the Church did not occur unti
the parish levies were definitely abolished in 1799,[8]
and the glebes confiscated three years later.   Man;

of the clergy were then forced to abandon their charges and the parishes 'one by one gave up the hopeless struggle and passed into the inanition of seeming death'.[84]

The organization of the new Diocese of Virginia in 1785 and the consecration in 1790 of Bishop Madison, the first Bishop, had contributed little to the revival of the Church which cannot be said to have begun until the election of Bishop Moore in May, 1814.[85] This good man did much by his personal influence to awaken a spirit of true religion in the people and through his efforts and those of Bishop Meade,[86] his successor, the foundations of the present Church in Virginia, were laid.

[1] An article by the writer of this book, entitled 'The Parishes and their History', was published in *Bulletin*, No. 3, of the Fauquier Historical Society, June, 1923.

[2] The parish at one time was also a quasi-political division with the privilege of sending one or two representatives to the General Assembly. An Act passed in 1656 provided that 'if any parish shall return a Burgess for their particular occasion, then the charge of the said Burgess to be levied in and by the parish that elected him'. (Hening, I, p. 421.)

[3] The fact seems to have been that the parishes had no desire for the appointment of a colonial bishop, as the support of such a functionary would have increased the local assessments. In an anonymous arraignment of Governor Andros 'as no real friend to the Clergy' the charge was made, that 'it is carefully buzzed into the people's ears that they must not encourage the coveteousness of the clergy, nor be priestridden, otherwise they shall soon have a Bishop with a salary to be raised by the Country and tythes, which the Church Government will allow'. (Perry, *Hist. Coll. Am. Colonial Churches*, I, p. 35.)

[4] Instructions to Thomas Lord Culpeper, Sept. 6, 1679. (*Ibid.*, p. 2.)

[5] Commissary James Blair, July 17, 1724, in answer to queries by the Bishop of London says: 'At first conventions were once a year. This was found inconvenient especially when the Country is in Parties, for, or against a Governor. They are now only upon extraordinary occasions, as the accession of a King or Bishop. I call none now because I had not my commission. The method of Proceeding has been; The Comy. preaches a Sermon; delivers what he has in charge from the Bishop. The Comy. presides; one of the Clergy is clerk, they have a free conference, concerning what the Comy. or any of the Clergy have to propose for the good of the Church in this Country.' (*Ibid.*, p. 257.)

[6] The arraignment of Sir Edmund Andros referred to in a previous note includes this statement: 'My Lord Bishop of London's authority residing there in his commissary is notoriously despised and under-valued. The said commissary having been called before the Governor and Council and restrained from proceeding against several enormities that do plainly belong to the ecclesiastical jurisdiction, such as incestuous marriages and the like, which being taken out of their hands, and ordered to be prosecuted before the Civil Courts were there so slightly handled that they escaped uncondemned. Nay so jealous is the Governor of the said Commissary's meddling in any thing, that if any vestry made their application to him upon occasion of any scandal concerning their minister or any other difference between them and him, they were sure to be reprimanded for it, so that now both ministers and country are very sensible that there is no surer way to lose the Governor's favour than by making any application to the Bishop of London's commissary'. (*Ibid.*, p. 35.)

[7] Jefferson says: 'The vestrymen are usually the most discreet farmers, so distributed through the parish that every part of it may be under the immediate eye of some one of them. They are well acquainted with the details and economy of private life, and they find sufficient inducements to execute their charge well, in their philanthropy, in the approbation of their neighbors, and the distinction which that gives them.' (Fiske, *Old Va. and Her Neighbors*, II, p. 31.)

[8] An act of March 23, 1662, provided: 'That for the making & proportioning of the Levys & Assessments, for building & repairing the Churches & Chapels, Provision for the poor, maintenance of the ministers & each other necessary Uses, & for the more orderly managing all parochial Affairs; Be it enacted that 12 of the most able men of each parish be by the major part of the s⁴ parish chose to be a Vestry out of which number the minister & Vestry to make choice of two Church Wardens yearly, & in Case of the Death of any Vestryman or his Departure out of the parish, that the s⁴ Minister and Vestry make Choice of another to supply his room; And be it further enacted that none shall be admitted to be of the Vestry, that doth not take the Oaths of Allegiance & Supremacy to His Majesty, & subscribe to be conformable to the Doctrine & Discipline of the Church of England'. (Perry, *Hist Coll. Am. Colonial Churches*, I, p. 243.)

[9] The persons in a parish who were 'tithable' and on whom the parish levy was laid were 'all Male persons of the age of sixteen and upwards, and all Negroe, Mulatto, and Indian Women of the same age not being free'. (*Ibid.*, p. 329.) The levy in Dettingen parish for th year 1745, was 28 lbs. tobacco for each tithable person. (*Dettinger Parish Register*, p. 6.)

[10] The oath administered to a churchwarden in 1643 required him 't present all who, to his knowledge, had been guilty of uttering "wicked oaths, violating the Sabbath, profaning the name of God or abusin his word and Commandment, contemning His Holy Sacraments, or any thing relating to His Worship, committing adultery, fornication, drunk eness or defamation, or remaining away from divine service'. (Bruc *Inst. Hist. Va.*, I, p. 81.)

[11] Hening, II, p. 45.

[12] *Ibid.*, IV., p. 475.

[13] *Ibid.*, I, p. 242.

[14] Rev. John Bagg of St. Ann's Parish, answering queries by t¹ Bishop of London in 1724 states: 'The Laws of Virginia allow t¹

Minister 16,000 lb. Tobacco (8 per Cent being deducted for Cask) as his yearly Salary, besides perquisites, which follow, (viz:) 50 lb. for Marriage, with the publication of banns, the fee for which is 15 lb., register 5 lb., if a marriage by licence 200 lb. Tob°. Register of births, Baptisms, and Deaths 3 lb. each; funeral Sermons 400 lb., 500 lb., or 600 lb., according to the custom of the Parish, that fee not being settled by Law. I judge my perquisites one Year with another to be about 1200 lb. Tob°.' (Perry, *Hist. Coll. Am. Colonial Churches*, I, p. 316.)

[15] The acreage of the glebes varied widely. That of Bristol Parish in 1724 consisted of '40 acres of barren land, not deserving of a house and consequently has none nor ever had.' (*Ibid.*, p. 267.) On the other hand Hungar's Parish had a glebe of 1,500 acres. (*Ibid.*, p. 273.)

[16] The minister of Southwark Parish in 1724, states that, 'Due care is not taken to keep the house in repair, on the precarious tenure I hold it, without induction I don't think it my business. Beside the buildings are of wood and require such expence to keep them tenantable that my poor salary would be exhausted that way. And the parish were unwilling to do it, so that I have been obliged to look out for a habitation elsewhere'. (*Ibid.*, p. 307.)

[17] *Ibid.*, pp. 302 and 272.

[18] Commissary James Blair says in a communication to the Bishop of London, July 17, 1724, 'I do not know above 4 ministers in all the Country that are inducted; the rest officiate like Chaplains without any assurance of holding their livings but during their good behaviour & the good graces of the Vestry, this I observe has the following evil consequences. 1st. It discourages the better sort of Clergymen who hear of it, from adventuring into this Country. 2nd. The glebes are much neglected & unimproved to what they would be if the Ministers were at a certainty as to the possession of them'. (*Ibid.*, p. 259.)

[19] *Ibid.*, pp. 261-318.

[20] Meade, *Old Churches*, II, p. 183.

[21] This clergyman was the son of the Rev. John Scott of Dipple Parish, Morayshire, Scotland. He was born July 20, 1686, and was ordained by the Bishop of London, who appointed him minister of Overwharton Parish in 1710. On his arrival in Virginia, he states in a report to the Bishop of London that he 'was received by the vestry without induction, that being not common.' Finding his glebe inconvenient he resided at his house on the Potomac which he called 'Dipple.' He acquired a considerable tract of land in what is now Fauquier county and died April 1, 1738. He married Sarah Gibson Brent 'six years after his arrival in Virginia'. (Perry, *Hist. Coll. Am. Colonial Churches*, I, p. 311 and *F. H. S. Bulletin*, No. 1, p. 78.)

[22] Meade, *Old Churches*, II, p. 197.

[23] This parish was named for Lord George Hamilton (1666-1737), Governor of Virginia until his death. He served under William III at the Battle of the Boyne and later as a general officer under Marlborough in all the great battles in Flanders. He was made Earl of Orkney on his marriage to Elizabeth Villiers in 1696. (*Old Prince William*, I, p. 302.)

[24] Hening, IV, p. 304.

[25] *Journal, Diocese Va.*, 1906, p. 315.

[26] Hening, IV, p. 303.

[27] *Ibid.*, p. 366.

[28] *Colonial Churches, Va.,* pp. 256-7.

[29] Hening, IV, p. 304.

[30] The glebe acquired at this time consisted of 300 acres of land, and may have been the tract which Col. Thomas Harrison, in his will dated Sept. 26, 1773, refers to as 'formerly the glebe of Hamilton parish'. It adjoined a tract of 938 acres on Dorrell's run, patented by Thomas Harrison, Sr., Oct. 13, 1710.

[31] This church was abandoned when the first Pohick Church, a simple frame structure situated on the south side of Pohick run in Fairfax county, was built. (*Colonial Churches, Va.,* p. 295.)

[32] Hening, IV, p. 369. This act also provided that the vestrymen of Hamilton parish at the time of the division, should continue to serve in the new parishes in which they respectively resided, and that the freeholders of each parish should then complete their vestries by the selection of the necessary number of new vestrymen.

[33] Hening, IV, p. 366.

[34] Meade, *Old Churches,* II, p. 209.

[35] Hening, V, p. 259.

[36] The location of the angle in the Dettingen parish line is established by a recently discovered survey of the Dettingen boundaries made by James Genn in 1745, and a tributary of Bull run known since 1782 as Young's branch, has been identified as the Bull Lick run mentioned in the act.

[37] Hening, V, p. 259.

[38] *F. H. S. Bulletin,* No. 4, p. 504.

[39] The first tract contained 208 acres and was conveyed by Tilman Weaver and Jacob Holtzclaw to John Wright and Joseph Blackwell, churchwardens, June 22, 1746. It is described as 'Beginning at a red oak saplin in Jeremiah Darnal's line and extending thence with Darnal's line North forty one degrees West eighty two poles thence North forty nine degrees East four hundred twenty seven poles to a white oak in Carter's line thence along Carter's line South forty one degrees East seventy four poles to a small red oak standing by the German rolling road on the West side, thence to the beginning'. (Pr. Wm. D. B., I, p. 127.)

The second piece of land was conveyed by Herman Fishback to John Wright and Joseph Blackwell, churchwardens, Oct. 16, 1746. It consisted of 50 acres of land 'lying and being in or near the German Town in the parish of Hamilton aforesaid on the East side of Licking run between the lands which the aforesaid John Wright and Joseph Blackwell purchased of John Rector, Elizabeth Marr and Tilman Weaver to and for the use of the said parish of Hamilton for a glebe'. (Pr. Wm. D. B., I, p. 230.)

Another conveyance is recorded July 28, 1746, but the quantity of land is not stated and as the glebe on its sale in 1770, when Leeds was created, is described as containing only 240 acres, this latter conveyance was evidently, for some reason, ineffective.

[40] The location is shown on the Fry and Jefferson map of 1755, as three miles north of Germantown.

[41] Meade, *Old Churches,* II, p. 216. Of the interior arrangement of the churches of this period Bishop Meade says, 'The old English custom (beginning with the Royal family in St. George's Church at Windsor) of appropriating the galleries to the rich and noble was

THE PARISHES AND THEIR CHURCHES

soon followed in Virginia, and, as we shall see hereafter, the old aristocratic families could with difficulty be brought down from their high lofts in the old churches, even after they became uncomfortable and almost dangerous. I find an entry on this vestrybook concerning payment to the sextons of these churches for making fires, which is the first of the only two instances I have met with, and I am in doubt whether the payment was for fire in the churches or vestry-rooms in the yard; for I have never seen where provision was made for fires in any of the old churches, either by open chimneys or stoves, if indeed stoves were then known in the land'. (*Ibid.*, p. 210.)

[42] The vestry of Dettingen parish Nov., 1748, consisted of Benjamin Grayson and Anthony Seale, churchwardens, Richard Blackburn, Valentine Peyton, Lewis Renno, John Baxter, Isaac Farguson, Robert Wickliff, Bertrand Ewell, William Tibbs, John Diskin, Charles Ewell (*Dettingen Parish Register*, pp. 1, 19 and 20), all of whose names appear on the test sheet.

[43] Other signatures to the test on this leaf are those of Joseph Hudnall, Benjamin Bullitt and William Rousau, who appear as members of the Hamilton vestry of 1757.

[44] *F. H. S. Bulletin*, No. 3, p. 290. The Rev. James Keith's daughter, Mary, married Thomas Marshall in 1754 and was the mother of Chief Justice John Marshall.

[45] Burton, *Annals Henrico Parish*, Vestry Book, p. 3.

[46] Commissary James Blair writing to the Bishop of London, March 24, 1734/5, says "There are two more vacancies occasioned by the removing of Mr. De Butts and Mr. Keith to Maryland. Of this last I gave your Lordship an account of the misfortune which occasioned it, tho' I did not then know what I have learned since that from some circumstance in his case, our Governor recommended him to the Governor of Maryland'. (Perry, *Hist. Coll. Am. Colonial Churches*, I, p. 358.)

[47] Meade, *Old Churches*, II, p. 216.

[48] This clergyman must not be confused with the Rev. John Brunskill, Senior, who came to Virginia in 1716 and appears as minister of Wilmington Parish in 1724. On June 18th of that year, answering queries by the Bishop of London as to the state of his parish, he asserts that he came out to 'the Plantations as a Missionary' eight years and six months before that date and that he had had no other church since then. April 9, 1719, he united in an address by the clergy to Governor Spotswood and October 30, 1754, he appears in 'A List of the Present Ministers of Virginia', as minister of St. Margaret's and St. Mary's Parishes in Caroline County. His name again occurs in a clergy list June 10, 1755, and on February 25, 1756, we find him heading a list of ten signatories to an address to the Bishop of London, as 'Jnᵒ Brunskill, Senʳ., in the 40th. year of my Ministry'. (Perry, *Hist. Coll. Am. Colonial Churches*, I, pp. 224, 277, 411, 429 and 446.)

[49] *Ibid.*, I, p. 406. This clergyman seems to have been presented by the vestry and regularly inducted by the Governor.

[50] The jurisdiction of the Governor in such cases was not accepted by the clergy, but taking issue in so flagrant a case of misconduct by one of their number, was obviously most injudicious. The whole incident seems to justify the vestries in their attitude of refusing to present ministers for induction.

[51] Perry, *Hist. Coll. Am. Colonial Churches*, I, pp. 449-55.

[52] *W. & M. Quarterly*, 2nd Series, IV, p. 46.

[53] Hening, VII, p. 245.

[54] *Old Prince William*, I, p. 296.

[55] Meade, *Old Churches*, II, p. 218.

[56] *Ibid.*, p. 216. Dr. T. Withers testified in court in 1841, that in 1803 or 1804 when a school boy at the Warren Academy under Parson O'Neil, he had often seen the Parish Register in the school building and that it had at that time been mutilated by the boys. From this Dr. Lindsay suggests that when rescued from Mr. O'Neil's unworthy guardianship and transferred to the Clerk's Office for safekeeping, its tattered condition may have produced the impression that it was valueless and led to its final destruction as Bishop Meade states. A later record of the parish fell a prey to the flames that destroyed the Warren Green Hotel, November 13, 1874. (Rev. John S. Lindsay in his Anniversary Discourse, August 6, 1876.)

[57] *Fauquier Court Minute Book*, 1759-63, p. 13.

[58] *Ibid.*, pp. 89 and 128.

[59] *Ibid.*, pp. 60 and 63.

[60] *Ibid.*, p. 116.

[61] *Journals H. B.*, 1766-69, p. 195

[62] Leeds parish took its name from the Manor of Leeds, the greater part of which lay in Fauquier at the foot of the Blue Ridge mountains.

[63] Hening, VIII, p. 403. This act was passed in November, 1769, to take effect May 1, 1770.

[64] Deeds, 1772, 1782, 1784, to land in the Court House settlement in some cases describe the property conveyed as in the parishes of 'Leeds and Hamilton,' in others in the 'Parish of Leeds', and in others again as in the 'Parish of Hamilton'. (*Fauquier D. B.'s*, 6, p. 248; 5, p. 69; 8, p. 233; 7, p. 412.)

[65] The Jesse Williams tract on the Rappahannock river passed from him to Samuel Porter, March 26, 1780, (*D. B.* 7, p. 258); from Samuel Porter to Martin Porter, March 12, 1819, (*D. B.* 23, p. 184); from Martin Porter to his son John Porter by will dated April 1, 1835, (*W. B.* "A", p. 84); from Ann Porter, widow of John Porter, to W. H. Gaines, Dec. 13, 1873, (*D. B.* 65, p. 341); and from W. H. Gaines to his daughter, Elizabeth Gaines Smith, Dec. 26, 1881, (*D. B.* 72, p. 217.) The dwelling house on this property is situated about half a mile from the east bank of the Rappahannock river opposite the mouth of Negro Run.

[66] Hening, VIII, p. 428.

[67] *Journals, H. B.*, 1770-72, p. 125.

[68] *Ibid.*, p. 225.

[69] Hening, VIII, p. 624.

[70] *Fauquier D. B.*, 4, p. 106.

[71] This tract was situated on Wild Cat run adjoining John Duncan's land, and was part of a tract patented by George Wheatley, Dec. 24, 1716. (*Fauquier D. B.*, 16, p. 467.) It is described in a later conveyance as 'lying on the waters and branches of the Elk Marsh Run'. (*Ibid.*, p. 634.)

By authority of an act of Assembly, Jan. 12, 1802, the Overseers of the Poor of Fauquier county, who at that time consisted of Augustine Jennings, James Withers, John Marr, John Grant, Benjamin Grigsby, Francis Payne, James Hunton, Thomas O'Bannon, Richard Rixey, George Lowry, George Marshall and Jeremiah Darnall, sold this property, Aug. 8, 1806, to Joseph Blackwell. (*Fauquier D. B.*, 16, p. 634.)

[72] *Fauquier Court Minute Book*, 1768-72, pp. 223 and 227.
[73] Meade, *Old Churches*, II, p. 219.
[74] *Fauquier D. B.*, 5, p. 401.
[75] *Ibid.*, p. 403.
[76] *Ibid.*, p. 522.
[77] Meade, *Old Churches*, II, p. 218.
[78] The following entry is found in Mr. Thompson's note book: 'I sailed from Hampton Roads with a fair wind for London, December 30, 1765, in the ship Molly, Cap't Brown'. (*Whittle Parish Leaflet*, April, 1906.)
[79] Meade, *Old Churches*, II, p. 219.
[80] *Colonial Churches, Va.*, p. 40.
[81] *Ibid.*, p. 42.
[82] *Old Prince William*, I p. 299.
[83] *Colonial Churches, Va.*, p. 41.
[84] *Ibid.*, pp. 41 and 45.
[85] Meade, *Old Churches*, I, p. 38.
[86] The Rt. Rev. William Meade, D. D., third Bishop of the Protestant Episcopal Church in Virginia, was born Nov. 11, 1789. He was ordained Feb. 24, 1811, made Asst. Bishop Aug. 19, 1829, and Diocesan Nov. 11, 1841. He died March 14, 1862.

CHAPTER VIII

Organization of the County.

THE county of Fauquier was formed from Prince William May 1, 1759.[1] Following the division of the original Northern Neck county of Northumberland by the erection of Lancaster on the Rapphannock riverside in 1651[2] and Westmoreland on the Potomac in 1653,[3] Old Rappahannock county had been created from Lancaster in 1656,[4] as we have seen, and Stafford from Westmoreland in 1664.[5] Subsequently Old Rappahannock had become extinct on its division into Essex and Richmond in 1692,[6] and from the latter county, King George on the western river had been formed in 1721.[7] Prince William had then been set up 'on the heads of Stafford and King George' in 1731,[8] immediately after the creation of Hamilton, its coterminous parish.

Fauquier was now taken from Prince William above 'a line to be run from the head of Bull run and along the top of the Bull run mountains, to Chapman's mill, in Broad run thoroughfare, from thence by a direct line to the head of Dorrell's run, and from thence by a direct line till it intersects the nearest part of the line dividing Stafford and Prince William counties'. The 'direct line' from the head of Dorrell's run to the Stafford-Prince William line was a short one of about a quarter of a mile, and the Stafford-Prince William boundary which became the eastern end of the southern boundary of Fauquier was, as shown in the last chapter, a south west line from the head of the north branch of Chipawansic creek to the head of Deep run. The course of Deep run, formerly the northern boundary of King George, then continued Fauquier's southern line to the Rappahannock, and that river became the western boundary of the new county.

The territory designated by these boundaries had, before the formation of Prince William, been included in Richmond (and afterwards King George) and Stafford, the interior dividing line being the drainage ridge, or 'forest' as it was described in land grants, between the two great rivers. Following the natural water shed this line after running north through the greater part of what became Fauquier, turned abruptly west where the head of the Rappahannock drainage is reached (approximately the present town of Marshall), and from thence followed the southern drainage of Goose creek, a tributary of the Potomac, back to the head springs of the Rappahannock.[9] In relation to this division land grants are recorded as in Richmond (or King George) and Stafford counties, respectively, prior to 1731.

Fauquier thus completed the western projection of the Rappahannock river counties and extended beyond the headwaters of that stream into the Blue Ridge mountains. There it commanded two important passes, Calmes' (Manassas gap) and Ashby's Bent, the latter originally an Indian thoroughfare through which the early pioneers found their way to the valley and over which later flowed an almost constant stream of westward emigration. Access to it through Fauquier was gained by

roads from Dumfries on the Potomac and Falmouth on the Rappahannock which united at Walnut branch of Cedar run. Afterwards a more direct
route from Falmouth was found in the Fredericksburg-Winchester road, the main highway of the
county.

At the time of its formation, Fauquier's population centered probably at the site of the future Elk
Run Church, to the west of which lay the Elk
Marsh settlement of small landholders who had
approached this region from the falls of the Rappahannock, while to the east of it the old tidewater
civilization, of which the brick church was an ex-
pression,[10] extended into the new territory from
the Potomac. Included in the latter penetration
were the men to whom the administration of the
new county was to be entrusted. Before they were
allowed to assume that responsibility, however,
several ineffectual efforts were made to obtain the
necessary legislation. Whether from a possible
survival of the turbulent spirit of 1732 among the
small planters, or from the fact that the unfavor-
able impression produced by the disturbances of
that year had not yet been effaced, the creation of
the county was delayed for fifteen years after the
reconstruction of Hamilton parish.

The first petition was presented in 1755 and, although at that time a bill to set off the new county
was passed by the House of Burgesses, the Council
refused its assent. Another attempt was made
two years later, but in this case opposition was encountered from Dettingen on the ground that the
proposed division would take too many tithables
from what remained of Prince William, and the
bill failed in the House. A third unsuccessful peti-

tion was offered in 1758, when Fairfax and Loudoun urged their claims to the territory between Bull Run and the Bull Run mountains and Dettingen again brought forward her objection on the score of tithables asking for assurances that 2,000 should be left in the old county.[11] Finally a bill was introduced in March, 1759, which was enacted April 14th of the same year to take effect May 1st.

The county was named for Francis Fauquier, Lieutenant Governor of Virginia, whom Jefferson describes as 'the ablest man who over held that office'.[12] He was appointed January, 1758, and the act creating the county which took his name was passed at the first Assembly held by him after his arrival in the colony. Fauquier was born in London in 1704 at the house of his father, John Francis Fauquier, a Huguenot physician, who had left his native town of Clairac, near Bordeaux in the south of France, after the revocation of the Edict of Nantes (1685) and sought refuge in England. There he found employment in the Mint and eventually became a Director of the Bank of England. The future governor first served in the British army and later after his marriage to Catherine, daughter of Sir Charles Dalston, was seated at Toteridge, in Hertfordshire, where he lived the life of a country gentleman. He was made a Director of the South Sea Company in 1751 and a Fellow of the Royal Society in 1753. In September, 1756, he published a pamphlet on a method of raising money for the prosecution of the Seven Years War with France,[13] which gained him some celebrity and which was probably the basis of his appointment two years later to the governorship of Virginia, although in his will he attributes his promotion solely to the good offices of his 'much esteemed and respected patron, George Montague Dunk, earl of Halifax', at that time President of the Board of Trade. That Fauquier had a 'good interest' among the politically powerful merchants in London may also have had some bearing on his appointment. He died and was buried at Williamsburg, March 3, 1768.[14]

The reputation left by him in Virginia with a reference to his besetting sin, is recorded by John Burke, the historian, as follows:[15]

"With some allowance Fauquier was every thing that could have been wished for by Virginia under a royal government. Generous, liberal, elegant in his manners and acquirements: his example left an impression of taste, refinement and erudition on the character of the colony, which eminently contributed to its present high reputation in the arts. It is stated on evidence sufficiently authentic that on the return of Anson[16] from his circumnavigation of the earth, he accidently fell in with Fauquier, from whom in a single night's play he won at cards the whole of his patrimony: that afterwards being captivated by the striking graces of this gentleman's person and conversation he procured for him the government of Virginia. Unreclaimed by the former subversion of his fortune, he introduced the same fatal propensity to gaming into Virginia: and the example of so many virtues and accomplishments alloyed but by a single vice was but too successful in extending the influence of this pernicious and ruinous practice. He found among the people of his new government a character compounded of the same elements as his own: and he found little difficulty in rendering fashionable a practice which had before his arrival already prevailed to an alarming extent. During the recess of the courts of judicature and assemblies he visited the most distinguished landholders in the colony, and the rage of playing deep, reckless of time, health or money, spread like a contagion amongst a class proverbial for their hospitality, their politeness and fondness for expence. In every thing besides Fauquier was the ornament and delight of Virginia."

The first court for the new county was held May 24, 1759.[17] There is no record of where it was held, but there is a persuasive tradition that it met at a house situated on the Marsh road at its junction with Frogg's road, about three quarters of a mile northwest from the present village of Morrisville. This property had until a few weeks before the first court belonged to Major John Frogg,[18] one of the justices of the new county, and its position on the Marsh road, then the main thoroughfare of lower Fauquier, with the fact that it was within a few miles of Elk Run Church or its antecedent chapel, lends credibility to the legend.

At the first session of the court, however, the justices reached the conclusion 'that the plantation of John Duncan is the most proper and convenient place for the courthouse of this county to be established on' and it was ordered that it be so 'certified to his Honour the Governour'. The land belonging to this John Duncan (there were two of the name in Fauquier at that time), included the junction of the Marsh road and the lower Dumfries road and lay in the immediate vicinity of the Turkey Run Church. It was about fourteen miles north of John Frogg's land and therefore much nearer the geographical center of the county. Here the second court (June 28th) was convened, but on a writ issued by the Governor June 13th, being read, it was learned that 'the house of William Jones on the lands of Richard Henry Lee'[19] had been selected as the temporary court house and thither the court adjourned on the same day. Jones' house was about a mile north of John Duncan's and the Governor's order in this respect practically confirmed the decision of the Fauquier justices to establish the county seat some miles north of what was then the center of population. The transfer of the court to the Jones' house meant only that Richard Henry Lee's political influence had been exerted to secure the selection of his own land for the future settlement.

The organization of the court was now effected. A commission of the peace was first read 'bearing Date at Williamsburg the seventh Day of May last' and directed to eighteen of the most influential residents of the new county, to-wit: Thomas Harrison, Joseph Blackwell, John Wright, William Blackwell, John Frogg, John Bell, William Eustace, John Churchill, William Grant, John Crump, Duff Green, Yelverton Peyton, Thomas Marshall, George Lamkin, Wharton Ransdall, Elias Edmonds, Thomas McClenahan and Richard Foote. They were by this commission jointly and severally assigned to keep 'our peace' and to keep and cause to be kept all the ordinances, statutes and laws of the Kingdom of England and Colony and Dominion of Virginia. The commission was accompanied by a *dedimus* which empowered those named to administer the appointed oaths, including the oath to 'His Majesty's Person and Government' prescribed by an Act of Parliament passed on the accession of George I in 1714. The purpose of this act was to 'further' secure the Protestant succession through the heirs of the reigning King's mother, the Princess Sophia, grand-daughter of James I and wife of Ernest Augustus, Elector of Brunswick-Luneburg. Another oath required of all colonial officials was the 'test', wherein disbelief of the Real Presence in the elements of the Lord's Supper was declared.

After the commission and *dedimus* had been read, Thomas Harrison was sworn as Justice of the Peace and Justice of the County Court in Chancery, by Yelverton Peyton and Thomas Marshall, and subsequently sat as presiding justice of the court.[20] Colonel Harrison was a member of a prominent Stafford county family and had long been active in public affairs. He was sheriff of Prince William in 1733, and appears in the commissions of the peace for that county in 1734 and 1742.[21] He succeeded his father, Thomas Harrison, Sr., as presiding justice in 1752, and represented Prince William in the Assembly from 1748 to 1755. He owned several tracts of land in Fauquier on its creation, including land on Dorrell's run which he had purchased from his father in 1740 and which he refers to in his will as 'The Old Plantation'.[22] It was on this property that he was living in 1759 (see Bertrand Ewell's survey of Prince William-Fauquier boundary, 1759).[23]

Colonel Harrison later served Fauquier as burgess continuously from 1760 to 1769,[24] and succeeded Henry Churchill as county lieutenant, April 23, 1761.

In following the proceedings of this court it must be borne in mind that the justices met in a newly built log house[25] situated at a backwoods crossroads remote from any town or village, in a country

recently opened by a system of rough roads; that
over these roads the inhabitants travelled on horseback or, with ox teams, transported their tobacco,
their only marketable product, to the rivers; that
the region was sparsely settled with a heteroge-
neous population in which English yeomen prepon-
derated, but which contained German settlers,
Scotch-Irish immigrants and ex-indentured servants, the two latter classes often cultivating their
tobacco with convict labor; and that dominating
these elements were the gentry of English descent
whose supremacy was not questioned and to whom
the social life of the community was confined. It was
this class whose plantations were worked by negro
slaves. The background to it all was supplied by
the enormous individual holdings of the great tidewater speculators whose lands were undeveloped
and settled, if at all, by an overseer and a slave
quarter. To complete the picture the glory of a
May morning in Northern Virginia must be considered, with the woods bright with dogwood
bloom and everywhere the radiance of early
summer!

The next step in the organization of the court
was to administer the oaths to such of the justices
as were present, and this Colonel Harrison proceeded to do.

Of the justices named in the commission, Thomas
Harrison, Joseph Blackwell, John Wright, William
Blackwell, John Frogg, John Bell, William Eustace,
John Churchill and William Grant were of the
'quorum', that is, the presence of one or more of
them was necessary in any quorum of four or more
justices constituting a court.

The justices on whom this responsibility was laid were all men of standing and experience in county administration. Captain John Wright,[26] for instance (whose name follows that of Joseph Blackwell afterwards sworn as sheriff), had presided at the court for Prince William at which the first petition for the formation of Fauquier was presented. The record[27] attests that,

"At a Court held at the Court House of Prince William County the 14th. day of April, 1755, For Receiving propositions and Grievances and for proof of Public Claims,
PRESENT John Wright, Bertrand Ewell, John Crumpe, Howson Hooe & Henry Peyton, gent Justices.
A PETITION signed by sundry Inhabitants praying a Division of the County being presented to the Court was ordered to be Certified to the General Assembly."

Captain Wright appears as a justice of Prince William as early as 1743, and held that office until July 4, 1751, when he was appointed sheriff. He was re-appointed in 1752 and afterwards returned to the bench and served again as justice of Prince William until the separation of Fauquier.[28] He was also of the original vestry of Hamilton and we find him serving as churchwarden in 1746[29] and as a member of the vestry in 1758, his service in the meantime probably having been continuous. Born in the 'great house' of his grandfather, Major Francis Wright, on the Lower Machodoc peninsula in Westmoreland, John Wright as a child of thirteen years had removed with his father to a plantation on the Potomac near Powell's run. After his father's death he had continued the westward movement of his family and March 23, 1741, he purchased of Jeremiah Darnall, a plantation called 'Pine View', consisting of 236 acres, in what was then Prince William, lying on the branches of Marsh run near the cross-roads settlement now known as 'Liberty'. There he passed the last fifty years of his life, and there he died and was buried in the winter of 1791-2.[30]

Of the other justices of the quorum, Colonel William Blackwell[31] was the son of Samuel Blackwell, of Northumberland, and a brother of the Joseph Blackwell, who was soon to be sworn as the first sheriff of Fauquier. Colonel Blackwell moved from Northumberland to Prince William (afterwards Fauquier), and appears as a vestryman of Hamilton parish in 1749. He was commissioned colonel of militia, August 23, 1759, and qualified as sheriff at the May court, 1766.

Major John Frogg sat as a justice of Prince William in 1744[32] and very possibly held office in that county until the formation of Fauquier. He also appears as a vestryman of Dettingen parish,[33] and as vestryman of Hamilton in 1747 and 1749. He had numerous land grants from the proprietor's office in 1742, 1743, 1745 and 1746, and early in 1759 we find him living on a tract of 167 acres taken up by John Morehead, September 10, 1740. This land with an adjoining tract of 386 acres on Brown's run,[34] which he had himself patented March 30, 1743, was the property on which court was being held.

Colonel John Bell had been a justice of Prince William in 1753 and 1754,[35] and had represented that county in the House of Burgesses in 1756, 1757 and 1758.[36] He appears as a vestryman of Hamilton parish in 1749 and churchwarden in 1759, 1760 and 1761. He was probably the son of Parson John Bell of Lancaster, who, October 17, 1724, patented 2,470 acres of land 'lying and being in the County of Stafford and on the Great Branch of Accaquan river called Ceader run and on the head Branches of the said run'.[37]

John Bell qualified as colonel of militia September 27, 1759, and he and Thomas Harrison sat as the first burgesses for Fauquier at the sessions of 1760 and 1761.[38] He is mentioned as living in 1764 on a plantation adjoining that of his brother-in-law, Captain William Edmonds, situated on the main road to Winchester above Fauquier Court House,[39] in all liklihood the land patented by his father.

Major William Eustace, who was living on Elk run at the time Fauquier was organized,[40] was a justice of Prince William in 1757, and a church-warden of Hamilton parish in 1749 and 1758[41] He was commissioned major of militia August 23, 1759, and was made sheriff of Fauquier, September 1, 1769.[42] During the Revolution he held the rank of captain in the 2nd Virginia Regiment and received a bounty of 1,000 acres of land for his services.

Colonel John Churchill was the second son of Colonel Armistead Churchill of 'Bushy Park', Middlesex, Va. The Churchills were an ancient family of co. Middlesex, England, the first of whom to settle in Virginia (about 1672) was Colonel William Churchill of 'Wilton'.[43] He sat as a burgess for Middlesex, in 1692 and 1704, and as a member of the Council in 1705.[44] He also appears as a churchwarden of Middlesex parish.[45] John Churchill served as a justice of Prince William county in 1753 and 1755. He was a large land owner in Fauquier, having, with his brothers, William and Armistead, inherited 'Pageland', a tract of 10,600 acres on Turkey run.[46]

William Grant, the last justice of the quorum, had been a justice of Prince William in 1757. At the Fauquier court held June 28, 1759, he produced his commission and was sworn as coroner and later, May 26, 1763, was made sheriff of the county.[47]

Such were the ranking justices of Fauquier, but these gentlemen were not all present when the first court met. William Blackwell, William Eustace, John Churchill and William Grant, however, were sworn, and they together with three of the junior justices, Yelverton Peyton,[48] Thomas Marshall,[49] and George Lamkin[50] took their places on either side of President Harrison as he called the court to order. Captain Wright came in later and being duly sworn took his seat with the others.

The court thus convened proceeded with the qualification of county officers and the appointment of minor officials. The clerk's credentials were first demanded and these Humphrey Brooke[51] submitted in the form of a commission to him under the seal of the deputy secretary of the colony and was forthwith sworn as county clerk, a position held by him for a period of thirty-four years with credit both to himself and to the county that he so faithfully served. On his retirement in 1793, he was succeeded by his son, Francis, who held the office for twelve years. One family, therefore, supplied the clerks of Fauquier for the first forty-six years of the county's history.[52]

The next office to be filled was that of sheriff which, from the emoluments and authority attaching to it, was the most important in the county. Under the statutes of Virginia the sheriff was chosen from the justices of the county court, but having accepted the appointment and taken the oath, he thereupon ceased to be a justice and could not resume office as such until the end of his shrievalty. In an organized county the justices were required each year to nominate three of their number to the Governor, from whom he selected one and commissioned him sheriff for the ensuing year.

Joseph Blackwell having previously received his appointment as sheriff 'from his Honor the Governor and under the seal of the Colony', had not qualified as a justice, and he now came into court, produced his commission and having acknowledged bond, took the usual oaths of allegiance and was sworn as sheriff.

The bond he offered on this occasion bound him and his sureties, William Blackwell and William Eustace, 'to our sovereign Lord King George the Second', in the sum of ten thousand pounds current money of Virginia, the condition being,

"That if the above bound Joseph Blackwell Sheriff of the aforesaid County of Fauquier shall well and truly collect and receive all and every sum and sums of money laid and assessed by an Act of Assembly Intituled an Act for raising the sum of Twenty Thousand pounds for the better protection of the Inhabitants on the Frontiers of this Colony and for other purposes therein mentioned or already laid and assessed or hereafter to be laid and assessed by any other Act of Assembly of this Colony and shall duly Account for and pay the same to the Treasurer of this Colony for the Time being on or before the tenth Day of June annually during the Time of the Sherivalty of the said Joseph Blackwell then this obligation to be void and of none effect otherwise to remain in full force and Virtue".[53]

Another bond in the sum of one thousand pounds current money of Virginia, was required of him, that he should 'well and truly collect all office fees and dues put into his hands to collect, and duly account for and pay the same' and 'execute and due return make of all processes and precepts to him directed'. This bond he entered into with the same sureties, at the August term of court,[54] and at the February court, 1760, he gave a third bond in the sum of eighty-one thousand, two hundred and sixty-four pounds of tobacco, in which William Grant and William Blackwell joined, and which recited that 'the above bound Joseph Blackwell is empowered to receive of and from the Tithable persons of the county of Fauquier their County Levies and of and from every other person or persons chargeable with the Paiment thereof all such sums of money and tobacco as upon them respectively are assessed for discharging the same'.[55]

Joseph Blackwell was of a prominent Potomac river family which became closely identified with the early history of Fauquier. His father, as we have seen, was Samuel Blackwell (1680-1732), of 'Walnut Lodge', Northumberland, who appears as a vestryman of St. Stephens parish in 1724, and his oldest brother, his father's 'heir-at-law', was Captain Samuel Blackwell (1710-1762), who served as a vestryman of St. Stephens in 1748[56] and sat as a burgess for Northumberland from 1742 to 1747.[57] Joseph Blackwell, with Colonel Thomas Harrison, had represented Prince William in the House of Burgesses from 1748 to 1755, and was for

many years a churchwarden of Hamilton.   He
owned land in various parts of the county and bequeathed that on which he lived at the time of his
death to his son, General John Blackwell.[58]

General military command in each of the counties
was vested in a county lieutenant, who in that respect acted as the representative of the Governor.
This office was invariably held by men of family
and position, and in the organization of Fauquier
it was filled by the appointment of Henry Churchill,
the youngest son of Colonel Armistead Churchill
and the brother of John Churchill, the Fauquier
justice. Henry Churchill, who enjoyed the unusual distinction among 18th Century Virginians
of having been called to the English bar, was only
27 years old when he received the appointment, but
he did not long survive the honor, succumbing to
an attack of pleurisy in the following winter.[59] He
has, however, left us in the inventory of his personal effects, an illuminating suggestion of the
manner of dress of a gentleman of that period and
one that carries with it the conviction that tidewater civilization had, in 1759 at least, penetrated
the 'lower end', of Fauquier. Among the articles
enumerated were: a blue cloth coat and breeches;
3 white cloth waistcoats; red velvet waistcoat and
breeches; white crepe coat and breeches; a blue
silk waistcoat laced; Virginia cloth vest; suit of
white cloth trimmed with vellum; 2 claret colored
coats and waistcoat; a great coat; old grey coat;
suit of sagathy; black shag waistcoat and
breeches; brown holland coat, 4 pairs breeches; old
silk waistcoat; 18 shirts; 9 bands and white waistcoat; a black silk band; 9 silk, worsted and thread
hose; 3 pairs shoes; 1 colored and 3 white cambric

handkerchiefs; a pair of gloves; 3 wigs; 2 sets shoe and knee-buckles; a band buckle; a gold watch; a gold ring set with topaz; a sword and belt; a pair of plated spurs. The inventory otherwise included saddles and saddle cloths, portmanteaus and bags, and a very considerable law library.[60]

The new court was not to lack advocates. At its first sitting three lawyers presented themselves and qualified. They were William Ellzey, James Keith and Cuthbert Bullitt. Of the former little is known except that he appears as a vestryman of Dettingen parish in 1749, and in a deed dated March 26, 1761, by which he and his wife, Alice, conveyed a tract of 309 acres 'lying on a branch of the Marsh Run called Marr's Run' to Daniel Bradford, he is described as 'William Ellzey Gent of Dettingen Parish in Prince William County and in the Colony of Virginia'. Of James Keith, a son of the Rev. James Keith and brother to the direct ancestor of that James Keith[61] who in later years shed lustre on the bench and bar of his native state, it may be surmised that during the short period of his practice at the Fauquier bar he upheld the traditions of an honorable family and took with him to another field of activity the respect of his former associates.

Of Cuthbert Bullitt of 'Mount View', Prince William county, there is a more definite record.[62] Born in 1740, he practiced law in Prince William and Fauquier, and sat with Colonel Henry Lee as a burgess for the former county in 1776.[63] He was also a member of the conventions of 1775, 1776, 1778 and of the Prince William Committee of

Safety. In a letter written to Governor Henry, December 30, 1784, he complains that he is 'con-demmed for bread to drudge on in the practice of the Law and applies to be appointed Attorney for the Commonwealth in one or more of the Districts on the Circuit where he lives'.[64] Later, December 27, 1788, he was appointed additional judge of the General Court of Virginia. He married about 1760, Helen, daughter of the Rev. James Scott of 'Dipple', Stafford County, and in 1765 was drawn into the unfortunate quarrel between his brother-in-law, John Scott, and Colonel John Baylis. Mr. Bullitt with much reluctance consented to act as young Scott's second and in attempting to effect a reconcilation on the field, provoked Colonel Baylis' resentment and eventually became involved in the duel as a principal. He acted with great magnanim-ity in withholding his fire when Baylis' pistol missed fire but in the exchange of shots that followed in-flicted a wound from which his adversary died.[65]

Cuthbert Bullitt owned land in Fauquier in ad-dition to his interests in Prince William. In his will he left 800 acres to his son, Thomas, 600 acres of which he bought of the widow of the Rev. John Scott after the year 1785, and the balance of John Waller.[66]

The attorneys having qualified, the organization of the county proceeded. Martin Pickett and Rhod-ham Tullos presented themselves before the court and were sworn as under sheriffs.

Martin Pickett at this time was a youth of nine-teen years, having been born in King George county in 1740. He was the son of William and Elizabeth (Cooke) Pickett, who afterwards removed to

Prince William. In later life he became prominent
in Fauquier and was made sheriff in 1785. He
served with distinction in the French and Indian
wars and during the Revolution rose to the rank
of colonel, succeeding Colonel William Edmonds in
command of a militia regiment in 1781.[67]

Rhodham Tullos was a man whose name frequently appears in land transactions in the early
Fauquier deed books, but who cannot be said to
have played any important part in the political life
of the county. Prior to 1759, he purchased a tract
of one hundred acres on Town run from John Boy-
stone,[68] on which he may have been living when
the county was organized.

The next business of the court was to divide the
county into districts for the purpose of listing persons subject to taxation. At that time property,
except in slaves, was not taxed and the county levy
laid by the court for the upkeep of court house and
jail, roads and bridges and for administrative expenses, was assessed per capita on the taxable population of the county, as in the case of the parish
levy. The official assigned to the first district was
Thomas Marshall, who was appointed 'to take a
list of the tithables below the Mountain Church to
the county line and it is ordered that he distinguish
the Tithables in Dettingen Parish'.

The church referred to as the 'Mountain Church'
was probably the Turkey Run Church, although it
is difficult to understand this designation, and the
county line was clearly the new Fauquier-Prince
William line surveyed by Bertrand Ewell in the
previous month. The instructions to 'distinguish'
the tithables in Dettingen could only have been
meant as an admonition to the assessor to observe

carefully the location of houses in respect to that line.

To Yelverton Peyton was deputed the task of listing the tithables from the Mountain Church to the Pignut, and George Lamkin was similarly directed to list all taxable persons from the Pignut to the 'county line', probably in this case the Fauquier-Frederick line.

After these officials had been appointed and their duties explained, Thomas Marshall, who had served under Washington in his surveys of the Fairfax lands, rose in his place among the justices and produced a commission 'from under the hands and seals of the President and Masters of the College of William and Mary', appointing him surveyor of the county. He then took the prescribed oath and acknowledged a bond 'to our Sovereign Lord and King' in the sum of £500, with his brother-in-law, James Keith, and Cuthbert Bullitt as sureties.[69]

At the time the county was created the roads were maintained by the tithables under the supervision of road surveyors, as they were called, a method seemingly more appropriate to early conditions than to the somewhat recent date to which it survived. The appointment of these officials was undertaken by the first court but the list was by no means completed at that session. Such sections of road, however, as were assigned can, in most instances, be identified. Thus, John Catlett,[70] who lived in the bend of Dorrell's run below Colonel Harrison, was given the road 'from Brent Town to the Stafford line,' a road that passed through Stafford county to the mouth of Aquia creek on the Potomac.

The second Prince William court house and the
one at which court was held when Fauquier was
created was situated on Philemon's branch of Cedar
run. Access to it by the 'back inhabitants' of Prince
William was had by the Court House road, the section of which from Marsh run to the Elk Run
Church was known as the Chapel road, and this
portion, 'from Marr's bridge[71] to Elk Run Church',
was assigned to Daniel Bradford. William Conway
was given the extension from Elk Run Church to
Town run and George Cosby from 'Town Run to
the [Prince William] County Line'.

The Marsh road, a branch of the Rappahannock
Falls road, was then the main north and south thoroughfare of lower Fauquier, and its maintenance
from the mouth of Deep run, where it entered the
county, 'to Coventons ordinary', was assigned to
Joseph Odor. Coventon's was situated at the cross
roads where the first court was then being held and
from that point to Marr's bridge, Alexander Bradford was made surveyor, while to the upper section,
which joined the lower Dumfries road, Joseph Hitt
was appointed 'in the Room of John Duncan'.

Between the Marsh road and the Rappahannock,
Benjamin Crump was given the road from the
mouth of 'the Marsh Run to Coventon's ordinary',
and John Allen, Jr., the road 'from Marsh Run to
Hedgman's Quarter', the latter situated between
Tin Pot run and the river. The lower end of the
Carolina road 'from the Marsh Run to Normans
Ford', was also assigned to Allen, while of the other
sections of this road as it passed northeast through
the county, Davis Holder was appointed surveyor
'from Licking Run (Germantown) to Turkey Run',

and Robert Singleton 'from the Mall Branch (Auburn) to the Cross Roads by Thomas Dodson's'.

Following the same line as the Falls road from the Rappahannock and branching with what became the Marsh road just beyond the new Stafford-Fauquier boundary, an old Indian trail, later known as the Shenandoah Hunting Path, had passed north by Elk Run Church and Walnut branch. This trail as far as Elk Run Church eventually became the southern end of the much traveled Fredericksburg-Winchester road, and its lower section 'from the Forks of the road above Deep Run to Bryants Breedings' was now assigned to Thomas Smith, and 'from Bryants Breedings to Elk Run Church', to John James. The extension of the future highway from Elk run to Germantown, which was then known as the 'German rolling road', was allotted to William Rust.

The road from Dumfries on the Potomac entered Fauquier at Walnut branch and continued to the present village of Auburn where it forked, the lower branch extending west to the Rappahannock, while the upper road passed north through the thoroughfare of the Rappahannock mountain to Ashby's gap in the Blue Ridge. The surveyors for the upper section were William Durham, whose land cornered with that of James Genn near Walnut branch, and who took the road 'from Mall Branch to the [Prince William] County Line'; Thomas Chapman 'from the Cat Tail to Cedar Run', no surveyor being appointed at this court for the road from Walnut branch to Cat Tail run; Jeffry Johnson 'from Cedar Run to David Barton's precinct'; David Barton 'from his precinct to Goose Creek'; Benjamin Ashby 'from Goose Creek to Crooked Run', where the

original road first touched the run; and William
Howard 'from Crooked Run to the [Frederick]
county line', in Ashby's gap.

A road that gave Chapman's Mill, in Thoroughfare gap of the Bull Run mountains, an outlet to
the Dumfries road, was assigned 'from Chapman's
Mill to the Thoroughfare of South Run' (New Baltimore) to William Barker, and 'from the Thoroughfare of South Run to the [Prince William]
County Line', to John Leachman.

Returning to the southern end of the county,
Brereton Jones was given the road 'from Town Run
(Bristersburg) to the Stafford Line', which crossed
that line about three miles northeast of the Marsh
road and later became the route of the main stage
road from Falmouth to Winchester.[72] Also two sections of a road that may have connected the Dumfries road with the Court House road just inside
the new Prince William line, were assigned to
Joseph Bullit 'from Cedar Run to Turners Quarter'
and to Rhodham Tullos 'from Turners Quarter to
Town Run'. Richard Hampton was given the road
'from Mall Branch to Lazarus Taylor's', the position of which cannot now be identified, and
Augustine Jennings and Joseph Hudnall were appointed to other roads too vaguely described to be
recognizable.

All of these men lived on the roads allotted to
them and the court ordered 'that they and every of
them with the several and respective tithable persons that belong to the said roads do clear and keep
the same in repair according to law'.

It can be imagined that the selection of responsible men for the important work of road mainte

nance, and of those who would be willing to
undertake it, consumed the last hour or two before
the court adjourned for such refreshment as the
nearby ordinary could afford and that fortified by
ham and eggs at least, preceded probably by a fairly
stiff toddy, the justices resumed their sitting prepared to make prompt disposition of the remaining
business which demanded their attention. Of this
the most important item was the selection of a permanent court house site and, as we shall presently
see, their decision was not arrived at without some
difference of opinion. Preliminary, however, to a
discussion of this question, Colonel Harrison was
appointed to provide weights and measures for the
use of the county, and the sheriff was instructed to
apply to the printer at Williamsburg for eighteen
copies (one for each justice) of the current code of
laws. Joseph Odor, John Duncan, William Roberts
and Stephen Bailey were then sworn as constables,
and Reginald Young and Peter Carter, who had
acted in that capacity before the county was separated from Prince William, were continued. One
or two wills were proved and appraisers appointed,
the churchwardens of Hamilton, Colonel John Bell
and Major William Eustace, were ordered to bind
two negro women to James Robinson, and Richard
Coventon's license to keep ordinary was renewed.

The court now took up the question of the location of the Court House, and the selection of a site
in the more thickly settled neighborhood in which
the court was then sitting, was evidently strongly
urged. To this location Colonel Bell, Elias Edmonds, Duff Green and Wharton Ransdall were
opposed and had refused to qualify as justices until
a decision was reached, the two former perhaps

being influenced by the fact that their land lay
nearer the center of the county. The plantation of
John Duncan which was eventually decided upon
seemed, however, to meet their approval and they
came into court prepared to take the oaths of office. These the court then refused to administer
and they did not qualify until a subsequent session
The matter being thus disposed of, the court ad
journed ' 'til the court in course'.

In the separation of Leeds parish from Hamilton
in 1769, the subsequent division of Fauquier county
by practically the same line was evidently contem
plated and after the Revolution an unsuccessful ef
fort was made to effect it. A petition was presented
in 1795, which set forth:

"That the said County of Fauquier from its great Exten
(being fully fifty six miles in Length) renders the attending
of Courts Extremely inconvenient and burthensome to you
Petitioners, when attending in Suits, Either as parties or wit
nesses as well as in other necessary calls for attendance at that
place, The Multiplicity of business in Court often occasion
your Petitioners, even as witnesses, to attend many days; When
they are obliged to submit to the Extravagent charges of the
Tavernkeepers, or to press on the Neighboring Farmers, where
it is often found difficult to obtain a Lodging and Entertain
ment. Add to this the delay of Justice occasioned by the num
ber of suits in the said Court; The Suits set for tryal the secon
day of the Court not being determined during the Continuan
of the Term; We humbly beg leave to observe to your Hono
that the County as it now stands contains between five and s
thousand Tithables, which we humbly apprehend are a sufficie
number to support the charges arising by a Division."

The proposed boundary was 'a line to begin
the mouth of Carter's Run, to Extend across the sa

County to Intersect the Line which divides Fauquier and Prince William Counties nearly Opposite the house of William Herndon'. From the maps which accompanied the petition Herndon's house appears at a point on the Fauquier-Prince William line 5¼ miles south of Chapman's mill, so that the boundary designated in the petition differed from the Leeds-Hamilton line only in that it included all of the Court House settlement in what was intended to be the lower county, which was not the case in respect to the parishes when Leeds was taken from Hamilton. This effort to divide the county failed. The inhabitants of the 'lower end' offered objections and the Assembly holding them to be 'reasonable', rejected the original petition.[78]

[1] Hening, VII, p. 311.

[2] *Bulletin Va. State Library*, IX, p. 83.

[3] Hening, I, p. 381.

[4] *Ibid.*, p. 427.

[5] *Bulletin Va. State Library*, IX, p. 87.

[6] Hening, III, p. 104.

[7] *Ibid.*, IV, p. 95.

[8] *Ibid.*, p. 303.

[9] *Old Prince William*, I, p. 337.

[10] The author of *Landmarks of Old Prince William* recognizes a contour line through the sites of the seven pre-Revolutionary brick churches, Pohick, Falls, Christs, Quantico, Payne's, Broad Run and Elk Run, as marking the high tide of the civilization of old Virginia in the Piedmont. He says 'their sites are enduring bench marks of the highest reach of the tide of the old civilization of Virginia. A contour line drawn through those sites may be taken as a boundary which, without changing his habit, the tidewater planter could not pass on his march to the Blue Ridge. For beyond that boundary began the America of today'. (*Old Prince William*, I, p. 300.)

[11] *Ibid.*, p. 330.

[12] Reference is made to an article entitled *A Portrait of Governor Fauquier*, published in F. H. S. *Bulletin*, No. 4, p. 343, *et seq.*

[13] *An Essay on Ways and Means for raising Money for the Support of the Present War without increasing the Public Debts*, London, Printed for M. Cooper at the Globe in Paternoster Row, 1756.

[14] He was buried in the north aisle of Bruton Church, in the floor of which a modern stone is set quoting the obituary which appeared in the

Virginia Gazette at the time of his death. (F. H. S. *Bulletin*, No. 4, p. 349.) He provided in his will that his slaves if they went to new masters of their own choice, should be sold at 25% less than their value. (*Old Prince William*, II, p. 657.)

[15] Burke, *History of Virginia*, III, p. 333.

[16] Lord Anson, First Lord Commissioner of the Admiralty, to whom Fauquier dedicated his pamphlet, *An Essay on Ways and Means, etc.*

[17] *Fauquier Court Minute Book*, 1759-63, p. 1.

[18] *Fauquier D. B.*, I, pp. 197 and 199.

[19] This was the 'Great Run tract' of 4,200 acres granted to Thomas Lee, the father of Richard Henry Lee, in 1718. (See Chapter V, *supra*).

[20] Thomas Harrison, known as the younger, was the son of Thomas Harrison (1665-1746) of Chipawansic, in Stafford, whose father was Burr Harrison, born Dec. 28, 1637, in the parish of St. Margaret's, Westminster. The latter became a justice of Stafford and appears in 1699 as one of an 'embassy' to the 'Emperor of the Piscataways'. His son succeeded him as justice of Stafford and represented that county and Prince William until his death in 1746. In Oct. 1710, he took up 938 acres on Dorrell's run, one quarter of which he conveyed to his son, Thomas² Harrison in 1740.

The latter, Thomas² Harrison, married Ann, the widow of John Quarles, and in his will, dated September 26, 1773 and proved January 25, 1774, he names sons William², Thomas³, Burr³, and Benjamin, and daughters Susannah Gibson, Mary Fowke and Ann Gillison; sons-in-law Jonathan Gibson and Chandler Fowke. The inventory of his property shows that his estate was a very large one and that he owned 73 negroes at the time of his death. (*Va. Mag.*, XXIII, p. 332.)

[21] *Old Prince William*, I, p. 339.

[22] F. H. S. *Bulletin*, No. 4, p. 376.

[23] This property was on the eastern side of Dorrell's run, and although in Fauquier county was within the curve of that stream which formed the western boundary of Dettingen parish. Thomas Harrison's name occurs among the signatures to the 'test' in 1749, on the loose leaf referred to in the last chapter, but he was not included in the Dettingen vestry of that year. Either he or his father appears in 1745, to have attended a chapel of that parish situated at the confluence of Broad and Cedar runs. At a meeting of the vestry of Dettingen held at the Quantico vestry house Oct. 14, 1745, it was 'ordered that Majr Thomas Harrison have the Liberty of Building a Gallerie for the use of himself & Family in Broad run Chapple not Discommodeing any of the Pews in the Chapple'. (*Dettingen Parish Register*, p. 7.)

[24] Stanard, *Colonial Register*, pp. 152-180.

[25] Tradition has it that the house was built in the expectation of the location being adopted as that of the permanent court house of the county.

[26] John Wright, born about 1710, was a younger son of John¹ Wright and his wife, Dorothy, of Stafford county. John¹ Wright was born about 1685 and in 1723 purchased of Col. Henry Lee, 1,000 acres in Stafford between Niapsco creek and Powell's run, which was part of an estate afterwards known as 'Leesylvania'. Col. Lee regained possession of this property in 1741, after John¹ Wright's death. John² Wright's grandfather was Major Francis Wright, of Lower Machodoc, Westmoreland county, Va., and his wife, Ann (Washington) Wright, daughter

of Col. John Washington and sister to Lawrence Washington, the grand-father of General George Washington. John[2] Wright, justice of Fauquier, was, therefore, George Washington's second cousin.

John[2] Wright married Elizabeth, probably daughter of Waugh Darnall and in that case sister to Jeremiah Darnall. His will, dated June 1, 1785 and proved February 27, 1792, mentions sons, James (afterwards known as Major James Wright), William and John; daughters, Mary Wright, Rosamond Wright and Elizabeth Parlow. (*Tyler's Quarterly*, IV, p. 210 *et seq.*).

[27] *Prince William Court Record Book*, II, pp. 219-20.

[28] *Tyler's Quarterly*, IV, pp. 231-33.

[29] *Prince William D. B.*, I, p. 127.

[30] *Tyler's Quarterly*, IV, pp. 210 *et seq.*

[31] See *The Blackwell Family*, F. H. S. *Bulletin*, No. 4, p. 489.

[32] *Tyler's Quarterly*, IV, p. 227.

[33] Meade, *Old Churches*, II, p. 215.

[34] This property was conveyed by John Frogg and his wife Elizabeth to Allen Macrae, a merchant of Dumfries, May 2, 1759. (*Fauq. D. B.*, I, pp. 197,199.)

[35] *Tyler's Quarterly*, IV, pp. 233, 247.

[36] Stanard, *Colonial Register*, pp. 141, 143, 145.

[37] *N. N. Grants*, A, p. 92.

[38] Stanard, *Colonial Register*, p. 152.

[39] F. H. S. *Bulletin*, No. 2, p. 147.

[40] *Fauquier D. B.*, I, p. 2.

[41] Major William[2] Eustace, born in Lancaster county in 1729, was the son of Capt. William[1] Eustace and Anne Lee (Armistead) Eustace, widow of William Armistead and daughter of Hancock and Mary (Kendall) Lee. He married, Dec. 11, 1749, Anne, daughter of Thomas and Mary (Conway) Gaskins. Major Eustace died in Fauquier county, Dec. 1800. He bequeathed to his son Isaac, 450 acres of land purchased from Col. John Lee and originally patented by Peter Byrum, March 1, 1731. Isaac Eustace later sold this tract to Elias Edmonds. Of Major Eustace's brothers, Hancock Eustace was a signer of the famous Westmoreland Resolutions drawn by Richard Henry Lee in 1765, and John Eustace was a vestryman of Wicomico parish, Northumberland, in 1770.

[42] *Fauquier Court Minute Book*, 1759-63, pp. 24, 110.

[43] Col. William Churchill's daughter, Priscilla, married first, Robert Carter of 'Nomini', by whom she had a son Robert, afterwards known as 'Councillor Carter', and a daughter Betty. She married second, Col. John Lewis of 'Warner Hall'. (*Va. Mag.*, XXIII, p. 162). Col. William[1] Churchill's eldest son, Armistead[1], married Hannah ,daughter of Col. Nathaniel Harrison of Wakefield, a member of the Council in 1713 (Stanard, *Colonial Register*, p. 45), and had sons, William[2], John (the Fauquier justice), Armistead[2], and Henry (county lieutenant). (Hayden, *Va. Genealogies*, p. 253.)

[44] Stanard, *Colonial Register*, pp. 44, 87, 96.

[45] Meade, *Old Churches*, I, p. 364.

[46] Col. Armistead[1] Churchill purchased this tract from Mann Page and on his death prior to 1765, he left it to his surviving sons, William, John and Armistead, subject to a mortgage executed in 1759 in favor of John Robinson and Lewis Burwell (*Fauq. D. B.*, 4, p. 189). William[2]

Churchill remained in Middlesex and Armistead[2], who married Elizabeth Blackwell, moved from Fauquier to Jefferson county, Kentucky, after the Revolution.

[47] *Fauquier Court Minute Book*, 1763-64, p. 33.

[48] Yelverton Peyton was a son of John Peyton of Stony Hill, Stafford county, and his first wife, Ann (Waye) Peyton. He lived on land in Fauquier inherited from his father, after whose death in 1760, he returned to Stafford and in 1768 kept an ordinary at Aquia. He appears as a justice of Stafford in 1769, and a member of the Revolutionary Committee of that county in 1774. He died intestate in 1794, and his widow, Elizabeth (Heath) Peyton, subsequently sold 270 acres on Broad run in Fauquier, which he had patented in 1779. (Hayden, *Va. Genealogies*, pp. 495 and 514).

[49] Thomas Marshall was born in Westmoreland county, April 2, 1730, and was thus 29 years of age when he was made a justice of Fauquier. His father, John Marshall 'of the forest', was a small planter, who in 1727, acquired 200 acres of very poor land on Appomattox creek originally granted to 'Jno. Washington & Thomas Pope, gents — — — & by them lost for want of seating'. (Beveridge, *John Marshall*, I, p. 13). Thomas Marshall inherited this property from his father but soon abandoned it and at the date of the first court for Fauquier was living on Licking run near Germantown, on land which he had taken up about the year 1754. In 1765 he leased 330 acres of land on Goose creek known as 'The Hollow', where he lived until 1773, when he purchased a tract of 1,700 acres on the Fredericksburg-Winchester road under the Little Cobbler mountain. At this time he was the leading man of Fauquier. He sat in the House of Burgesses 1761 to 1767, when he was appointed sheriff of the county. He was made a vestryman of Leeds on the creation of that parish in 1769 and again represented Fauquier in the Assembly 1769 to 1773. He also sat as a member in 1775 and supported Patrick Henry in the Convention of that year. He had some military training in the Indian wars and served successively as ensign, lieutenant and captain of militia. When the Culpeper Minute Men were formed and mustered Sept. 1, 1775, Marshall, representing Fauquier, was made major. When his battalion was discharged after the battle of Great Bridge, he was transferred to the 3rd Virginia Line and marched north to join Washington. He was made lieut. colonel Aug. 13, 1776, and on Christmas night of that year took part in the battle of Trenton. He took command of this regiment on his promotion to colonel, Febr. 21, 1777, and fought with the greatest gallantry at the battle of the Brandywine, having two horses shot under him. A few months later he was elected colonel of the Virginia State Reg't of Artillery. Before the Revolution, Marshall owned 2,000 acres in Fauquier and 22 negroes. He married Mary Randolph Keith, daughter of the Rev. James Keith, in 1754, and by her had nine children, the eldest being John, the future Chief Justice of the United States, born on Licking run, Sept. 24, 1755. Thomas Marshall died in Kentucky in 1802. (See *Thomas Marshall*, F. H. S. *Bulletin*, No. 2, p. 134 *et seq.*)

[50] George Lamkin, 'Gent', was a man who apparently did not always see eye to eye with those among whom his life was spent. He applied for permission to keep ordinary at the Court House in 1760, which was refused, but in the following year he was granted a licence to keep ordinary 'at his house'. July 23, 1761, he 'came into court and desired it might be certified to his honor the Governor that he was desirous he might not be in any future Commission of the Peace for this County'.

(*Fauq. Court Minute Book*, 1759-63; pp. 114, 129, 190). The court records show that he was constantly engaged in litigation.

⁵¹ Humphrey Brooke was born in 1728 and probably resided at Dumfries before Fauquier was formed. His father was Humphrey Brooke, who married Elizabeth Braxton, and his grandfather was Robert Brooke (born 1654), of Old Rappahannock county (now Essex), who married Catherine, daughter of Humphrey Booth. Humphrey² Brooke acted as clerk of the upper house of the Virginia Assembly in 1786, and from 1791 until his death in 1802. He was a delegate to the conventions of 1788 and 1798, and appears as colonel of militia in 1779 and 1780.

Humphrey² Brooke married 1st, Ann Whiting and had issue: Francis, Married Ann, daughter of Martin Pickett; Matthew Whiting, married Cecilia Gustavus Brown; Ann, died unmarried; Catherine, married Burr Powell; Lucy, married Thomas Ingram; Elizabeth, married Thomas Digges, and George, who married Judith Marshall, sister of Chief Justice John Marshall.

Humphrey² Brooke married 2nd, Mildred, widow of Col. Francis Tomkins, of Gloucester, no issue. (Letter of Hon. James V. Brooke, Cando, N. D.).

⁵² Johnson, *Memorials of Va. Clerks*, pp. 176, 130.

⁵³ *Fauquier D. B.*, I, p. 1.

⁵⁴ *Ibid.*, p. 30.

⁵⁵ *Ibid.*, p. 60.

⁵⁶ Meade, *Old Churches*, II, p. 468.

⁵⁷ Stanard, *Colonial Register*, pp. 123, 139.

⁵⁸ *Fauquier W. B.*, II, p. 216.

⁵⁹ Col. James Gordon of Lancaster, who married Mary Harrison, the aunt of John, Armistead and Henry Churchill of Fauquier, noted in his diary, '1760 Dec. 24. Last night Mr. Spann came with the news of Henry Churchill's death with pleurisy; my wife went to the Court House store to get mourning for Col. C's family'. (Hayden, *Va. Genealogies*, p. 253).

⁶⁰ *Fauquier W. B.*, I, p. 57.

⁶¹ See *James Keith of Fauquier* by Katherine Isham Keith, F. H. S. *Bulletin*, No. 3, p. 287.

⁶² Cuthbert Bullitt was the son of Capt. Benjamin and Elizabeth (Harrison) Bullitt of Prince William and Fauquier. His grandfather was Joseph Bullitt of Maryland, who held land on Mattioman creek where his remains were interred. Capt. Benjamin Bullitt was evidently married twice, as in his will dated May 3, 1766, and proved October 27th of that year, he mentions sons Joseph, Thomas and Cuthbert, and daughters Seth Combs, wife of John Combs, and Elizabeth Bullitt, all of whom had been provided for and who were apparently the children of his first wife. He then bequeathes to his loving wife Sarah and his six sons, 'William Burditt alias Bullitt', John, George, Benoni, Parmanus and Burwell, 'all the rest of my estate real and personal that I have before mentioned to support and bring up my above named six sons on'. (*Fauq. W. B.*, I, p. 108.)

⁶³ Stanard, *Colonial Register*, p. 209.

⁶⁴ *Cal. State Papers, Va.*, III, p. 639.

⁶⁵ Hayden, *Va. Genealogies*, pp. 597, 607.

⁶⁶ *Ibid.*, p. 597.

[67] F. H. S. *Bulletin*, No. 2, pp. 148, 209.

[68] *Prince William D. B.*, B, p. 506.

[69] *Fauquier D. B.*, I, p. 1.

[70] His house on the Brent Town road is shown on Bertrand Ewell's survey of the Fauquier-Prince William line in 1759. This John Catlett was a descendant of Lederer's companion who entered the county on an exploring expedition in 1670.

[71] John Marr in 1712, took up land in the Elk Marsh on a branch of the Marsh run first known as the Horsepen, but which afterwards acquired Marr's name. This was the stream flowing into the Marsh run from the east next above Brown's or Hopper's run, the latter being shown as Harper's run on the map of Fauquier County, 1914. It was where Marr's run crossed the Marsh road, that Marr's Bridge (referred to as the Marsh Bridge in the minutes of the Prince William court of 1753), was probably situated.

[72] Martin, *Gazetteer of Va.*, 1835, p. 174.

[73] *Old Prince William*, I, p. 333.

CHAPTER IX

Roads and Towns.

THE history of the early occupation and subsequent colonization of a country might be learned from its roads, if only the record imprinted by the restless feet that passed in their making could be read. In Fauquier the courses of the roads, controlled by the obstacles imposed by nature, were as obvious to the buffalo and the savages who hunted them, as they were to the pioneers of our civilization and are today to the drivers of high-powered motor cars. Trails at first, worn by files of roving Indians, on the coming of the white man widened into roads and as successive bands of straggling immigrants pushed on to find new homes in the wilderness, settlements were established in the political organization of which a system of road upkeep and betterment was eventually adopted. Today the surfaces of the highways are metalled or laid in concrete. That the roads of Fauquier, however, were, to the end of the eighteenth century, often undistinguishable and always so bad in places as to make traffic hazardous, is attested by the journals of many travellers, but in their most primitive state they served at least for the prevailing horseback travel and, where access to market was required, for the transportation of tobacco.[1] Later they were used by passenger vehicles,[2] the four-wheeled carriage or coach of the period and the two-wheeled chaise.[3]

The Carolina road which, as has been explained
in an earlier chapter, originated in the 'plain path'
established by the Susquehannocks in their trade
with the Carolina Indians, was for many years an
important route of travel and commerce between
the northern and southern colonies. From the
mouth of the Monocacy on the Potomac, it traversed the northern Piedmont country east of the
Bull Run mountains and, passing through the future
county of Fauquier, crossed the Rappahannock
below the Great Fork and the James at Manakin
Town, whence it proceeded south to Occaneechi
island in the Roanoke. When the conquering Iroquois drove the Susquehannocks from Maryland,
they adopted this trail for their marauding expeditions. At that time it entered Fauquier's territory above Walnut branch and crossing Cedar run at
Weaversville[4] followed the course of Elk run to the
site of Elk Run Church, from which point it passed
south by Bryant's Breedings and *Goldvein*, leaving
the county at *Rockford*. The Brent Town block
house was built in 1686 to 'overlook' this path, as
William Fitzhugh testifies, and the Iroquois, whose
activities were not such as to welcome publicity,
then made a detour in their route by which they
crossed what was to be the Fauquier-Prince William boundary opposite *Greenwich* and passed Cedar
run above the Mall branch (*Auburn*), where George
Neavil was later to establish his widely known ordinary. From thence they proceeded by *Casanova*,
Germantown and *Bealeton* to Norman's ford of Rappahannock river, and on by the Germanna ford of
Rapidan to the same crossing of the James that had
been used by the Susquehannocks. This became the
route of what was described in deeds of a later

period as the Carolina or 'Jersey' road, an important
highway during the eighteenth century.

The original Susquehannock trail was given the
name of the 'Shenandoah Hunting Path' by the
white settlers who pushed in after it had been abandoned by the 'Senecas', and this designation adhered
to it as late, at least, as 1742, when it was so described in a grant of land in the neighborhood of
Elk Run Church.[5] When the Iroquois finally transferred their trail to the Valley and their detour by
Auburn and *Germantown* was taken over as the Carolina road by the colonists, the Shenandoah Hunting
Path became the resort of cattle thieves and other
gentry of ill repute and acquired the name of the
'Rogues road', by which it is shown on Bertrand
Ewell's survey of the Fauquier-Prince William line
in 1759. Later similar practices earned this designation for the Carolina road and corrective legislation was attempted in 1742. The assembly in that
year passed an act, the preamble to which recited,
that,

"Whereas divers vagrant people travel through this colony,
from the northern provinces to the southern, peddling and selling horses; and either buy or steal great numbers of neat
cattle which in their return back they drive through the frontier counties; and often take away with them the cattle of
the inhabitants of the said counties under pretence that they
cannot separate them from their own droves."[6]

The act then provided that drovers should carry
with them a bill of sale of their cattle and produce
it on demand by any justice of the peace: a law
which resulted in a decided mitigation of the evils
of cattle thieving, although in the following year

the practice of horse stealing was reported to be 'much increased'.

It was by the Carolina road that Governor Spotswood's miners in 1720 travelled from Germanna to establish on Licking run one of the first settlements in Fauquier, and the first record of inter-colonial travel over it is found in the annual visits to that congregation of John Bartholomew Rieger, pastor of the German Church at Lancaster, Pennsylvania, which were inaugurated in 1739. Other Moravians followed him, notably Bishop Spangenberg and his companions who, in July, 1748, on their return journey to the Potomac, failed to identify the road at some point and lost their way. They then 'had to follow the compass northeast over hills and valleys. When night set in they were compelled to camp in the forests. On the next day they continued their former course until they found the right way and finally came to a large plantation. But they could get nothing there to satisfy their hunger, 'for there are very unkind people down there in Virginia.' Without supper, breakfast and dinner, they continued till they reached a public house on Goose Creek where they were able to satisfy their hunger and thirst'.[7]

During the Revolution, in the tread of marching feet on the Carolina road could be heard the promise of coming victory. In January, 1779, the Saratoga Convention prisoners passed over it on their way to Charlottesville, and two years later 'Mad' Anthony Wayne followed with his brigade of the Pennsylvania Line to reinforce Lafayette's army in the campaign that ended at Yorktown.

The march of the British and Hessian prisoners
has been recorded by Thomas Anburey, a lieutenant
in Burgoyne's army, and its route laid down on a
map prepared by him, which shows 'Nevils Plant".
(*Auburn*), 'Farquier Court House' and 'Carter's
Plantation' at Norman's ford. He describes the
hardships of winter travel at that time:

"The difficulty of crossing the Potomac was only a forerunner of the hardships and fatigues we were to experience
on our entering Virginia: for on our march to this place
[Charlottesville] the men experienced such distresses as were
severe in the extreme: the roads were exceedingly bad from
the late fall of snow which was encrusted, but not sufficiently
to bear the weight of a man, so we were continually sinking
up to our knees and cutting our shins and ancles: and, perhaps, after a march of sixteen or eighteen miles in this manner, at night the privates had to sleep in the woods. After
their arrival at the place of destination the officers [usually]
had to ride five or six miles to find a hovel to rest in."[8]

On this march the Baroness Riedesel accompanied her husband, who had commanded the
Brunswick troops in the British army, and in her
journal amplifies Anburey's account of the roads
and inveighs bitterly against the inhospitality she
met with on the way.[9] She says:

"Before we passed the so-called Bull Mountains we were
forced to make a still further halt of eight days that our troops
might have time to collect together again. In the meantime
such a great quantity of snow fell that four of our servants
were obliged to go before my wagon on horseback in order
to make a path for it. We passed through a picturesque portion of the country which, however, by reason of its wildness,
inspired us with terror. Often we were in danger of our lives
while going along these break-neck roads: and more than all
this, we suffered from cold and, what was still worse, from a

lack of provisions. When we were only a day's journey from
the place of our destination we had actually nothing more remaining but our tea, and none of us could obtain anything
but bread and butter. A countryman whom we met on the
way gave me only a hand full of acrid fruits. At noon we
came to a dwelling where I begged for something to eat. They
refused me with hard words, saying there was nothing for dogs
of Royalists. Seeing some Turkish [i. e., corn] meal lying
around, I begged for a couple of hands full that I might mix
it with water and make bread. The woman answered me, 'No,
that is for our negroes, who work for us, but you have wished
to kill us'. Captain Edmonston offered her for me two guineas
for it, as my children were so hungry, but she said, 'Not for
a hundred would I give you any, and should you all die of
hunger it will be so much the better'."[10]

General Wayne with his brigade marched from
York, in Pennsylvania, May 26, 1781. The diary
of one of his officers states that the troops crossed
the Potomac May 31st 'in Squaws', one of which
loaded with artillery and quartermaster's stores
was sunk. The weather during the next two days
being wet they lay on the south bank of the river
until June 3rd, when they resumed the march and
passing through Leesburg encamped at Goose
creek. The next day they arrived at the Red House
(*Haymarket*) and from there by successive stages
reached the North Branch of the Rappahannock
(at Norman's Ford) on the morning of the 8th
whence they proceeded south, still by the Carolina
road, across the Rapidan to the James.[11]

Meanwhile the Moravian Church, ever mindful of
its brethren on the southern frontiers, had sent John
Frederick Reichel from Bethlehem, Pennsylvania
in May, 1780, to visit the congregation at Salem in
North Carolina. He went and came by the Caro
lina road, and of his return journey, after crossing

into Fauquier, he says, 'we had a very bad stony road, especially in the place known as the Devil's Race Ground where we saw rock enough. About five o'clock we passed the place where Germantown once stood, but little of it is now to be seen.' At sunrise on the following day 'we passed Capt. Nevills', and so by Goose creek and Noland's Ferry on the Potomac back to Pennsylvania.[12]

The next traveller by the Carolina road whose journal survives was Dr. Johann David Schoepf, a German scientist who in 1784, entered Fauquier by the old Shenandoah Hunting Path and passed the night at the house of one 'Capt. B. H.' (probably Benjamin Harrison), below Cedar run. He discourses pleasantly on the entertainment offered the traveller at public and private houses in Virginia. Of the ordinaries, as the wayside inns were called, he says:

"It is not always the custom to hang shields before taverns, but they are easily identified by the great number of miscellaneous papers and advertisements with which the walls and doors of these public houses are plaistered: generally, the more of such bills are to be seen on a house, the better it will be found to be. In this way the traveller is afforded a many sided entertainment and can inform himself as to where the taxes are heavy, where wives have run away, horses have been stolen, or the new Doctor has settled. . . . Along the chief roads these ordinaries are commodious enough when they are not too many guests, but coffee, ham and eggs are commonly the sole entertainment. Ham is the great delicacy to the Virginian."[13]

He then compares such resorts with private houses where lodging could be had for pay:

"We spent a night at a plantation where, although no tavern is kept, the traveller is entertained for pay. There are disadvantages about this sort of inn, but on the one hand the proprietor escapes the payment of a liquor license and the trouble of catering to a crowd of idlers, and on the other hand the guest must answer *only a few times* the usual questions as to where he is going, where he came from, and what his business is."[14]

That the ordinary also had its disadvantages may be gathered from the chronicle of an English lady who journeyed through the country a few years after Dr. Schoepf and who supplements his description of the road taverns.

"We scarcely pass ten or twenty miles", she says, "without seeing an ordinary, as they call inns in this country. They all resemble one another, having a porch in front, the length of the house, almost covered with hand bills: they have no sign but take their name from the person that keeps the house, who is often a man of consequence; for the profession of an inn keeper is far more respected in America than in England. Instead of supplying their guests as soon as they arrive, they make everybody conform to one hour for the different meals. There are always several beds in every room and strangers are obliged to sleep together. The sheets are mostly brown and seldom changed."[15]

The keepers of these public houses were usually land-owners and men of standing in their communities and their attitude toward their customers was much more independent than that of 'mine host' of the English inn. They were licensed by the county courts which, in granting licenses, were enjoined to see that,

"the Petitioner is of Ability to provide Travelers with Lodging, Diet, Provender, Pasturage and other Necessaries; but must not grant License to poor Persons under pretence of Charity but to such only who are able to keep good Houses and a Constant Supply of all necessary Entertainments."[16]

The tariff of charges was also fixed by the court. In Fauquier the following schedule was established for the year 1760,[17] from which it will be seen that the traveller had it in his power to go to bed oblivious of the color of his sheets.

"The Court doth set & rate the following Prices to Liquor, Diet etc. at and for which the several Ordinary keepers are to sell for the ensuing year viz:

Rum the Gallon	12.6
French Brandy the Gallon	12.6
Peach or Apple Brandy, the Gallon	8.0
For a Quart of Rum Punch with Loaf Sugar	1.3
For a Quart of Brandy do. with do.	1.0
Port Wine the quart bottle.	2.6
Sherry the Quart Bottle	4.0
Madeira Wine the quart	3.6
Tyall Wine the Quart	2.0
Claret the Quart Bottle	5.0
Virginia Strong Beer, the quart bottle	1.0
English Strong Beer Quart Bottle	1.3
For a hott diet	1.0
For a cold do.	0.8
For a nights Lodging with clean Sheets	0.6
Pasturage for a Horse 24 Hours	0.6
Stableage & Fodder for Horse 24 Hours	0.6
For a gallon of Corn or Oats	0.6
Virginia Cyder the Gallon	1.0

And so in proportion for a greater or less Quantity."

Of the ordinaries within the territory of Fauquier, the most important was George Neavil's situated on Cedar run where the Carolina road was intersected by the Dumfries road. Neavil's appears to have been a place of public entertainment as early as 1748 when George William Fairfax and George Washington spent the night at 'Mr. George Neavil's in Prince William County' on their way from Belvoir to the Valley. On the organization of Fauquier in 1759, the records of the court show that in that year, Neavil applied for a license to keep ordinary and that his license was renewed in 1761 and again in 1770. He died in 1774, but the ordinary was continued by his widow, Mary Neavil, who took a license in her own name in the following year. After her death the place, still known as Neavil's, was conducted by a son-in-law, Ambrose Barnett, who obtained licenses in 1778 and 1780, and again in 1792.[18]

Another early ordinary was that kept by Martin Hardin on the Shenandoah Hunting Path, or Falmouth road, one and a half miles north of Elk Run Church. This was a cross roads of local importance at which the road from the Elk Marsh settlement to the court house, then of Prince William county, crossed the Falmouth road and at which the latter road was joined by the 'German Path', passing south from Germantown. Hardin received a license from the Fauquier court to keep ordinary 'at his house' in August, 1759, but there is no record of the renewal of the license and Hardin, about the year 1765, removed from the county. His place is shown on the Fry and Jefferson map of 1755.[19]

Norman's Ford, where the Carolina road left the county, although never the location of an ordinary, was late in the eighteenth century adopted as a town site. This crossing of the Rappahannock, then known as Hedgman's river, took its name from one Isaac Norman, who in 1726 patented land on the Spotsylvania (Culpeper) side, which he afterwards sold to Robert Carter. It was on this plantation that Colonel Carter established his 'Normans Ford Quarter', and on his death the property passed to

his son, Charles Carter of Cleve, who in 1736 inaugurated a ferry service at the ford[20] to the great
convenience of those who travelled by this route.
Landon Carter, Charles Carter's son, succeeding to
the title, undertook in 1785, to establish a town on
the Fauquier bank of the river, and for that purpose
laid off 50 acres, 'being part of a large tract belonging to Landon Carter, gentleman, lying at a place
called Norman's Ford in the county of Fauquier'.
The town was to be known as Carolandville[21] and
the act of Assembly authorizing the project, named
as trustees, John Blackwell, Humphrey Brooke,
George Fitzhugh, William Pickett and Thomas
Helm.[22]

Under the system of 'establishing' towns by act
of Assembly 'for the cohabitation of those who are
minded to settle there', the trustees named in the
application were given title to the land set apart as
the town site, with authority to lay it off in lots and
streets; to sell the lots; make public improvements,
and thereafter 'to maintain a proprietary municipal
government under direct responsibility only to the
Assembly'.[23] They filled vacancies in their own
body and issued their 'Rules and Orders' for repairing and mending the streets and in other respects
for the orderly administration of the town.

Carolandville was the first municipality attempted in lower Fauquier, but the enterprise failed
and the name is not recorded on any map. A bridge
across the river built by Landon Carter in 1787 to
connect the town with the Culpeper shore, is, however, shown on the 1807 edition of Bishop Madison's
map and is recited in an act of 1819, as 'a point on
the Rappahannock river formerly called Norman's
Ford, now Carter's Bridge'.[24]

Another road, of more importance to the early settlers of Fauquier, was the road from the mouth of Quantico creek on the Potomac, in a fork of which the second Prince William court house was established in 1742.[25] Branching half a mile west of the court house it crossed the Shenandoah Hunting Path, or Falmouth road, at Elk Run Church and gave the 'back inhabitants', at that time of Prince William, access to the county court by what became known as the Court House road.[26] The main road, however, entered Fauquier above Walnut branch, where it intersected the Shenandoah Hunting Path and passed on to cross the Carolina road at the site of George Neavil's ordinary (*Auburn*).   When a few years later the Scotch trading settlement which grew up about the tobacco warehouses and wharves on the Quantico, was 'established' as the town of Dumfries (1749), this road became known as the Dumfries road, although still frequently referred to in contemporary conveyances as the 'road to Quantico'.

The policy of the Glasgow merchants, who before the Revolution controlled the tobacco trade of the upper Piedmont and the Valley, was to promote the building of roads and to establish stores at convenient points where their agents could distribute their merchandise and buy tobacco.[27] The Dumfries road was thus extended beyond Neavil's by two forks, the lower, or Dumfries-Rappahannock road, passing by Turkey Run Church and crossing the head of the Marsh road, proceeded to the mouth of Carter's run (*Waterloo*) on the Rappahannock river. It was on this road that Alexander Cunninghame, one of the Dumfries merchants, built his 'Red

Store' which became the nucleus of the court house village.[28]

The upper branch of the Dumfries road continued by *Chestnut Forks*, where it crossed the future Alexandria turnpike, to *Bethel* and thence through the thoroughfare of the Rappahannock mountain, north by the foot of the Cobblers, to a ford of Goose creek. (*Delaplane*). From there it followed the course of Crooked run, between foothills of the Blue Ridge (Bushy mountain and Lost mountain), and passed into the Valley by the old buffalo trail through Ashby's gap. The ultimate destination of this road explains the name of 'Shenandoah road' given to the Dumfries road by Bertrand Ewell as it crossed the eastern boundary of Fauquier.[29]

The upper Dumfries road was the early route from the Potomac to the Valley and, as we have seen, the youthful Washington travelled it in 1748, while Lord Fairfax, on his journeys from Greenway Court to the lower counties of the proprietary, must also have passed that way. The entry in Washington's journal is:[30]

"Fryday, March 11th, 1747/8. Began my Journey in Company with George Fairfax, Esq. We travell'd this day 40 Miles to Mr. George Neavil's in Prince William County.

"Saturday, March 12th. This Morning Mr. James Genn, the Surveyor, came to us. We travel'd over the Blue Ridge to Capt. Ashby's on Shannondoah River. Nothing remarkable happen'd."

George William Fairfax, Washington's companion on this journey, was evidently not impressed with the condition of this road as it approached Ashby's gap from the east, for at the next session of the Assembly, as a representative of the county of Frederick, he procured the passage of an act which recited that:

"Whereas the clearing of a road from a place called the Pignut Ridge in the County of Prince William so far as to meet the road already cleared in the County of Frederick by the inhabitants thereof to that part of the said County of Prince William which is next to the mountains will be very convenient to travellers; but forasmuch as the distance of the said road will be so great and the places on which it is to be made are so rocky, mountainous and full of grubs that the persons living near to and by law obliged to clear the same are not able to do it:"[81]

It was then provided that the road should be cleared by order of the Prince William Court, the cost being distributed among all the tithables of that county.

Another traveller of the upper Dumfries road was Archdeacon Burnaby in 1760. He, however, entered it at George Neavil's, having come from Fredericksburg by the Falmouth road to Elk Run Church and thence by Germantown to Auburn. He describes his itinerary and discourses on the beauties of the way:[32]

"May 30. I left Fredericksburg and having ferried over the Rappahannock at the falls, travelled that night to Neavil's ordinary, about thirty four miles.

May 31. I passed over the Pignut and Blue Ridges; and crossing the Shenandoah, arrived, after a long day's journey of above fifty miles, at Winchester". [Here he appends a foot note: 'Greenway Court, the Seat of the venerable Lord Fairfax, is situated a few miles on the left of the road, about half way between the Appalachian mountains and Winchester. His Lordship being absent, I was prevented from paying my respects to him'.]

He continues, "The Pignut ridge is a continuation of the southwest mountains. It is nowhere very high; and at the gap where I passed, the ascent is so extremely easy, owing to the winding of the road between the mountains, that I was scarcely sensible of it. * * * *

"The Blue Ridge is much higher than the Pignut: though even these mountains are not to be compared with the Alleghany. To the southward, I was told, they are more lofty; and but little, if at all, inferior to them. The pass, at Ashby's Gap, from the foot of the mountains on the eastern side to the Shenandoah, which runs at the foot on the western, is about four miles. The ascent is no where very steep; though the mountains are, upon the whole, I think, higher than any I have ever seen in England. When I got to the top, I was inexpressibly delighted with the scene which opened before me. Immediately under the mountain, which was covered with chamoedaphnes in full bloom, was a most beautiful river: beyond this an extensive plain, diversified with every pleasing object that nature can exhibit; and, at the distance of fifty miles, another ridge of still more lofty mountains, called the Great, or North Ridge, which inclosed and terminated the whole."

The travellers' resorts on this road beyond George Neavil's, were Joseph Neavil's and Watts' ordinaries. No connection can be established between Joseph Neavil and the inn keeper at *Auburn,* and it is an odd coincidence that two taverns in such close proximity should have been kept by persons of the same name, and one that has caused some geographical confusion. Joseph Neavil's house was situated on the head waters of Cedar run in the thoroughfare of the Rappahannock mountain, on land originally granted to John Hudnall in 1728 and noted on the Fauquier map of 1914 as the 'Rockingham' estate. The Prince William records show that Neavil received licenses to keep ordinary 'at his house' in the years 1752 and 1753,[33] and his place appears on the route surveyed by Dalrymple in 1754, as 'Nevill's Ord'. There is no other historical reference to it nor was his license renewed after the creation of Fauquier.

Watts' ordinary, a place of more importance, is shown by Dalrymple as twelve miles north of Neavil's, where the village of *Delaplane* now stands. It was kept by Thomas Watts, who was granted a license by the Prince William court in 1753 'for the ensuing year'.[34] There is no record of the license being continued by the Fauquier court, but that Watts' house remained a local landmark is shown by the fact that John Wood in 1761 was appointed surveyor of the road from 'Watts to the head of Goose creek', and again in the same year, 'from Thomas Watts to the Top of the Ridge on the Manassas Road'.[35] The road thus indicated was obviously the road from Delaplane leading up Goose creek to its source in the Manassas gap of the Blue Ridge.

Between these ordinaries on the upper Dumfries road, or the Fredericksburg-Winchester road as it had become known by that time, the town of Salem (*Marshall*) was chartered in 1796. Before the Revolution and during Dumfries' pre-eminence as a tobacco port, another road serving that town was pushed north on the eastern side of the Bull Run mountains from the second Prince William court house, and passing by *Haymarket,* entered Fauquier through the thoroughfare of Broad run (*Thoroughfare gap*). It then proceeded west above the Pignut and merging with the original Dumfries road crossed into the Valley by Ashby's gap as 'the road to Shenandoah'.

It was at the point where these Dumfries roads came together that Salem was established on land belonging to John Monroe, a useful man in his com-

munity who combined the vocations of physician
and Baptist preacher. The act which Dr. Monroe
procured,[36] provided that,

"Thirty acres of land the property of John Monroe, in the
county of Fauquier, shall be and they are hereby vested in
John Monroe, William Brown, John Robinson, Joseph Smith,
Minor Winn, William S. Pickett, Alexander Scott, John Dear-
ing and Daniel Floweree, gentlemen, trustees, to be by them,
or a majority of them, laid off into lots of half an acre each,
with convenient streets, and establish a town by the name of
Salem".

The town was laid off April 27, 1797, by John
Mauzy.[37] The site was part of a small tract of 142
acres lying 'on the main road to Winchester' and
was originally included in the grant to the Rev.
Alexander Scott, July 10, 1727, of 2,823 acres,[38] afterwards known as 'Gordonsdale'.

Another municipal venture, earlier than that of
Salem and indeed the first made in the county, was
one promoted by John Rector in 1772. In that year
Rector petitioned the assembly for authority to lay
out a town on his land, alleging that 'several trades-
men have already settled at this place and others
are willing to settle there in case a town is established'. The Assembly considering the location to
be 'convenient for an inland town', by an act of the
same year established the town of Maidstone, with
Rector as trustee.[39] It was situated on 'Rector's
road' about four miles north of Salem and survives
today as the village of Rectortown.

The map of Virginia drawn by Joshua Fry and
Peter Jefferson and first published in 1751, was subsequently revised and republished in 1755. In the

latter edition data collected by Captain John Dalrymple in 1754 was added, which included certain roads, with the towns, ordinaries and other places of note, occurring along their courses. Between these points Dalrymple shows the distances in figures and the accuracy of his measurements between places that can now be identified, justifies their acceptance in other cases where the routes of his roads are somewhat obscure. He shows, for instance, a Fredericksburg-Winchester road which he personally surveyed, made up of sections with which we are already familiar, namely, the Falmouth road from the Falls to Elk Run Church, the German path thence to Germantown, and the upper Dumfries road from Joseph Neavil's ordinary to Ashby's gap. Between Germantown and Joseph Neavil's, however, his route is indefinite, but as George Neavil's ordinary is not shown, it is evident that he took the more direct route over the hill on which, a few years later, the court house village was built. His avoidance of the more travelled road may have been due, as has been suggested in *Landmarks of Old Prince William,* to his purpose of showing the shortest route for the movement of troops from Fredericksburg to the Valley. Three miles north of Germantown, Dalrymple places the Hamilton parish parsonage, occupied at that time by the disreputable Brunskill, and thirteen miles further on, Joseph Neavil's tavern. The total distance thus given of sixteen miles from Germantown to Neavil's would have been covered in travelling by a road crossing from the latter point to an early established mill[40] (shown as *Shumate's Mill* on the map of Fauquier, 1914) on the Marsh road; from there by that road and path over the Warrenton hill to *Bethel* on the upper Dumfries road; and thence to Neavil's, which we may assume to have been his route. With the exception of a more direct route from German-town to Warrenton after the court house was estab-lished, this is the present line of the Fredericksburg-Winchester road.

The Marsh road, by which access to what became Fauquier was gained by the early Elk Marsh set-tlers, left the Falmouth road at *Goldvein* and pass-ing north by *Morrisville, Bealeton* and *Raytown,* joined the Rappahannock-Dumfries road above Tur-key Run Church. On it, as we have seen, Richard Coventon's ordinary near *Morrisville* was situated, and the first court for the new county was held. That the neighborhood of Coventon's did not also include a trading post of the Scotch tobacco mer-chants was due to its abandonment as the court house site, for a few weeks prior to the date of the first court, Allan Macrae purchased from Captain John Frogg[41] the property on which the court was held with this object evidently in view.

The Marsh road, denied the court house settle-ment, claimed a town site several miles north of Coventon's and at its junction with a road that led to one of the upper fords of the Rappahannock. Here the establishment of the town of Fayettesville was undertaken in 1798.[42] The Assembly in that year authorized trustees appointed for the purpose, to lay off thirty acres of land belonging to Austin Miskell, John Overall, Benjamin Bronaugh, Peter Lucas, Howson Duncan and Armisted Blackwell. The trustees named in the act were, Robert Lewis, William Brent 'senior', James Weathers, 'son of Cain', John Blackwell and Robert Hunton. The

enterprise, however, was unsuccessful, although
Fayettesville still appears as a place name on the
county map.

Warrenton, the county seat, had its origin in the
selection of a court house site in the vicinity of
Alexander Cunninghame's 'Red Store'. The second
court for the county, June 28, 1759, had been adjourned from John Duncan's house on the Rappahannock branch of the Dumfries road near its junction with the Marsh road, to the house of William
Jones 'upon the lands of Richard Henry Lee'. The
Jones land lay northwest from the Duncan house
and within half a mile of the crossing of Dalrymple's
road and the Dumfries road, where the Red Store
was situated. It was included in the 'Great Run
tract' of 4,200 acres patented in 1718 by Thomas
Lee, the father of Richard Henry Lee to whom the
property had descended.

After its adjournment to the Jones house, the
court at the same session made provision for the
erection of the necessary county buildings. The
sheriff was ordered to advertise that the court at
its next session would 'agree with workmen' to build
a court house of wood, and that John Bell, William
Eustace and Yelverton Peyton should receive bids
for building a prison for the use of the county of
the same dimensions as the prison of Stafford
county.[48] To provide a site for the proposed buildings, the next court, July 26, 1759, at which Lord
Fairfax presided, directed John Bell and Yelverton
Peyton 'to lay off two acres of land belonging to
Richard Henry Lee for the court house and prison
of this county to be erected on'.[44] Thereupon Elias
Edmonds undertook to build at once 'a prison of

wood to be 12 feet square in the clear with a brick
or stone chimney', for the sum of seventy-three
pounds and fifteen shillings,[45] and this building was
completed and accepted April 24, 1760. Although
there is no record of a court house having been con-
tracted for at that time, a small temporary building
was evidently constructed, as on August 29th of the
same year (1760), the sheriff was ordered to pay
John Bell twenty-four pounds, eighteen shillings
and eleven pence, 'being the sum the Court House
was built for'.[46] These buildings stood below the
Rappahannock road, between the present Culpeper
street and the cemetery.

In the meantime the erection of a permanent
court house was under consideration, and June 27,
1760, the sheriff gave notice that at the August
court, the court would agree with an 'undertaker'
to build a court house of brick, to be 36 feet long
and 20 feet wide in the clear.[47] Subsequently the
advisability of erecting a frame building was considered, and at the next court John Wright and
John Bell were appointed to receive bids for a court
house of clapboards, to be 24 feet long, 16 feet wide
and 10 feet pitch, with a partition of 10 feet at one
end, and to have a bench and a bar.[48] Eventually,
however, the justices decided to build a court house
of brick and August 29, 1760, John Bell undertook
to construct a building of this material, '26 feet long
and 20 feet wide in the clear; the walls to be 18 feet
high from the surface and 18 inches thick from the
water table; 6 sash windows, below, 14 lights in
each, 12 by 10; two dormers, 18 lights in each, 12
by 10; a partition of 12 feet at one end for a justices'
room, with a chimney; the plank used to be of pine,
and shingles of chestnut, sapped; the doors to have

good locks and hinges and in all other respects to be finished in a complete and workmanlike manner, after the manner of the court house of Lancaster County'; all for the consideration of three hundred and thirty-nine pounds, and to be finished by November 20, 1762.[49]

The position of the second court house was opposite that of the first, east of Culpeper street and about a quarter of a mile below the Dumfries-Rappahannock road on the upper side of which stood the Red Store. A tavern had been opened by Andrew Edwards, to whom a license was granted at the July court, 1759;[50] a blacksmith shop was built; a few houses sprang up, and the locality, under the name of Fauquier Court House, soon became a thriving cross-roads settlement.

It was not until 1790, however, that any attempt was made to lay off a town. By that time the brick court house built in 1762, had become inadequate to public needs and the county, May 26, 1790, purchased Thomas Maddux's life lease of the present site[51] 'for the purpose of erecting thereon a Court House, Prison, Pillory, Whipping post and stocks'. The buildings when completed were said to have been 'spacious and handsome and erected at a cost of $30,000'.[52]

Improvements of so extensive a character suggested the adoption of a town plan and James Routt, December 4, 1790, by Richard Henry Lee's direction, laid off eight acres which he divided into twelve lots lying on either side of the Rappahannock road, a section of which by this survey became the 'Main Street' of the village.[53] Lot No. 2 on this plan included the original Red Store and drawn to it, as to a magnet, the court house had now ap-

proached to within 150 yards on the western pro-
longation of Main street.

Early in its history Warrenton appears to have
been chosen as a school location and significantly its
name is derived from that given to the first 'academy' established there. In 1777, Hezekiah Balch,
a graduate of Princeton College, organized a classi-
cal school in Fauquier[54] and conducted it with such
success that in 1786 Martin Pickett and other influential citizens of the county, addressed Richard
Henry Lee with a view to obtaining from him the
gift of two acres of land near the court house as an
endowment, suggesting for the purpose one or the
other of 'several beautiful situations on Spicer's
tenement'.[55] Colonel Lee having signified his assent,[56] the property was duly conveyed, January 15,
1787,[57] to Martin Pickett, William Edmonds, Humphrey Brooke, William Pickett, Edward Digges,
Thomas Digges, Francis Whiting, Gustavus Brown
Horner and John Blackwell, Jr., trustees 'for the
Academy or Seminary of Learning at Fauquier
Court House'. A 'large and costly' school building
was said to have been erected on the lot and the
institution was incorporated November 28, 1788,[58]
as the 'Warren Academy', named in honor of the
hero of Bunker Hill. From this academy the town
apparently took its name. It was referred to in a
local deed as early as 1797 as 'Fauquier Court House
now called the Town of Warrenton',[59] although it
was not 'established' as a municipality until January
5, 1810.[60]

The Warren Academy in the meantime flourished,
and by 1802 had gained a wide reputation. John
Davis, the English traveller and novelist, writing in
that year of a small school he was about to open at

Occoquan, says, 'I was to occupy a log house which
however homely would soon vie with the sublime
College of William and Mary and consign to ob-
livion the renowned Academy in the vicinity of
Fauquier Court House'.[61]   Mr. Balch was succeeded
as teacher of the school by 'Parson' O'Neill, probably in 1800, who held the position until 1805 when
he removed to Dumfries.[62]

The act chartering Warrenton, named as trustees, Edward Digges, Jr., John Scott, William Horner, John A. W. Smith, George B. Pickett, George
Pickett, Jr., John Kemper, Daniel Withers and
Hugh R. Campbell, and the town was laid off to
include seventy-one acres, May 8, 1811.   In this
survey the old roads were absorbed by the streets
of the new town.   The Fredericksburg-Winchester
road was straightened to conform to the new plan
and became the Winchester street of today; the
Dumfries-Rappahannock road which followed Main
street to the court house, passing west from that
point took the name of Jail street, now known as
the Waterloo road; the road to Culpeper Court
House was changed to Culpeper street; and the
road to Churchill's mill (shown as White's mill on
the map of Fauquier, 1914) which existed as early
as 1768, became Court Lane and was subsequently
adopted as the line of the Alexandria turnpike.[63]

---

[1] The method of transporting tobacco from plantations above navi-
gation to the river wharves, was to attach shafts to each individual
hogshead, to which horses or oxen were then hitched and the cask rolled
over the roads.   Roads used in this way were termed 'rolling' roads and
were intermediate between the original trail and the roads later used
for vehicular traffic.   (*Old Prince William,* II, p. 466.)

[2] The passenger vehicles used at first were all privately owned.   It
was not until the very end of the 18th century that the public stage
was introduced.   (*Ibid.,* II, p. 445.)

³ The fiscal statistics of Fauquier, 1799-1810, show that in the year 1799, 60 coaches and 16 chaises were owned in the county. The slave holders of about that time (1782) numbered 672, of whom 88 owned 15 or more negroes. The wheeled vehicles supplied only the families of the latter class, the rest of the white population of over 12,000 still travelled on horseback or on foot. (F. H. S. *Bulletin*, No. 4, pp. 426-34.)

⁴ For convenience of description the routes of original paths and roads are explained by reference to modern place names which appear on the map of Fauquier county published in 1914. The places so cited are printed in italics.

⁵ *N. N. Grants*, E, p. 362.

⁶ *Old Prince William*, II, p. 456, citing Hening, V, p. 176.

⁷ *Va. Magazine*, XI, p. 242.

⁸ *Old Prince William*, II, p. 459.

⁹ That this attitude was due to partisanship on the part of the women of the Piedmont rather than to inhospitality, may be deduced from the experience of the Marquis of Chastellux a few years later. "He spent a night at a humble Virginia cabin * * * and was hospitably entertained. As he left he offered his host two louis in payment for his lodging and asked if it was enough. 'Much too much', was the answer, 'you have come from France to succor and defend my country and I should receive you better than I have and take nothing for it'." (*Ibid.*, p. 502.)

¹⁰ *Ibid.*, p. 459.

¹¹ The diary of Capt. John Davis. (*Va. Magazine*, I, p. 2.)

¹² *Old Prince William*, II, p. 463.

¹³ *Ibid.*, p. 485.

¹⁴ Morrison, *Travels in Virginia in Revolutionary Times*, p. 51.

¹⁵ *Old Prince William*, II, p. 485.

¹⁶ *Ibid.*, p. 488.

¹⁷ F. H. S. *Bulletin*, No. 1, p. 72.

¹⁸ *Ibid.*, p. 69.

¹⁹ *Ibid.*, p. 67.

²⁰ *Old Prince William*, II, p. 500.

²¹ Hening, XII, p. 217.

²² *Old Prince William*, II, p. 664.

²³ *Ibid.*, p. 661.

²⁴ *Ibid.*, p. 500.

²⁵ *Ibid.*, II, p. 468. The location of the second Prince William Court House on Philemon's branch of Cedar run, was in the vicinity of the modern village of Orlando.

²⁶ The Court House road from Elk Run Church to the Marsh road was known as the 'Chapel' road.

²⁷ *Old Prince William*, II, p. 387.

²⁸ F. H. S. *Bulletin*, No. 1, p. 75.

²⁹ See Bertrand Ewell's survey of the Fauquier-Prince William boundary, 1759.

³⁰ Journal of *My Journey over the Mountains*.

³¹ *Old Prince William*, II, p. 471.

³² Burnaby, *Travels, etc.*, 1904, pp. 71-3.

[33] *Old Prince William*, II, p. 490.

[34] *Ibid.*, p. 493.

[35] F. H. S. *Bulletin*, No. 1, p. 70.

[36] Shepperd, II, p. 30.   The name of this town was changed December, 1881, to Marshall, in honor of Chief Justice John Marshall, whose boyhood had been passed at 'Oak Hill' nearby.

[37] A plat presented to the county court in July, 1803, and ordered to be recorded, shows that 'the boundaries of the town as surveyed formed a rectangle one half mile long and about 502 feet wide. Through the centre of the site the main street, 66 feet wide, was laid off in a straight course running northeast and southwest. At a right angle to the main street two cross streets, 60 feet wide and 800 feet apart, were run. The site was then divided into 52 lots, each having a frontage of 100 feet on the main street. On the south side of that street the lots were numbered, from the northeast boundary to the southwest boundary, from 1 to 26. On the other side of the street they were numbered from the southwest boundary, from 27 to 52. From the southwest boundary line of the site to the first cross street, there were ten lots on each side of the main street, while the other cross street divided evenly the rest of the lots.

'The first lots built on lay near the cross street in the western end of the town, and the first dwelling house appears to have been erected on lot No. 30. This lot, with the house, was sold by John Monroe in April, 1799, to George Chriesman, who bought four years later all the unsold lots in the town. In January, 1805, George Chriesman and his wife, Sally, sold to Charles Bennett and Peyton C. Thompson, merchants of Alexandria, lots Nos. 1 to 15 inclusive, and lots Nos. 39 to 52 inclusive. This firm, in 1811, appointed John A. W. Smith, attorney, to sell the 31 lots bought of Chriesman. Chriesman also bought lot No. 18. John Scatterday bought lot No. 35; Ludwell Rector lot No. 17, and William Elgan, lots Nos. 37 and 38, in 1799. George Elgan purchased lot No. 16, in 1800, and in the same year he bought of John Monroe and his wife Eleanor, that part of the Monroe farm remaining after the town was laid out, in all 112 acres, with the dwelling house and out buildings.' (Curtis Chappelear, in F. H. S. *Bulletin*, No. 3, p. 305).

[38] This property was ultimately found to contain 3,533 acres as stated in a previous chapter.

[39] *Old Prince William*, II, p. 664.

[40] Originally known as Ball's Mill.

[41] This property consisting of a tract of 167 acres patented by John Morehead, Sept. 10, 1740, and another tract of 386 acres, on Brown's run adjoining it, patented by John Frogg, March 30, 1743, was conveyed by Frogg to Allan Macrae, May 2, 1759. (*Fauq. D. B.*, 1, pp. 197-99.)

[42] *Old Prince William*, II, p. 666.

[43] *Fauquier Court Minute Book*, 1759-63, p. 12.

[44] *Ibid.*, p. 20.

[45] *Ibid.*

[46] *Ibid.*, p. 94.

[47] *Ibid.*, p. 77.

[48] *Ibid.*, p. 87.

[49] *Ibid.*, p. 96.

[50] *Ibid.*, p. 13.

[51] Title in fee simple to this property was later obtained from Martin Pickett or his heirs. (F. H. S. *Bulletin*, No. 1, p. 76.)

[52] The court house on this site has been twice destroyed by fire and twice rebuilt, once in 1853 and again in 1889. (*Ibid.*)

[53] *Ibid.* See insertion, 'Plan of Warrenton', showing surveys of 1790 and 1811, by Richard N. Brooke. By Routt's survey the Main Street was 55 ft. 7 in. wide and was intersected by three cross streets 30 ft. wide.

[54] Alexander, *Princeton College in the XVIII Century.*

[55] F. H. S. *Bulletin*, No. 2, pp. 224-5.

[56] Ballagh, *Letters of Richard Henry Lee*, II, p. 411

[57] *Fauquier D. B.*, 9, p. 423.

[58] Hening, XII, p. 685

[59] It is also shown as the town of Warrenton on Bishop Madison's map of 1807.

[60] Acts, 1809-10, ch. 41, p. 37. Warrenton was incorporated in 1816. (Acts, 1815-16, ch. 84, p. 203.)

[61] John Davis, *Travels, etc.*, p. 396.

[62] The Rev. Charles O'Neill was not one of the shining lights of the church, nor would his disciplinary methods as a school master have commended him to the parents of this generation, certainly not to their sons. Bishop Meade says of him: 'Mr. O'Neill was an Irishman, and a man of ardent temperament and of ardent temper. We have often heard him spoken of by elderly persons, but more as a teacher than as a preacher. He was of that class of teachers that adopted not only the theory, but the practice also of the old *regime,* as the best for the government of boys. Flogging was a main ingredient in the practice of his system. He had a summary method of reducing and gentling a refractory youth. Mounting him upon the back of an athletic negro man, whom he seems to have kept for the purpose, the culprit was pinioned hand and foot as in a vise, and with the unsparing application of the rod to his defenceless back, was taught the lesson, if not the doctrine, of passive obedience'. (Meade, *Old Churches*, II, p. 90.)

[63] This road was finished in 1826. Mr. William Horner, writing from Warrenton, April 12, 1826, says: 'William Bell's damages have been fixed at $16. for the road passing by his door and the contractors are trying to get off and to bring the road the old way and up the Academy Hill.' Under date of January 29, 1827, he writes: 'Our road is finished and we have two stages per week to run from Alexandria to Orange Court House'. (F. H. S. *Bulletin*, No. 2, p. 199).

CHAPTER X

Dissolution of the Proprietary.

A S Fauquier emerged from its colonial stage the Northern Neck proprietary was entering upon its last phase, the incidents of which are as noteworthy as any in its earlier history. Vigorously as the proprietary privileges had at first been resisted by the colonists the territory was to be the last in Virginia in which the feudal land system was abolished, a remarkable tribute to the justice and moderation with which Lord Fairfax had administered the property and to the respect in which he was held by all classes of the community. The proprietary, indeed, had become an accepted institution in Virginia and even after its dissolution the tradition of the Northern Neck as a distinct territory persisted until the latter half of the nineteenth century in that all grants by the Commonwealth during that period continued to be recorded in the same series of land books which Philip Ludwell, as agent of the proprietors, had opened in 1690.[1] Finally this royal grant, surviving the Revolution, gave rise to litigation in which a decision by the Supreme Court of the United States is held to have definitely established the appellate jurisdiction of that court over the highest tribunal of any State.

Of the events that led to the partition of the Northern Neck lands Lord Fairfax's death was, of course, the forerunner. When hostilities against

Great Britain began in 1775, he was a very old man, too old to be a factor in the politics of the time, and although naturally concerned in the effect on his tenure that a possible change in government might have, he was too wise to antagonize the patriotic party by openly displaying sympathy with the Tories. Burnaby says of him at this time, 'So unexceptional and disinterested was his behavior, both public and private, and so generally was he beloved and respected, that during the late contest between Great Britain and America, he never met with the least insult or molestation from either party, but was suffered to go on in his improvement and cultivation of the Northern Neck; a pursuit equally calculated for the comfort and happiness of individuals and for the general good of mankind'.[2]

Lord Fairfax's legal status during the Revolution was that of a citizen of Virginia[3] and not that of a British subject, so that the confiscatory acts which were then passed[4] had no application to him, and his rights and privileges were in no way curtailed. Moreover, when the Commonwealth abolished feudal land tenures in 1777 and the lands were exempted from the further payment of quit-rents, the Northern Neck was specifically excepted and no attempt was made to interfere with the collections of Lord Fairfax's rents. Indeed, to equalize the benefits of the act without disturbing him in this privilege, his tenants were allowed to reimburse themselves by deducting from their taxes the sum of two shillings six pence for every one hundred acres on which quit-rents had been paid.[5]

The Declaration of Independence, disavowing monarchical rule in America, freed the Virginia lands of the supreme overlordship of the Crown,

and when quit-rents were also abolished in all parts
of the Commonwealth except the Northern Neck,
the feudal system of land tenure which had so long
prevailed, gave place to allodial tenures, or absolute
ownership, subject only to the right of eminent do-
main inherent in the State.   This status was confirmed by an act of May, 1779, entitled 'An act for
Establishing a Land Office, etc.', which, after premising that land owners should no longer be 'subject
to any servile, feudal or precarious tenure and to
prevent the danger to a free state from perpetual
revenue', provided 'that the reservation of royal
mines, of quit-rents, and all other reservations and
conditions in the patents or grants of land from the
Crown of England, or of Great Britain, under the
former government shall be and are hereby declared null and void; and that all lands thereby
respectively granted shall be held *in absolute and
unconditioned property*, to all intents and purposes
whatsoever, in the same manner with the lands
hereafter to be granted by the Commonwealth, by
virtue of this act'.[6]   In the Northern Neck the land
was still held of the proprietor by feudal tenure but
he, no longer a Crown tenant, held his ungranted
lands as a private owner and in the case of lands
to which he had passed title, collected his quit-rents
only by favor of the Assembly.

Lord Fairfax died December 9, 1781,[7] in his
eighty-ninth year, not, it is now believed, at Greenway Court in senile despondency over the news of
Cornwallis' surrender, but after a two hours ride
into Winchester to visit his local physician.   He had
been ill a few years before, 'bowed down to the
grave', as George Washington put it in a letter to

George William Fairfax in 1778,[8] and possibly a recurrence of the symptoms had induced him to see the doctor at whose house he died. This, at all events, is a pleasanter picture of the end of a long and vigorous life than that presented in the Kercheval-Weems tradition.

The news of his death was communicated to Bryan Fairfax (younger brother to George William), in a letter from Thomas Bryan Martin, February 3, 1782, in which he stated that, 'his lordship died December the 9th, and is interred in the Church in Winchester'. The original place of burial was the parish church of Frederick in the town of Winchester, a stone building erected by Lord Fairfax in 1762, and there a marble tablet was set up with the inscription, 'In memory of Thomas, Lord Fairfax who died 1782 [sic] and whose ashes repose underneath this church which he endowed.'[9] Later his remains were removed to Christ Church, Winchester, where in 1925, a new bronze tablet was erected, which, under the arms of Fairfax of Cameron quartered with Culpeper and the motto 'Fare Fac', bears the legend:

"Under this Spot repose the Remains of Thomas, sixth Lord Fairfax of Cameron, Son of Thomas, fifth Lord Fairfax and Catherine Culpeper, his wife. Born at Leeds Castle, County Kent, England, October 22, 1693. Died at his proprietary of the Northern Neck in Virginia, December 9, 1781, in the eighty-ninth year of his age. He was buried in the original Frederick Parish Church at the corner of Loudoun (Main) and Boscawen (Water) Streets, whence his remains were removed to this church in 1828; where they were reinterred in 1925, when this tablet was erected by the Vestry of Christ Church."

In Lord Fairfax's will dated November 8, 1777, and proved May 5, 1782,[10] he devised 'all that my undivided sixth part or share of my lands and Plantations in the colony of Virginia, commonly called or known by the name of the Northern Neck of Virginia * * * * being formerly the estate of the Hon. Alexander Culpeper, Esq., deceased; *Together with all other lands and tenements I have, am possessed of, or have a right to, in the said colony of Virginia'*, to his nephew, the Rev. Denny Martin, of county Kent, England, on the condition that he should procure an Act of Parliament to take the name of Fairfax and the Fairfax coat of arms. Should Denny Martin not survive him, the property to pass to Thomas Bryan Martin and then to Philip, the youngest of the Martin brothers. To Thomas Bryan Martin '600 acres purchased of John Borden and all stock of cattle, sheep, horses, implements of husbandry, household goods and furniture on the Farm or plantation whereon I now live called Greenway Court', and to the three Martin brothers jointly all his negro slaves.[11] This latter bequest, however, was modified in a codicil dated November 27, 1779, by which he left one-fourth of his slaves to Bryan Fairfax, afterwards eighth Lord Fairfax. Various legacies were contained in the will, among which was one of £500, to his brother Robert. Denny Martin was made residuary legatee and Thomas Bryan Martin, Peter Hog and Gabriel Jones were named as executors.

It will be seen that by this will Alexander Culpeper's interest, which Lord Fairfax had inherited from his grandmother in fee, was devised by him in the form in which it was received, that is, as an undivided one-sixth share in the proprietary, and that the separate bequest of his other lands could refer only to those in which he had acquired property in the soil by conveyance and re-conveyance. The undivided five shares in the proprietary which he held as tenant in tail under his mother's will, passed on his death, to his brother, Robert, who succeeded to the title as the seventh Lord Fairfax.

Denny Martin took the name of Fairfax by royal license, August 10, 1782,[12] under the terms of his uncle's will, and prepared to urge his claims although the situation in Virginia at the time offered little encouragement to their successful prosecution.

The Assembly had in May, 1779, passed an act, entitled 'An act concerning escheats and forfeitures from British Subjects',[13] which declared in its preamble that when the people of the United States 'were obliged to wage war in defence of their rights, and finally to separate themselves from the rest of the British empire, to renounce all subjection to their common prince, and to become sovereign and independent states, the said inhabitants of the other parts of the British empire, became alien and enemies of the said states; and as such incapable of holding the property, real or personal so acquired therein, and so much thereof that was within the Commonwealth, became, by the laws, vested in the Commonwealth'. The act then repealed so much of a previous act (1777) 'as may be supposed to have suspended the operation of the laws of escheat and forfeiture', and provided, that all lands belonging to any British subject 'shall be deemed to be vested in the Commonwealth; the lands, slaves, and other real estate by way of escheat, and the personal estate by forfeiture'. The act further defined those who should be considered British subjects within its meaning as 'all persons subjects of his Brittanick majesty, who on the nineteenth day of April, in the year 1775, when hostilities were commenced at Lexington between the United States of America and the other parts of the British Empire, were resident or following their vocations in any part of the world, other than the United States, etc.'

Denny Martin Fairfax was a British subject and as such not capable of taking under his uncle's will, a status that applied to his inheritance of the manor lands as well as the ungranted lands, although in the former case no attempt was made to dispossess him in the legislation that followed. In respect to the unappropriated lands, however, the position of the Commonwealth was made plain in two acts which undertook the regulation of these lands evidently on the presumption that complete title to them had been vested by the act of 1779.[14] The first of these acts, passed in October, 1782,[15] a few months after Lord Fairfax's will had been recorded, declared that, 'there is reason to suppose that the said proprietorship hath descended upon alien enemies', and provided that all landowners in the Northern Neck 'shall retain sequestered in their hands all quit-rents which are now due, until the right of descent shall be more fully ascertained and the general assembly shall make final provision thereon', and that all quit-rents which became due after the passage of the act should be paid into the public treasury, 'for which quit-rents the inhabitants of the said Northern Neck shall be exonerated from the future claim of the proprietor'. The other act passed at the same time,[16] after premising that the death of Lord Fairfax 'may occasion great in-

convenience to those who may incline to make entries for vacant lands in the Northern Neck',
provided 'that all entries made with the surveyors
of the counties within the Northern Neck and returned to the office formerly kept by the said
Thomas Lord Fairfax, shall be held, deemed and
taken as valid in law as those heretofore made
under the direction of the said Thomas Lord Fairfax until some mode shall be taken up and adopted
by the general assembly concerning the territory of
the Northern Neck'.

The Treaty of Peace with Great Britain which
closely followed this legislation materially changed
the situation, however, and seemed to offer the Fairfax heirs an opportunity to regain their proprietary
privileges. By its terms the protection of land titles
in the United States was assured to British subjects,
and on its ratification, September 3, 1783, and its
confirmation by the Virginia Assembly in October,
1784,[17] Denny Martin Fairfax came out to America
to claim his rights. On the advice of John Marshall,
then a rising young lawyer, he asserted title to both
the manor lands and the unappropriated lands, and
in 1786 filed *caveats* against all grants by the Virginia government in the Northern Neck territory,[18]
thus precipitating litigation that was destined to
have far-reaching results.

With Denny Martin Fairfax's one-sixth interest
in the lands in dispute, was involved, of course, Robert Lord Fairfax's five-sixth share which had passed
to him on his brother's death as tenant in tail under
the will of his mother, Catherine Lady Fairfax. To
protect this interest Robert Lord Fairfax had given
George William Fairfax a power of attorney to act
for him and subsequently in May, 1783, appointed

Bryan Fairfax as agent for the Northern Neck,[19] an arrangement in which Denny Martin Fairfax apparently concurred; but by that time the legislation of 1782 had reduced the proprietorship to a mere claim and the activities of the last agent were confined to a futile memorial to the Assembly. Thomas Bryan Martin, acting with the other executors of his uncle's will had, however, been more effective. He had protested against the sequestration of quitrents due at the time of Lord Fairfax's death and in May, 1783, obtained the passage of an act remedying that injustice.[20]

Prior to the interposition of Denny Martin Fairfax's *caveats* the Assembly had sought to conclude the disposition of the proprietary interests left uncompleted by the acts of 1782. On October 17, 1785, it passed an act under the title of 'An act for safe keeping the land papers of the Northern Neck, etc.',[21] which provided for the transfer of all records, documents and entries for lands in the Northern Neck to the land office of the Commonwealth; that, as no mode had heretofore been adopted for making entries for waste or unappropriated lands since Lord Fairfax's death, such lands should now be granted under the hand of the Governor and seal of the Commonwealth 'in the same manner as is by law directed in cases of other unappropriated lands', that upon grants issued under this act on entries previously made, a composition of thirteen shillings and four pence for every hundred acres should be paid to the register of the land office; and 'that the landholders within the said district of the Northern Neck shall be forever hereafter exonerated and discharged from composition and quitrents, any law, usage, or custom, to the contrary notwithstanding'. The provisions of this act apparently did not violate the terms of the Peace Treaty as they completed legislation adopted prior to its execution and the state government, holding this view and considering the question now definitely disposed of, began to issue patents for land in the Northern Neck in the following year.[22] The title to the manor lands, on the other hand, had evidently been conceded to the Fairfax heirs, for Thomas Bryan Martin, acting as attorney for his brother, Denny Martin Fairfax, granted leases in the Manor of Leeds from April 14, 1786, until the sale of that property was agreed upon in 1793.[23]

A case arising from Denny Martin Fairfax's action in support of his claims and reported in the Court of Appeals as *Hunter* v. *Fairfax's Devisee* (Munford I, pp. 218 *et seq.*) came up in the Winchester District Court in 1791.[24] It appeared that Governor Beverley Randolph for the Commonwealth, April 30, 1789, had made a grant of 788 acres of unappropriated land in Shenandoah county to one David Hunter, a well-to-do citizen of the State. Denny Martin Fairfax claimed possession of this tract as his uncle's devisee on the ground that the confiscatory acts of 1777 and 1782 had not been completed prior to the Treaty of Peace, and that their provisions, therefore, could not be enforced against him. Hunter brought suit in ejectment and on the case being decided against him, April 24, 1794, carried it to the Court of Appeals.[25] The case was first argued in that court, May 3, 1796, but although no decision was rendered at the time, it appears to have been taken to the Supreme Court of the United States in the same year. (Dallas, III, p. 305.)

In the meantime, while this and other suits over
titles to the unappropriated lands were pending,
John Marshall had proposed to his client, Denny
Martin Fairfax, that he, Marshall, should purchase
from the Fairfax heirs the manor lands and what
remained of the ungranted lands of the Northern
Neck. The proposal was made during the period of
enormous land speculations following the Revolution, in which Robert Morris of Philadelphia, the
financier of the war and one of the wealthiest men
in America, was a leading figure. Morris was in
close relation with John Marshall, who had for several years acted as his attorney in Virginia, and it
is supposed that he instigated the purchase of the
Fairfax lands. At any rate he undertook to finance
the speculation. John Marshall in this transaction
represented a syndicate composed of himself and his
brother, James M. Marshall, who shortly afterwards married Robert Morris' daughter;[26] his
brother-in-law, Rawleigh Colston; and General
Henry Lee, who, however, appears to have dropped
out before the purchase was completed.

The price offered was about £20,000 and an agreement on these terms was reached with Denny Martin Fairfax, May 17, 1793,[27] but deeds could not be
executed until title to the lands under negotiation
had been cleared. The case of *Hunter* v. *Fairfax's
Devisee* was then before the Supreme Court and
John Marshall, early in 1796, went to Philadelphia
to endeavor to have the cause advanced so that an
early decision could be reached and an immediate
and permanent settlement of the matter obtained.[28]
In this effort he failed, and although the case came
on in regular course during the fall term, it was not

argued, Hunter on the death of his counsel, Alexander Campbell, having obtained a continuance.[29]

About this time, however, a great number of petitions from the counties of Hampshire, Hardy and Shenandoah were received by the Assembly, reciting the hardships the settlers sustained through failure to secure patents for their lands owing to the controversy between the Commonwealth and the devisee of Lord Fairfax, and praying for a settlement of the dispute. These petitions were indicative of the general dissatisfaction and unrest throughout this region and the State government decided to act on them and forestall the result of pending litigation by making a compromise, if possible, with the Fairfax interests. With this end in view the Assembly passed a resolution in the following terms: 'That in case the devisees of Lord Fairfax, or those claiming under them, will relinquish all claims to lands supposed to lie within the Northern Neck, which were waste and unappropriated at the time of the death of Lord Fairfax, that it would be advisable for this Commonwealth to relinquish all claim to any lands specifically appropriated by the said Lord Fairfax to his own use, either by deed or actual survey'.[30] This proposal, if accepted, confirmed title to the manor lands under the designation of 'lands specifically appropriated by Lord Fairfax to his own use', which had already been conceded, and apparently secured the unappropriated lands to the State beyond the chance of adverse judicial decisions. The Marshall syndicate, on the other hand, recognized in the proposed compromise an opportunity to obtain an immediate settlement of the disputed titles even if it restricted the extent of their purchase and decided to accept the terms of the resolution. John Marshall, accordingly, November 24, 1796, wrote a letter to the Speaker of the House of Delegates, in which he, 'as one of the purchasers of the lands of Mr. Fairfax and authorized to act for them all', acceded to the resolution of the Assembly and agreed to execute deeds to the unappropriated lands as soon as he received a conveyance from Denny Martin Fairfax, 'provided an act passes during this session, confirming, on the execution of such deeds, the title to those claiming under Mr. Fairfax, to lands specifically appropriated and reserved by the late Thomas Lord Fairfax, or his ancestors, for his or their use'. This agreement was confirmed by an act of Assembly passed December 10, 1796,[31] and on Robert Morris being advised of the settlement, he wrote John Marshall from Philadelphia, 'altho you were obliged to give up a part of your claim yet it was probably better to do that than to hold a contest with such an opponent [the State of Virginia]. I will give notice to Mr. Jas. Marshall of this compromise'.[32]

Before the purchase of the Northern Neck lands could be completed, however, Robert Morris found himself in serious financial difficulties and unable to help the Marshalls, and it was not until James M. Marshall succeeded in negotiating a loan in Europe[33] that they were able to make the first payment of £7,700 to Denny Martin Fairfax,[34] January 25, 1797. The latter then executed a deed under date of August 30, 1797,[35] by which he conveyed to James M. Marshall 'all and every those divers tracts, pieces and parcels of land, being part and parcel of the proprietary of the Northern Neck of Virginia, and all and every the now remaining real estate and beneficial right and interest of him, the said Denny

Martin Fairfax, of whatsoever nature the same may be, of, in, to, or to arise out of, or from the same; and all or any other lands within the Commonwealth of Virginia, with their, and every of their rights, members and appurtenances; save and except, nevertheless, etc., *the Manor of Leeds and all and every tract, pieces or parcels of land lying within or reputed to be part or held of that manor.*'[36] This conveyance put the Marshalls in a position to discharge their obligation to the Commonwealth under the compromise agreement of 1796, and perfected their title to the lands specifically appropriated to Lord Fairfax's use. Afterwards, James M. Marshall seems to have retained individual title to the manor lands included in the conveyance,[37] probably by agreement with John Marshall and Rawleigh Colston, as a part of his individual share in the purchase. These lands consisted of the South Branch Manor containing 54,596 acres, and certain small manors and farms aggregating 4,363 acres which, from time to time, had been conveyed to Thomas Bryan Martin and reconveyed by him. Lots in the town of Winchester were also included and in a case involving title to them, an early application of the compromise agreement was made by the Court of Appeals.[38]

Denny Martin Fairfax, shortly after this transfer, died in England (April 3, 1800) and by his will, dated May 19, 1798, and proved before the Prerogative Court of Canterbury August 13, 1800,[39] left 'all manors, etc., in the Colony or State of Virginia devised to me by will of my uncle Thomas late Lord Fairfax, which shall remain undisposed of at my death and which I now have power to dispose of, also all manors in co. Kent, etc., (my oldest brother

Thomas Bryan Martin being otherwise amply provided for) to my younger brother, Major General
Philip Martin, in fee etc.' The will also contained
a legacy of £1,000 to Thomas Bryan Martin and
made provision for the testator's three sisters who,
with Philip Martin, were appointed executors. The
manor lands referred to as undisposed of at the time
of his death, comprised the Manor of Leeds which
was now all that remained of the Fairfax interests
in Virginia except some arrears of quit-rents which
he had reserved in the deed of 1797,[40] and to collect
which he had appointed James M. Marshall his ad-
ministrator with the will annexed.[41]

The financial burden entailed by the purchase of
the Fairfax lands without the assistance promised
by Robert Morris, pressed heavily on the Marshall
brothers, and John Marshall, who had hitherto consistently declined office, was constrained to accept
the appointment offered him by President Adams
in 1797, as a member of the mission then being sent
to France. Thomas Jefferson relates on Marshall's
return the following year, that 'Mr. John Marshall
has said here, that had he not been appointed minister [envoy] to France, he was desperate in his
affairs and must have sold his estate [the Fairfax
purchase] & that immediately. That that appointment was the greatest God-send that could ever
have befallen a man'.[42] The salary he received from
this appointment[43] and other sums raised by his
brother and brother-in-law, finally enabled the Marshall syndicate to complete payments under the
agreement of 1793 with Denny Martin Fairfax and
to acquire title to the Manor of Leeds. On October 18, 1806, Lieutenant-General Philip Martin, de-

scribed as of Leeds Castle in the county of Kent, England, executed a deed to Rawleigh Colston, then of Frederick county, and John Marshall and James Markham Marshall, of the city of Richmond, for the three tracts which constituted the Manor of Leeds and the lands held therewith. The amount paid for the 160,382 acres of land included in the purchase was £14,000 sterling, or about one shilling and nine pence per acre. The sale was made subject to leases executed prior to May 17, 1793, and the property was charged with the payment of three annuities of £100 each to the children of Bryan 8th Lord Fairfax, as provided in a codicil to the will of Thomas 6th Lord Fairfax.[44] By this transaction the dissolution of the proprietary was practically concluded, for although claims to the obsolete quit-rents had not definitely been written off, no further attempt was made to prosecute them, and the only questions at issue were titles to certain tracts of the unappropriated lands which still remained in litigation.

One of these cases was that of *Hunter* v. *Fairfax's Devisee* which, as we have seen, was first argued before the Court of Appeals in 1796. Now, on the appellant's demand, it was again taken up and re-argued after a lapse of thirteen years. In this case the title of the Fairfax heirs to a tract of the ungranted lands was in dispute, but since the suit was first brought the compromise act of 1796 had apparently disposed of the question and Denny Martin Fairfax in 1797, had conveyed his holdings in the Northern Neck, the Manor of Leeds only excepted, to the Marshall syndicate. When the Marshalls had, under the conditions of the compromise, executed deeds passing title to the unappropriated lands, this and other tracts, then in litigation, had presumably not been included and the Fairfax heirs had continued in possession. It would be difficult, otherwise, to explain what interest they now had in defending this suit and in subsequently taking appeals to the Supreme Court of the United States. That the Martin interests were involved in these actions and not those of their assignees, seems to be shown by the fact that Philip Martin in his conveyance to the Marshalls of the three tracts constituting the Manor of Leeds, reserved 'all and every such tracts and parcels of land and other estates late of the said Thomas Lord Fairfax in Virginia as are not comprised and comprehended within the aforesaid three respective surveys, bounds, limits and descriptions of the said Manor of Leeds'.[45]

The state court finally delivered judgment in *Hunter* v. *Fairfax's Devisee*, April 23, 1810. Judge Roane, in the opinion pronounced by him, held that the acts of Assembly passed subsequent to Lord Fairfax's death and prior to the Treaty of Peace, had definitely confiscated the lands of his devisee, whose status was that of an alien enemy, and that the act of 1785 constituted a sufficient inquisition of escheat or forfeiture, the terms of the Treaty of Peace being inapplicable to a condition antecedent to its ratification; but that, in any case, the compromise of 1796 disposed of the matter and confirmed Hunter's title. Judge Fleming, on the other hand, although concurring in his colleague's opinion that the act of 1796 was conclusive, held that except for it the appellee would have been entitled to judgment, as the acts of 1782 had not been completed by the inquest of office specifically provided for in the act entitled 'An act concerning escheators', passed in May, 1779. 'At this period (October, 1782)', he said, 'the legislature was quite undetermined on the subject of this territory, and had done nothing that squinted at an inquisition of office; and therefore there was, from any act of government at that time, scarce a semblance of a title vested in the Commonwealth; as the clauses just above recited seem to have been enacted merely for the convenience of those who were resident, and had acquired permanent titles to their lands within the territory, and also of those who were taking steps to acquire titles to lands therein'. The judgment of the lower court was thereupon reversed and a decision entered in favor of Hunter.[46]

In this and similar decisions, the Court of Appeals recognized the compromise agreement of 1796 as a contract definitely partitioning the Northern Neck lands between the parties in interest, and that the statute confirming it was conclusive in cases pending at the time of its enactment. The Supreme Court, on the other hand, held that titles existing before the confiscatory acts of the Virginia Assembly, had not lapsed as the technicalities of seizure under those acts had not been completed by the Commonwealth prior to the Treaty of Peace, and the Jay Treaty of 1794[47] by which British subjects were confirmed in their titles. In its decisions the intervention of the contract of 1796, entered into expressly for the purpose of escaping litigation, was practically ignored, and in deciding the cases on a construction of the Federal treaties the new court seems to have gone out of its way to assert its jurisdiction. Some such view of the matter was evidently taken by John Marshall, who in a letter to his brother stated his opinion that 'the case of Hunter v. Fairfax is very absurdly put on the treaty of '94'.[48]

The case of *Hunter* v. *Fairfax's Devisee* was taken to the Supreme Court under the title of *Fairfax's Devisee* v. *Hunter's Lessee*,[49] on a writ of error, and on March 15, 1813, Justice Story delivered the opinion. John Marshall, now Chief Justice,[50] had refused to sit during the arguments or to participate in the conclusions of his associates, stating that because of 'an opinion formed when he was very deeply interested [alluding to the partition of Lord Fairfax's lands], he could not consistently with his duty and the delicacy he felt, give an opinion in the cause'.[51] The court held that Lord Fairfax had absolute property of the soil in the land in controversy, that is, in the unappropriated lands; that Denny Martin Fairfax was capable of taking by devise under his uncle's will and that his title could only be divested by an inquest of office; that by the various acts of the Virginia Legislature no inquest of office and seizure could be considered to have been taken; that Denny Martin Fairfax was, therefore, in complete possession when the suit then before the court was commenced in the Winchester court in 1791; and that 'that possession and seizen continued up to and after the treaty of 1794, which being the supreme law of the land, confirmed the title to him, his heirs and assigns, and protected him from any forfeiture by reason of alienage'. Judgment was then entered reversing that of the Virginia Court of Appeals and affirming that of the District Court of Winchester, with an order remanding the case to the former court 'with instruc-

tions to enter judgment for the appellant Philip
Martin'.[52]

On receiving the mandate of the Supreme Court,
the judges of the Court of Appeals were highly incensed and notwithstanding the fact that they had,
in response to a Federal writ, certified the record of
this case to the Supreme Court, they now refused
to acknowledge that court's jurisdiction. The mandate was discussed in an assumed case (*Hunter* v.
Martin, Devisee of Fairfax, Munford, IV, p. 1, *et
seq.*) for six consecutive days (March 31 to April
6, 1814), during which time all the members of the
State bar were given an opportunity to ventilate
their views, but it was not until December 16, 1815,
a year and a half later, that the judgment of the
court was rendered. This was to the effect that,
'the court is unanimously of the opinion that the
appellate power of the Supreme Court of the United
States does not extend to this court, under a sound
construction of the Constitution of the United
States; that so much of the 25th section of the act
of Congress [1789] to establish the judicial courts
of the United States as extends the appellate jurisdiction of the Supreme Court to this court, is not
in pursuance of the Constitution of the United
States; that the writ of error in this case was im-
providently allowed under the authority of that act;
that the proceedings thereon in the Supreme Court
were *corum non judice* in relation to this court, and
that obedience to its mandate be declined by this
court.'

This decision gave rise to a controversy of nation-
wide importance in the settlement of which the ad-
judication of the Fairfax claims sank into insignifi-
cance. Was there to be a supreme federal court

with appellate jurisdiction over the state courts, or were the national laws and treaties to be interpreted by each state separately as the highest tribunal of that state saw fit? With these questions now at issue the case of *Hunter* v. *Fairfax's Devisee* was again brought before the Supreme Court, this time appearing on the docket as *Martin, Heir at Law and Devisee of Lord Fairfax* v. *Hunter's Lessee* (Wheaton, I, p. 304, *et seq.*).

The case was argued March 20, 1816, by Walter Jones for the appellant against St. George Tucker of Virginia, and Samuel Dexter of Massachusetts, for Hunter. Both Tucker and Dexter called attention to the fact 'that the decision of the court of appeals did not rest exclusively on the Treaty of Peace which alone in this case would have authorized an appeal to the Supreme Court'.[58] John Marshall had again refused to sit and the opinion of the court, all the justices concurring, was again delivered by Justice Story. 'The questions involved in this judgment,' he declared, 'are of great importance and delicacy. Perhaps it is not too much to affirm that upon their right decision, rest some of the most solid principles which have hitherto been supposed to sustain and protect the Constitution itself'. He then exhaustively reviewed the constitutionality of the act under which the Supreme Court's jurisdiction was created and announced the court's conclusion *that Congress had the right to confer appellate jurisdiction upon the Supreme Court in all cases involving the laws, treaties and constitution of the United States.* In regard to the Fairfax claims, he held that 'the case decided on a former record is not now before the court. * * * The question now litigated is not upon the construction of a treaty, but upon the constitutionality of a statute of the United States, which is clearly within our jurisdiction'. From 'motives of a public nature', however, the court would re-examine the grounds of its former decision. This he proceeded to do. 'It has been asserted at the bar, he said, 'that, in point of fact, the court of appeals did not decide either upon the treaty or the title apparent upon the record, but upon a compromise made under an act of the Legislature of Virginia. If it be true, as we are informed, that this was a private act, to take effect only upon a certain condition, namely, the execution of a deed of release of certain lands, which was matter *in pais,* it is somewhat difficult to understand how the court could take judicial cognizance of the act, or of the performance of the condition, unless spread upon the record. At all events, we are bound to consider that the court did decide upon the facts actually before them. The treaty of peace was not necessary to have been stated, for it was the supreme law of the land, of which all courts must take notice. And at the time of the decision in the court of appeals and in this court, another treaty had intervened, which attached itself to the title in controversy, and, of course, must have been the supreme law to govern the decision, if it should be found applicable to the case. It was in this view that this court did not deem it necessary to rest its former decision upon the treaty of peace, believing that the title of the defendant was, at all events, perfect under the treaty of 1794'. In conclusion, he delivered the opinion of the court, 'that the judgment of the Court of Appeals of Virginia, rendered on the mandate in this cause, be reversed, and the judgment of the District Court, held at Winchester, be, and the same is, hereby affirmed'.[54]

The last important case in which title to the Northern Neck lands was involved thus ended in a decision favorable to the Fairfax heirs, but this and the former decision of the Supreme Court, cannot be regarded as materially affecting the partition of Lord Fairfax's estate. That had been accomplished through the agency of John Marshall by the compromise act of 1796.

[1] *Va. Land Grants*, p. 121.

[2] Burnaby, *Travels, etc.*, 1798, App. 4.

[3] *Hite* v. *Fairfax*, Call IV, p. 55, and *Marshall's Lessee* v. *Foley, et al.*, *Fauquier Record of Land Causes*, B, p. 271.

[4] The act of Oct. 1777, entitled 'An act for sequestering British property, etc.', and the act of May, 1779, entitled 'An act concerning Escheats and Forfeitures from British Subjects'. (*Rev. Code*, 1819, II, pp. 484-6). For an opinion on this subject see *Fairfax's Devisee* v. *Hunter's Lessee*, Cranch (U. S.) VII, p. 623.

[5] *Rev. Code*, 1819, II, p. 351.

[6] *Ibid.*, p. 375.

[7] *Proprietors*, p. 130.

[8] *Ibid.*

[9] *Ibid.*, pp. 132-3.

[10] *Frederick W. B.*, 4, p. 583.

[11] The writer is indebted to Mr. Fairfax Harrison for the following memorandum:

"From the printed record of *Woodcock's adm.* v. *Macky's adm.*, adjudged in Frederick court in 1839, it appears that when Thomas Bryan Martin died, in 1798, his executors (Dr. Robert Macky and John Sherman Woodcock) found at Greenway Court an iron chest containing gold and silver. Not sure whether this belonged to Martin's estate or Lord Fairfax's, they held it intact. Physically it remained in Woodcock's possession until his death, in 1808, when it was transferred to Dr. Macky, who in turn deposited it in the Bank of the United States at Philadelphia. After Macky's death (1815) the proceeds of the chest seem to have been liquidated and mingled with Martin's estate.

'In Woodcock's accounts, this chest and its contents are described as follows, viz:

1808

Nov. 11 [Voucher No.] 96. To cash del'd Doct. R. Macky by R. Dunbar [adm. of Woodcock] and contained in an iron chest found in the house of T. B. Martin, deceased, as per Macky's receipt, viz:
730 crowns ($18,873.80);
Cut silver, 307½ ounces;

English and Portugese gold, 256 ounces, 18½ pennywts.;
Spanish and cobb. [i. e. the old Spanish 'piece of eight'] gold
63 ounces and two dwts;
French and Spanish gold, 137 ounces and 11½ dwts.;
German gold, 50 ounces and 12 dwts.; amounting to £8,683,
3, 7½'.

[12] *Proprietors*, p. 142.

[13] Hening, X, p. 66.

[14] Justice Story, in the opinion delivered in *Fairfax's Devisee* v.
Hunter's Lessee, says, 'The real fact appears to have been that the
legislature supposed that the commonwealth were in actual seizin and
possession of the vacant land of Lord Fairfax, either upon the principle that an alien enemy could not take by devise, or the belief that
the acts of 1782 had already vested the property in the commonwealth.'
(Cranch, U. S., VII, p. 626).

[15] Hening, XI, p. 128.

[16] *Ibid.*, p. 159.

[17] *Rev. Code*, 1819, II, p. 495.

[18] *Proprietors*, p. 142.

[19] *Va. Land Grants*, p. 118.

[20] Hening, XI, p. 289.

[21] *Ibid.*, XII, p. 111.

[22] The first grant by the Commonwealth was made by Gov. Patrick
Henry, Nov. 15, 1786, and is recorded in the same book of N. N. Grants
(S: 194) in which the last grant made by Lord Fairfax, April 3, 1780,
(S: 192) is entered.

[23] *Marshall's Lessee* v. *Foley, et al., Fauquier Record of Land Causes,*
B, p. 297.

[24] This case was argued in the Winchester court under an ancient
form of procedure, as *Timothy Trititle, Lessee of David Hunter* vs.
Denny Fairfax, Devisee of Thomas Lord Fairfax. When the case was
brought before the Court of Appeals the fictitious name was omitted
but in the case agreed Hunter was still referred to as the 'lessor'
(Munford, I, p. 222). The fiction was further reflected in the titles
of the case in the Supreme Court, as *Fairfax's Devisee* v. *Hunter's
Lessee* (Cranch, U. S., VII, p. 603) and *Martin's etc.* v. *Hunter's Lessee*
(Wheaton, I, p. 304.)
The court referred to as the Winchester District Court was the
Superior Court for the district composed of Frederick, Berkeley, Hamp-
shire, Hardy and Shenandoah counties. (Beveridge, *John Marshall*,
IV, p. 148.)

[25] *Hunter* v. *Fairfax's Devisee.* Munford, I, p. 218.

[26] April 19, 1795. Hester Morris at the time of her marriage to
James M. Marshall was considered to be the second greatest heiress in
America. (Beveridge, *John Marshall*, II, p. 203.)

[27] The deed by Genl. Philip Martin to the Marshalls and Rawleigh
Colston, Oct. 18, 1806, for the Manor of Leeds was made subject to
leases executed prior to this date. (*Marshall's Lessee* v. *Foley, et al.,
Fauquier, Record of Land Causes*, B, p. 267.)

[28] Robert Morris wrote to his son-in-law, James M. Marshall, March
4, 1796, 'Your brother has been here as you will see by a letter from
him forwarded by this conveyance. He could not get your case brought

forward in the Supreme Court of the U. S. at which he was much dissatisfied & I am much concerned thereat, fearing that real disadvantage will result to your concern thereby'. (Beveridge, *John Marshall*, II, p. 207.)

²⁹ *Hunter* v. *Fairfax's Devisee*, Dallas, III, p. 305.

³⁰ *Rev. Code*, 1819, I, p. 352.

³¹ *Ibid.*

³² Beveridge, *John Marshall*, II, p. 209.

³³ The loan was made in Amsterdam, and in James M. Marshall's personal account with Morris, the entry stands, 'Jany. 25 '97 to £7700 paid the Rev'd. Denny Fairfax & credited in your acc't with me'. (Beveridge, *John Marshall*, II, p. 210.)

³⁴ Denny Martin had assumed the name of Fairfax by royal license in 1782, but before the deed to the Marshalls was executed John Marshall had insisted that he should comply literally with the terms of the will of his uncle, Thomas Lord Fairfax, and procure an act of Parliament confirming his change of name and authorizing him to bear the arms of Fairfax. This he did in 1797. (*Proprietors*, p. 142.)

³⁵ Robert 7th Lord Fairfax died July 15, 1793 (Burke's Peerage, 1914, p. 754), two months after the agreement covering the sale of the Northern Neck lands to the Marshall syndicate. By his will, proved August 15, 1793 (*Proprietors*, p. 138), he devised his interests in Virginia and his estates in England, in fee to his nephew, Denny Martin Fairfax, who thus succeeded to the full proprietary title and became competent in himself to execute deeds disposing of the Fairfax holdings in America.

The family title passed to Bryan Fairfax, son of William Fairfax, of Belvoir, as the eighth baron, but with no provision from the Culpeper inheritance for its support. Robert Fairfax seems to have been willing at one time to make some compensation for the alienation of the Fairfax estates in Yorkshire, but his extravagant habits left him without means to carry out his purpose. He died in straitened circumstances, an allowance of £13,758 received by him in 1792 under an act of Parliament for the relief of American Loyalists, having been quickly swallowed up by creditors. (*Proprietors*, pp. 137-8.)

³⁶ *Marshall* v. *Conrad*, Call. V, p. 370.

³⁷ James M. Marshall and his wife Hester, made conveyances of land in Shenandoah and Berkeley counties from Nov. 12, 1798. (*Frederick D. B.*, 3, p. 364.)

³⁸ *Marshall* v. *Conrad*, Call, V, p. 406. Suit was brought by James M. Marshall to recover possession of a lot in Winchester on non-payment of rent. The case was decided against him in the lower court and he appealed, the appellee contesting Marshall's title. The opinion of the Court of Appeals, one judge dissenting, declared that 'it is unnecessary to pursue the inquiry; because the act of compromise in 1796, made during the pendency of a suit in this court, where all the points arose, has put an end to the controversy. For it makes Denny Fairfax capable; and relinquishes to the appellant all claim, on the part of the Commonwealth, to lands which had been appropriated by Lord Fairfax; and it is impossible to maintain, that the lot in question, which he had actually sold and was in the receipt of an annual rent for, had not been appropriated'. Judgment for the appellant was accordingly entered October, 1805.

³⁹ From an abstract of the will. (*Proprietors*, p. 143.)

⁴⁰ In this deed he excepted 'all and every quit rents reserved on grants of and for all and every part of the lands of the said Northern Neck'. (*Marshall* v. *Conrad*, Call, V, p. 370.)

⁴¹ Superior Court of Frederick Co., *Order Book*, III, p. 721.

⁴² Beveridge, *John Marshall*, II, p. 211.

⁴³ The amount paid Marshall by the U. S. Government for this service was $19,963.97. (*Ibid.*, p. 372.)

⁴⁴ *Marshall's Lessee* v. *Foley, et al., Fauquier Record of Land Causes,* B, p. 272. Partitions of the land included in this purchase were later made by the Marshall partners. Nov. 10, 1807, Rawleigh Colston received a conveyance from the Marshall brothers of the tract surveyed for Lord Fairfax by John Warner, Nov. 29, 1736, containing 26,535 acres and lying between Ashby's gap and Snicker's gap; and a tract of 13,465 acres, 'adjoining Ashby's gap' (evidently the so called Goony Run Manor), surveyed for Lord Fairfax by William Green, March 10, 1748. On August 22, 1816, John Marshall executed a deed to James M. Marshall for 21,187 acres lying in Fauquier on the north bank of the Rappahannock river, between that river and the eastern fork of Thumb run and skirting the Oven Top and Rattlesnake mountains. This conveyance, with the 58,959 acres originally conveyed to him by Denny Martin Fairfax, gave James M. Marshall 80,146 acres, and his lots in the town of Winchester as his share in the Marshall syndicate's purchase of the manor lands and left 98,740 acres of the original Leeds Manor tract in the possession of John Marshall.

⁴⁵ *Marshall's Lessee* v. *Foley, et al., Fauquier Record of Land Causes,* B, p. 283.

⁴⁶ *Hunter* v. *Fairfax's Devisee*, Munford, I, p. 219 et seq.

⁴⁷ The Treaty of London, negotiated by John Jay in 1794, confirmed and amplified the provisions of the Treaty of Peace in respect to non-confiscation of the property of British subjects.

⁴⁸ Beveridge, *John Marshall*, IV, p. 164.

⁴⁹ Cranch (U. S.), VII, p. 603.

⁵⁰ President Adams appointed John Marshall Chief Justice of the United States, January 20, 1801.

⁵¹ Beveridge, *John Marshall*, IV, p. 153.

⁵² *Hunter* v. *Martin*, Munford, IV, p. 6.

⁵³ Beveridge, *John Marshall*, IV, p. 161.

⁵⁴ The Supreme Court in this case, to avoid further friction with the Virginia Court of Appeals, decided to issue its process directly to the Winchester District court.

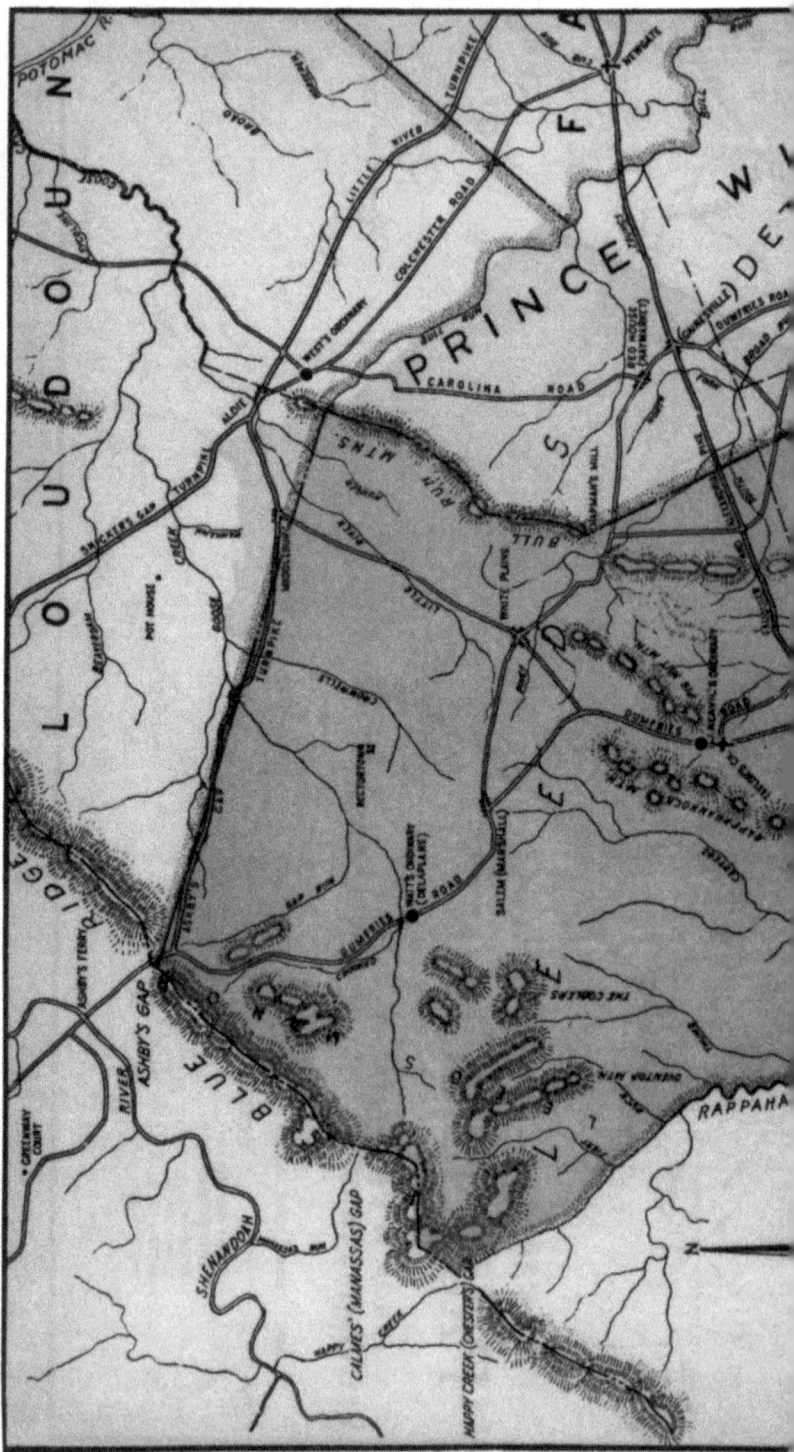

POTOMAC R.

BROAD RUN

LITTLE RIVER

COLCHESTER ROAD

PRINCE WILLIAM

FA...

DET...

DUMFRIES ROAD (CHESTNUT HILL)

CAROLINA ROAD

RED HOUSE (BRENTSVILLE)

BULL RUN

BULL RUN MTNS

LITTLE RIVER

WHITE PLAINS

L O U D O U N

SNICKER'S GAP

POT HOUSE

SNICKERSVILLE TURNPIKE

CAMPBELL

DUMFRIES

RAPPAHANNOCK MTN.

TO ...

BLUE RIDGE

ASHBY'S GAP

GAP RUN

WHITE CHURCH (DELAPLANE)

DUMFRIES ROAD

RAPPAHANNOCK

F A U Q U I E R

THE CRUMS

QUINTO MTN.

RIVER

SHENANDOAH

CALMES' (MANASSAS) GAP

HAPPY CREEK (CHESTER) GAP

RAPPAHA...

N

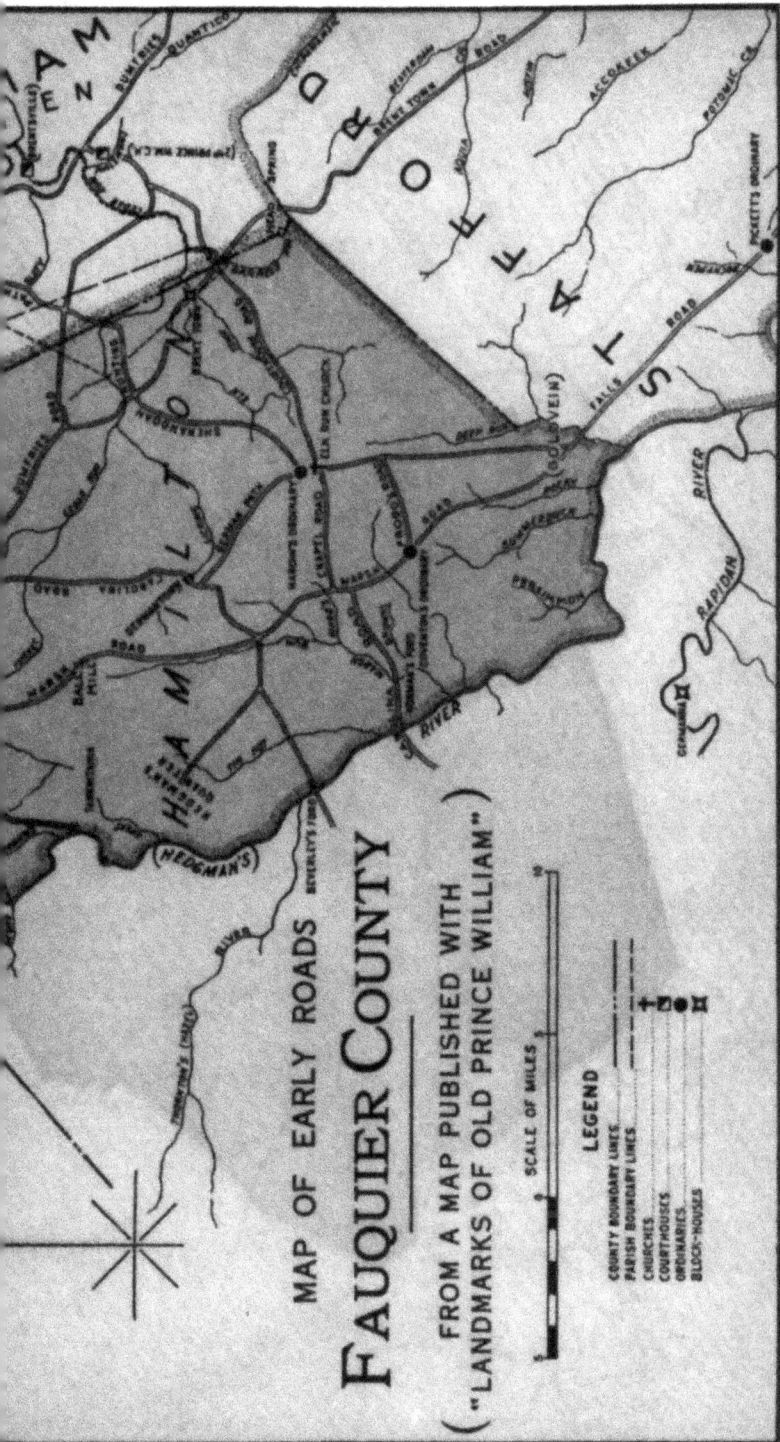

MAP OF EARLY ROADS

FAUQUIER COUNTY

(FROM A MAP PUBLISHED WITH "LANDMARKS OF OLD PRINCE WILLIAM")

SCALE OF MILES

LEGEND

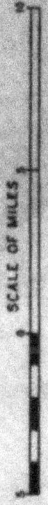

COUNTY BOUNDARY LINES
PARISH BOUNDARY LINES
CHURCHES
COURTHOUSES
ORDINARIES
BLOCK-HOUSES

INDEX

Act of Oct., 1777, 219, 240.
Act of May, 1779, 223.
Act of Oct., 1782, 224, 225.
Act of Oct., 1785, 226.
Act of Dec., 1796 (Compromise Act), 230, 242.
Albrecht, J. Justice, master miner, 114.
Allen, John, land grant to, 93
Allen, John, Jr., road surveyor, 180.
Allen, William, land grants to, 84 90, 92, 93.
Amoroleck, brother to Hassinunga chief, 5, 6.
Anburey, Thomas, lieutenant in Burgoyne's army, 195.
Anderson, Walter, land grant to, 102.
Andros, Sir Edmund, governor, 153, 154.
A r e t k i n, William, proprietary agent, 42.
Argall, Samuel, explorer, 8, 9, 18.
Arlington, Henry Bennett, Earl of, 38.
Aquia church, 137.
Ashby, Benjamin, road surveyor, 181.

Bacon, Nathaniel, treacherous attack, 9; rebellion, 39.
Balch, Hezekiah, schoolmaster, 213.
Ball, Capt. James, land grant to, 108.
Ball's (Schumate's) mill, 208.
Bailey, Stephen, constable, 183.
Baltimore, Charles, Lord, 11.
Barber, Charles, land grant to, 103.
Barber, Thomas, land grant to, 103.
Barker, William, road surveyor, 182.
Barrow, Edward, land grant to, 86.
Barton, David, road surveyor, 181.
Barton, Valentine, land grant to, 106.
Baylis, Col. John, 177.
Beach, Alexander, land grant to, 90.

Belfield, Joseph, land grant to, 83.
Bell, Alexander, land grant to, 103, 107.
Bell, Col. John, mentioned, 141, 145, 166, 183, 210, 211; notice of, 170.
Bell, Rev. John, land grants to, 100, 171.
Belvoir, 66, 69.
Berkeley, Sir William, governor, 19, 39.
Berry, Thomas, land grant to, 100.
Berryman, James, land grant to, 89.
Beverley, Henry, 47.
Beverley, William, commissioner, 63, 65.
Bilborough, Fairfax estate, 55, 78.
Bivings, Maurice, land grant to, 93.
Blackwell, John, vestryman, 149, 209, 213.
Blackwell, Joseph, churchwarden, 140, 144; J. P., 166; sworn as sheriff, 173; notice of, 174.
Blackwell, Samuel, 174.
Blackwell, William, mentioned, 141, 144, 149, 166; notice of, 170.
Blair, James, commissary, 153, 155, 157.
Bland, James, 98, 99.
Blowers, John, land grants to, 101, 106.
Bradford, Alexander, road surveyor, 180.
Bradford, Daniel, vestryman, 149; road surveyor, 180.
Brent, George, of Woodstock, partner in Brent Town tract, 22, 24; plans Catholic settlement, 25; proprietary agent, 45; died, 46.
Brent, William, 209.
Bristow, Robert, partner in Brent Town tract, 22.
Broad Run tract, 94.
Brooke, Humphrey, vestryman Leeds, 149; clerk, 172; notice of, 189; trustee, 213.

Brooke, Francis, clerk, 172.
Brooks, Thomas, land grant to, 111.
Brown, John, land grant to, 84.
Brown, William, 207.
Brunskill, Rev. John, minister of Hamilton, 142; removed, 142; refused to recognize order of Council, 143.
Brunskill, Rev. John, Sr., 157.
Brunswick county, 86.
Bryants Breedings, 192.
Buffalo, hunted by Siouan tribes, 8; seen by Argall in 1613, 9, 18.
Bull Run tract, 95.
Bullitt, Benjamin, 144.
Bullitt, Cuthbert, notice of, 176; family, 189.
Bullitt, Joseph, road surveyor, 182.
Burgess, Col. Charles, land grants to, 108.
Burnaby, Archdeacon Andrew, 80, 204.
Burwell, Lewis, land grant to, 95.
Butler, William, 140.
Byrd, Col. William, 9, 29, 63.
Byrn, George, land grant to, 110.
Byrnley, 110.
Byrum, Peter, land grant to, 107.

Cage, Col. William, trustee, 57.
Campbell, Hugh R., 214.
Carter's bridge, 202.
Carter, Col. Charles, mentioned, 63; land grants to, 83, 94; bequeaths land, 95; establishes quarters at Norman's Ford, 201.
Carter, Charles, son of Robert, land grant to, 94.
Carter, George, son of Robert, land grant to, 108.
Carter, John, son of Robert, land grant to, 94.
Carter, Landon, land grants to, 84, 95, 107; lays out Carolandville, 201; vestryman, 149.
Carter, Peter, constable, 183.
Carter, Col. Robert (King), proprietary agent, 28, 43, 46; address to Crown, 45; resumes agency, 57; revives feudal privileges, 58; protests grants by governor, 59; his death, 61, 68; income from N. N., 78;

success of his agency, 82; manorial grants to him, 94, 95, 107.
Carter, Robert, son of Robert, land grants to, 91, 95.
Carter, Capt. Thomas, land grant to, 100.
Catlett, Col. John, 19, 20, 29.
Catlett, John, land grant to, 29; road surveyor, 179.
Cedar Grove, 104.
Chalfee, Henry, land grant to, 100.
Chambers, Joseph, land grant to, 86.
Chapman, Nathaniel, land grant to, 110.
Chapman, Thomas, road surveyor, 181.
Chastellux, Marquis de, traveller, 215.
Chesapeake bay, Smith's explorations in, 3; N. N. boundary, 33, 64.
Chevalle, Clement, land grant to, 92.
Chicacoan, 34.
Chickahominy river, 2.
Chilton, John, vestryman, 150.
Chinn, Charles, 149.
Chinn, Rawleigh, land grant to, 109.
Chotanck, 137.
Chriesman, George, 216.
Church, disestablishment of, 152.
Churches:
  Dumfries, 138; Elk Run, 140; Goose Creek, 150; Old Bull Run, 150; Piper's, 150; Pohick, 156; Quantico, 140; Taylor's, 150; St. Mary's (Turkey Run), 140, 178.
Churchill, Col. Armistead, 94, 187.
Churchill, Armistead, Jr., 94, 146, 149, 187.
Churchill, Henry, county lieutenant, 175, 189.
Churchill, John, mentioned, 94, 146, 166; notice of, 171; family, 187.
Churchill's mill, 214.
Churchill, William, 94, 187.
Churchwardens, duties of, 133; how chosen, 154; requirement of oath, 154.
Clarke, John, land grant to, 110.
Clement, Alexander, land grant to, 100.

Mountjoy, Edward, land grant to, 83, 111.
Mt. Vernon tract, 42, 51.

Neavil, George, 144, 199, 200.
Neavil, Joseph, 102, 205.
Nelmes, Samuel, land grant to, 106.
Nelmes, William, land grant to, 106.
New Berne, 114.
Newport, Capt. Christopher, commands first expedition to Va., 1; explores James river, 2.
Nichols, William, land grant to, 111.
Nicholson, Francis, governor, 27.
Norman's Ford, 82, 200.
Norman, Isaac, 200.
Northern Neck, geographical position of, 30; land titles in, 30 et seq.; charter of 1649, 33; grantees, 33, 34; charter of 1663, 34; charter of 1669, 34; grantees, 34; tenure of lands, 36; proprietors 1674, 38; charter of 1688, 41; land books opened, 43; charter of 1688 confirmed 1694, 43; changes in proprietorship, 45; boundary dispute, 47; survey of disputed boundaries, 63; boundaries defined, 64; counties included, 65; back line run, 65; proprietary office at Belvoir, 73; office removed to Greenway Court, 73; land laws in proprietary, 73, 74; tenure in manors, 74, 75; income from, 78; quit rents maintained until after the Revolution, 220; commonwealth issues patents, 227; compromise of 1796, 230.
Northumberland county, 34, 160.
North Wales, 86.
Norwood, Sir Henry, 50.

Obanon, Bryan, land grant to, 106.
O'Bannon, John, 149.
Occaneechi island, 192.
Odor, Joseph, road surveyor, 180; constable, 183.
Old Rappahannock county, 35, 58, 160.
O'Neill, Rev. Charles, 214, 217.
Opechancanough, Indian chief, holds Smith prisoner, 2.

Ordinaries, described, 197, 198; tariff, 199; Coventon's, 180, 209; Hardin's, 200; George Neavil's, 199, 200, 208; Joseph Neavil's, 102, 205, 208; Watt's, 205, 206.
Orear, John & Daniel, land grant to, 91.
Overwharton parish, 135, 137.
Owsley, Capt. Thomas, ranger, 29.

Page, Carter, land grant to, 95.
Pageland tract, 94.
Page, Col. Mann, land grant to, 94, 95.
Patapsco river, 3.
Patuxent river, 4.
Peter Pocum's Pulpit, 90.
Perry, Micajah, London merchant, 46, 116.
Peyton, Henry, 149.
Peyton, John, land grant to, 110.
Peyton, Valentine, land grant to, 93; churchwarden, 140.
Peyton, Yelverton, mentioned, 166, 172, 179; notice of, 188, 210.
Pickett, George B., 214.
Pickett, George, Jr., 214.
Pickett, Martin, purchases Hamilton glebe, 149; vestryman of Leeds, 149; undersheriff, 177; notice of, 178; obtains endowment Warren Academy, 213.
Pickett, William, 149, 213.
Pickett, William S., 207.
Piedmont Plateau, region defined, 1.
Plantation, organization of, 85.
Pocahontas, daughter of the Powhatan, saves Smith's life, 3.
Poison field, 86.
Potomac river, 3, 64, 77.
Powell, Nathaniel, 16.
Prince William county, formation of, 160.
Prince William insurrection, 98, 99.

Quarters, described, 85.
Quirriough (Potomac) river, 33, 49.

Rangers, 27.
Randolph, Beverley, governor, 227.
Ransdall, Wharton, 144, 166, 183.

Rapidan river (South Fork, Conway), 7, 21, 64, 65.
Rappahannock river (Indian, Cannon, North Fork, Hedgman's), Smith enters, 4; shown on Smith's map, 7; described by Strachey, 16; headwaters reached by Cadwalader Jones 1670, 21; boundary of N. N., 60; Manor of Leeds on north bank, 75; settlement from falls north, 82 et seq.
Rector, Jacob, 122, 126.
Rector, John, land grant to, 106; will proved, 130; establishes Rectortown, 207.
Rector, Ludwell, 216.
Red Store, 202, 210, 212.
Reichel, John Frederick, 196.
Reno, Lewis, land grant to, 92.
Richmond county, 58, 160.
Richland tract, 83.
Riedesel, Baroness von, 195.
Rieger, Rev. John Bartholomew, 127, 194.
Roads:
  Brent Town, 24, 192.
  Carolina, 97, 192 et seq.
  Chapel, 180, 215.
  Court House, 180, 202, 215.
  Dumfries, 28, 202 et seq; 206, 208, 212.
  Falmouth, 208.
  Fredericksburg-Winchester, 76, 109, 128, 162, 181, 206, 208, 214.
  Frogg's, 165.
  German Path, 128, 181, 208.
  Marsh, 165, 180, 209 et seq.
  Shenandoah Hunting Path, 128, 181, 192, 193.
Roane, Judge Spencer, 234.
Roanoke river, 9.
Roberts, William, constable, 183.
Robinson, John, 63, 207.
Rousau, William, 144.
Rout, James, 212.
Rout, Peter, land grant to, 104.
Russell, William, land grants to, 88, 101, 103, 111.
Rust, William, road surveyor, 181.
Ryley, Edward, land grant to, 92.

Sandys, Sir Edwin, 32.
Saratoga prisoners, 194.
Scatterday, John, 216.
Schlatter, Rev. Michael, 127.

Schoepf, Dr. Johann David, 197.
Scotch-Irish settlers, 96.
Scott, Alex., trustee Salem, 207.
Scott, Rev. Alex., land grants to, 89, 102; minister of Overwharton, 136.
Scott, James, 149.
Scott, John, 177, 214.
Shenandoah county, 66.
Shenandoah river, 75, 76.
Shenandoah valley, 60, 82.
Shuemack, John, 99.
Siegen, Germany, emigrants from, 114.
Singleton, Robert, road surveyor, 181.
Sioux, pre-historic home among western foothills of Alleghany m'ts., 8; not agricultural, 8.
Skinker, Samuel, land grant to, 101.
Skrein, William, land grant to, 90.
Smith, Capt. John, lands with Newport, 1; explorations, 2, 3, 4; at falls of Rappahannock, 4; encounters Manahoacs, 5, 6; biographical sketch, 14; members of his party, July 24, 1608, 16.
Smith, John, tanner, land grant to, 89.
Smith, John A. W., 214.
Smith, Joseph, 207.
Smith, Thomas, road surveyor, 181.
Somers Islands co., 33, 50.
Spangenberg, Bishop, 127, 194.
Spencer, Col. Nicholas, proprietary agent, 12, 42, 43, 87.
Spillman, John, named in warrant for Germantown tract, 122.
Spillman v. Gent, 123.
Spotsylvania county, 58, 86, 126.
Spotswood, Alexander, governor, mentioned, 9, 11; applied to by Graffenried, 115; finances importation of Germans, 116; reports to Lords of Trade, 117; establishes Germans on Rapidan, 117; obtains act exempting then from payment of levies, 118; states terms of their employment, 120; finds iron ore at Germanna, 121.
Stafford county, 35, 160.
St. George parish, act creating, 118, 119.
St. Mary parish, 119.
Stone, Thomas, land grant to, 100.

Withers, James, land grant to, 92.
Withers, John, 137.
Woodstock, John Sherman, 240.
Wright, James, 149.
Wright, Capt. John, mentioned,
    140, 144, 166, 168, 211; notice
    of, 169, family, 186.
Wright, Joseph, land grant to, 101.

Wyatt, Sir Francis, governor, 33.
Wynn, Minor, 207.

Young, Reginald, constable, 183.

Zollicoffer, Jacob Christopher, 124,
    126.

* 9 7 8 0 8 0 6 3 4 9 5 3 4 *